THE NEW
AMERICAN ARTS

EDITED BY RICHARD KOSTELANETZ

FILM   *Harris Dienstfrey*

THEATRE   *Richard Kostelanetz*

PAINTING   *Max Kozloff*

POETRY   *Jonathan Cott*

DANCE   *Jill Johnston*

FICTION   *Richard Kostelanetz*

MUSIC   *Eric Salzman*

COLLIER BOOKS, NEW YORK

COLLIER-MACMILLAN LTD., LONDON

Acknowledgments

For permission to include material published by them, grateful acknowl-
edgment is made to the following: Ted Berrigan, editor of *C* ("Sonnet
XXXIV" by Ted Berrigan); Lurton Blassingame (from *The Sot-Weed
Factor* Copyright © 1960 by John Barth. Reprinted by permission.);
Bureau of American Ethnology, Smithsonian Institute ("Papago Dream
Song of a Woman" in *Papago Music* by Frances Densmore); Doubleday
& Company, Inc. (lines from "Night Crow" Copyright 1947 by
Theodore Roethke and "Open House" Copyright 1941 by Theodore
Roethke; "Parachutes, My Love, Could Carry Us Higher" in *Poems*
by Barbara Guest; lines from *The Sot-Weed Factor* by John Barth.
Copyright © 1960 by John Barth; "The Geranium" and "The Moment"
Copyright © 1963 by Beatrice Roethke as Executrix of the Estate of
Theodore Roethke in *The Collected Poems of Theodore Roethke.*
Reprinted by permission.); *Encounter* ("The Flaw" by Robert Lowell);
Faber & Faber Ltd. ("Exeunt" by Richard Wilbur in *Poems 1943-1956*;
"The Geranium" and "The Moment" by Theodore Roethke. Copyright
© 1963 by Beatrice Roethke as Executrix of the Estate of Theodore
Roethke in *The Collected Poems of Theodore Roethke;* lines from
"Colloquy in Black Rock" by Robert Lowell in *Poems 1938-1949*);
Farrar, Straus & Giroux, Inc. (extracts from *Dream Songs* by John
Berryman Copyright © 1959, 1962, 1963, 1964 by John Berryman;
from *Homage to Mistress Bradstreet* by John Berryman Copyright ©
1956 by John Berryman; lines from "Skunk Hour" in *Life Studies*
by Robert Lowell Copyright © 1956, 1959 by Robert Lowell; "Heine
Dying in Paris," "Sparrow Hills," and "Sappho" in *Imitations* by
Robert Lowell Copyright © 1958, 1959, 1960, 1961 by Robert Lowell;
Grove Press (lines from "Invincibility" in *Meditations in an Emergency*

by Frank O'Hara; *Ko, or a Season on Earth* by Kenneth Koch Copyright © 1959 by Kenneth Koch; "Summery Weather" and "Fresh Air" in *Thank You and Other Poems* Copyright © 1962 by Kenneth Koch); Harcourt, Brace & World, Inc. ("Exeunt" in *Things of This World* © 1956 by Richard Wilbur; lines from "Colloquy in Black Rock" in *Lord Weary's Castle* by Robert Lowell); Harper & Row, Publishers ("Reporting Back" Copyright © 1962 by William Stafford; "In the Night Desert" Copyright © 1962 by William Stafford; fragments of poems from "The Poets' Annual Indigence Report" and "Conservative" in *Traveling Through the Dark* by William Stafford; lines from "Daddy" Copyright © 1963 by Ted Hughes and "Lady Lazarus" Copyright © 1963 by Ted Hughes in *Ariel* by Sylvia Plath. Reprinted by permission.); Marvin Josephson Associates, Inc. (lines from *Some Trees* by John Ashbery); Alfred A. Knopf, Inc. ("The Manor Garden" Copyright © 1960 by Sylvia Plath, "The Colossus" Copyright © 1961 by Sylvia Plath, "Watercolor of Grantchester Meadows" Copyright © 1960 by Sylvia Plath in *The Colossus* by Sylvia Plath. Reprinted by permission. "Watercolor of Grantchester Meadows" first appeared in the *New Yorker*.); Kenneth Koch (lines from "When the Sun Tries to Go On" in *The Hasty Papers*; "The Poem of the 48 States" in *Second Coming*); Longmans, Green & Co., Limited ("In a Cold House," "Arriving in the Country Again," "Rain," and "The Jewel" in *The Branch Will Not Break* by James Wright); Meridan Books (lines from "The Cloud in Trousers" and "To His Beloved Self" in *The Bedbug and Selected Poetry* by Vladimir Mayakovsky, edited by P. Blake); New Directions Publishing Corp. (lines from "The Prime Minister Kintsune" in *One Hundred Poems from the Japanese* by Kenneth Rexroth. All rights reserved. Reprinted by permission.); the *New Yorker* ("The Amnesiac" by Sylvia Plath); Frank O'Hara (extract from *The School of New York* by B. H. Friedman, published by Grove Press); Ron Padgett and *C* ("I'd Give You My Seat If I Were Here . . ." by Ron Padgett); Partisan Review ("Water" by Robert Lowell); Alan Swallow, Publisher, Denver, Colorado ("Aspen's Song" and "Noon" in *Collected Poems* © 1952, 1960, by Yvor Winters); Totem Press in association with Corinth Books (lines from *Second Avenue* by Frank O'Hara Copyright © 1962 by Frank O'Hara); Wesleyan University Press ("In a Cold House," "Arriving in the Country Again," "Rain," and "The Jewel" © 1963, 1960, 1962 by James Wright in *The Branch Will Not Break* by James Wright; lines from "Europe," "The New Realism," "Our Youth," and "To a Young Girl" © 1960, 1961, 1957, 1961 by John Ashbery in *Tennis Court Oath* by John Ashbery); George Wittenborn, Inc. ("Ravenna" in *Mediterranean Cities* by Edwin Denby).

CONTENTS

THE NEW AMERICAN ARTS

INTRODUCTION:

ON THE NEW ARTS IN AMERICA

RICHARD KOSTELANETZ

I

The famous "modern break with tradition" has lasted long enough to have produced its own tradition.

Harold Rosenberg, *The Tradition of the New* (1959)

The history of modern art has demonstrated that the desire to create new forms and embody new themes, an ethos that has motivated Western artists particularly since the time of Baudelaire, has been and continues to be a prime force influencing artists, critics and audience alike. What prompts modern artists to create works which are distinctly new is, first, a dissatisfaction with what other artists are doing and, second, their truly felt need to engage the evolving spirit of their times. Thus, in the past hundred years, all the important painters, film-makers, dancers, composers and writers, in Europe and America, have created works that were decisively and propitiously original and, in turn, their new styles and/or themes influenced their artistic successors and, of course, also provided the young with an "old" against which to rebel.

Moreover, history itself seems to be an accomplice of the impulse to create new styles; for with each great historical change in the twentieth century, in America as well as Europe—World War I, the Depression, World War II—an era of art came to an end only to be followed in all arts by styles appreciably different. In this respect, the twentieth century epitomizes art's entire history in which, as the cultural historian Meyer Schapiro has observed, "Important economic and political shifts . . . are often accompanied or followed by shifts in the centers of art and their styles."

In recent years, the two-fold processes of social and esthetic change have, I believe, accelerated considerably—instead of passing through an overhauling change every fifty or twenty years, the world seems to be transformed every ten; and contemporary art, with each year, departs more rapidly and radically from the past. This acceleration is a key reason why newness as such has, in recent years, become a more important value in our understanding of art and in art's understanding of itself. Given the influx into art of new ideas and new compositional materials, given a contemporary historical predicament rapidly distinguishing itself from those of the far- and near-past, given the widespread esthetic cross-fertilization that the tradition of the new produces, one must say that no artist today or tomorrow will be considered significant unless his work either offers an expansion of formal range, an original reordering of materials within the spectrum of possibility, or a new perception of the changing esthetic and/or human situation of our time. Thus, when confronted with two recent artworks of equal substance, most modern artists and critics will usually consider an achieved newness to be the crucial criterion that distinguishes the competent from the imaginative, the enjoyable from the invaluable, the acceptable from the brilliant.

For several reasons, then, to understand the over-all direction of today's art and to appreciate the best recent works in Europe and America, an onlooker cannot depend upon modes of perception and criteria of judgment based on the past—he will surely wallow in misapprehension and confusion. Rather, he must slough off esthetic commitments to prior work to gain the open-minded attitude that initiates a rapport with new art.

II

What I would describe as realism—
the humble subordination of the art-
ist before the natural phenomenon
—is very rare in America.

Sir Herbert Read, "Some Observa-
tions on Art in America."

After many years of cultural isolation, American artists are no longer exempt from the dynamics of European art; for although Americans until 1920 seemed unaffected by European modernist developments (and vice versa), since that date American culture, in becoming a major contributor to world art, has assumed many of the characteristics and values of the international scene, among them a commitment to the tradition of the new. Despite the recent proclamations of conservative and theory-haunted native critics that the age of revolt has exhausted itself or is stalled in esthetic dead ends, American artists continue to produce works of dance and literature, cinema and music that have no precedent in our culture or, sometimes, that of the world. These artists have, in short, enlivened and extended America's participation in the modernist tradition. Moreover, the continuing receptiveness to true originality is affirmed, on one hand, in statements by the artists themselves— John Barth's and Saul Bellow's on the recent novel, Edward Albee's on the development of American theatre, and Merce Cunningham's on the dance—and, on the other, by the impact that the work of these and other original artists have upon sophisticated segments of the American art public.

Though the impact of the tradition of the new spread from its European origins to America, avant-garde arts in America assume a cast quite different from those abroad, largely because the isolated working environment of the experimental American artist both defines his condition and influences the character of his work. Just as the individual pitted against an indomitable Nature was a frequent protagonist in nineteenth-century painting and literature, so, in fact, this same aloof, eccentric, impatient, perhaps Faustian personality, wrestling with art's limits, inhabits the major American artists. If nearly all European avant-garde artists gravitate toward the cultural centers—usually Paris, but often one of several German cities—and develop their originality in an atmosphere of camaraderie and criticism, American artists start their careers as rather isolated figures scattered around the country, out of touch with the centers of established modern art, unapprenticed to recognized masters. Often in their later success they reaffirm the isolation of their youth, as William Faulkner clung to Mississippi, Charles Ives to northwest Connecticut, Robinson Jeffers to his California cliff, and William Carlos Williams to his New Jersey medical practice.

Today, although nearly all the leading figures in the non-literary arts and theatre live in New York, the gravitational center of the cultural mainstream that runs from Boston to Philadelphia, only a few were born or educated there (while, in contrast, most of the important critics are A-to-Z New Yorkers); the prime activity in creative literature is widely scattered—John Barth writes about his native Eastern shore Maryland from a Western Pennsylvania university town; James Wright and Robert Bly live in Minnesota; William Stafford, in Washington; Thomas Pynchon, as a recluse in Mexico; John Ashbery, in Paris; Vladimir Nabokov and William Burroughs, in Europe and North Africa; and Sylvia Plath, until her death, had been living in England. Also, largely because culture in New York is so diffuse, young artists achieve a kind of isolation there, apart from universities, cliques, alliances of sympathy and promotional establishments. For its first ten years in Manhattan, The Living Theatre was hardly noticed, and Merce Cunningham, who has lived there for twenty years, still suffers the indignity of infrequent New York recitals. In short, the alienation that European artists of the twentieth century "discovered" had, from the start, defined the American cultural condition.

This isolation, in turn, influences the character of our advanced arts; for our archetypal creative artist is the "pathfinder" who leaves, often with naïve motives, the confines of "civilization," a metaphor for conventional, largely European notions of artistic possibility, to explore the uncharted frontier, sometimes achieving a "breakthrough" into esthetic country that Europe had never seen before. America becomes Europe's artistic virgin land, for so many of the compositional ideas that have strongly influenced the organized European avant-gardes, from Edgar Allan Poe's symbolist poetic theory, through Henry James' and Faulkner's fictional techniques to John Cage's notions of aleatory music, have been American in origin; and this tradition accounts for why America's greatest representational arts, fiction as well as painting, tend to be more visionary and mythic—penetrating to the hidden essences of life—rather than concrete and realistic—encompassing a wealth of verifiable experience.

In an age when the quest for and response to the "new" moves artists everywhere, what particularly characterizes the American's explorations is his willingness to pursue esthetic ideas literally, wholeheartedly and unselfconsciously to ultimate and unprecedented ends. In a country where politics is very much the art of the possible, art is the politics of the impossible. Thus, not until The Living Theatre's production of Kenneth H. Brown's *The Brig* (1963) were the influential, semi-mad ideas of the Frenchman Antonin Artaud's *The Theatre and Its Double* fully realized—ideas which Europeans had pondered over, discussed, re-interpreted and faintly reproduced in the nearly quarter-century since the book's publication. It is similarly appropriate that the most radical experiments at both extremes of the compositional spectrum in music, consciously arbitrary and totally planned, should be attempted by American composers—respectively, Morton Feldman and Milton Babbitt; that the notion of using the products of technology for artistic purposes which had remained dormant since constructivism and the prime of Marcel Duchamp should blossom again in the American Pop artists; that the literary tradition of irony should be so *inclusively* utilized in cinema by Stanley Kubrick in *Dr. Strangelove,* that John Cage should provide a rationale for "composing" a piece of four minutes and thirty-three seconds of sheer silence (though no one has yet claimed its visual analogue, cellophone, is "art"), and that the French idea of absurd literature, which has permeated European theatre, should father a school of fiction unlike any other, anywhere—the absurd novels of Joseph Heller, Thomas Pynchon and John Barth.

Of course, this passion to follow a suggestive idea to its extreme conclusion reflects, in general, a certain innocence about fixed ideas—the naïve belief that they can be true and ultimate—but out of this obsession has sprung that peculiarly American tradition of works of art whose originality and imaginative strength exceed and eventually transform the going notions of artistic appropriateness and possibility. Walt Whitman, Herman Melville, Albert P. Ryder, Charles Ives, William Faulkner, Jackson Pollock, John Cage, D. W. Griffith, Isadora Duncan all pushed their art into new realms, single-handedly initiating changes that influenced scores of younger artists in America and (but for Ives) Europe.

What the Europeans find so appealing in American art, I think, is its seemingly untutored, law-defying, concentrated (rather than broad), somewhat violent imaginative energy. As the American critic Kenneth Rexroth once tellingly characterized the enthusiastic French response to American action painting, "[They] got hold of the wrong catalogue and were under the impression the pictures were painted by Wyatt Earp and Al Capone and Bix Beiderbecke." But Wyatt Earp is an apt metaphor of the American artist, for the optimistic spirit of the frontier lawman—performing old tasks in new ways by taking the laws of form into one's own hands, with little awareness of the tragedy of *hubris*—still dominates avant-garde American art. Once Europeans can understand and reproduce the American's rule-defying, original techniques, they often show up, in more pre-planned forms, in their own works. Out of Faulkner, for instance, come the cerebral novels of Claude Simon; out of Cage, the systematized chance and indeterminacy of Karlheinz Stockhausen. For another example, the tone-cluster (the sounding of whole blocks of notes simultaneously) was invented by Charles Ives and independently re-invented by Henry Cowell, only to be more shrewdly used by Bela Bartók. (Perhaps this trick, along with John Cage's prepared piano, belongs in the great American tradition of inspired gimmickry.) Indeed, some American artists, such as John Cage and Barnett Newman and, perhaps, Henry Cowell and Ezra Pound, are more important for the original esthetic ideas they propagate than for any single realized work they create.

The origins of this risk-taking individualism probably lie in the singularities of the American experience—in the exploitation of the frontier, in our inclination toward ideologies of untragic optimism, in our belief that in America everything is very possible and, more deeply, in the self-help capitalist ethos that atomizes rather than syndicates a society, coupled with the Protestant inclination for individual revelation which produces so many religious sects and which contrasts with the European Catholic tradition of communal revelation. In America, most of the very successful artists, moguls, salvationists and secular reformers are, particularly early in their careers, inspired independent operators, each stamping his achievement with a highly individualized mark.

Just as capitalism and Protestantism are responsible for both the achievements and disasters of American life, the pioneering stance is paradoxically the source of the key achievements and most disappointing deficiencies in the American artistic experience. On one hand, the American art scene as a whole or the scene in each of the arts is generally not as broadly sophisticated or significant as that in European countries—surely, for instance, neither American theatre nor cinema is one-half as rich as the French; on the other hand, in each American art are works which in crucial respects completely transcend anything in the European arts today— the paintings of Jasper Johns, Robert Rauschenberg and Frank Stella, Jack Smith's *Flaming Creatures,* the fiction of John Barth, the productions of The Living Theatre, the poetry of John Berryman, the dance of Merce Cunningham and the Judson Church movement, the great static spatial conceptions of Stepan Wolpe, Ralph Shapey (particularly *Evocations*) and Earle Brown.

Similarly, the careers of nearly all the greatest American artists are uneven, characterized by sporadic achievements amidst masses of debris, loss or severe diminution of creative talent, sometimes a lack or slowness of recognition, and early decline or death.

So many of our most significant novels from *Moby Dick* to *The Sound and the Fury,* from *The Great Gatsby* to *The Sun Also Rises,* are written by men about 30 who never do as well again. Charles Ives did little composing after he turned 45; after publishing at 30 his great novel *Call It Sleep* Henry Roth finished little else. Jackson Pollock, Isadora Duncan, Stephen Crane, and Nathanael West all died much too young. H. L. Mencken, much-quoted and perceptive at 45, was unread and irrelevant at 55. In what other culture do so many major artists voluntarily expatriate themselves, their work usually suffering a falling off; and where else do so many great imaginations, from Griffith to Melville, spend their last years in undeserved obscurity. In an essay on the jazz guitarist Charlie Christian, who died at 23, Ralph Ellison, himself the author of one and only one great novel, so perceptively noted, "Jazz, like the country which gave it birth, is fecund in its inventiveness, swift and traumatic in its development, and terribly wastefull of its resources."

Similarly, just as American art reflects the virtues of unsophistication—an originality stemming from a certain kind of innocence—it also embodies the perils of naïvety—a general inability to fashion neat wholes and an obsession in even the best artists with pursuing ideas to ridiculously unsuccessful ends. Charles Ives spent nearly forty-five years thinking about, and many of his last years working on, an unfinished *Universe Symphony* in which, write his biographers Henry and Sidney Cowell, "Several orchestras, with huge conclaves of singing men and women, were to be placed about in valleys, along hillsides, and on mountain tops." Who else but The Living Theatre, for example, would attempt with utter failure a theatrical work constructed on principles of chance. Who else but an American, Kenneth Koch, would produce an interminable poem of such arbitrary meaninglessness as *When the Sun Tries To Go On.* Where else could a composer like La Monte Young claim that his burning of a violin was a piece of music (because it made a noise?) and, like the most preposterous backwoods preacher, attract a small but vociferous following.

III

For all the inventive arts maintain, as it were, a sympathetic connection between each other, being no more than various expressions of one internal power, modified by different circumstances.

Percy Bysshe Shelley

Along with their commitment to the tradition of the new, most of the new American artists continue the modernist tradition of non-causal and spatial, rather than syllogistic and narrative-linear, relations—the artwork's basic connections coalesce across space, rather than in immediate, chronological succession—and, thus, of the unhindered exploration of abstract relational possibilities. As the structure of plays and films has become flat, as opposed to the pyramid of classical five-act drama, so painting in recent years, from the color fields of Morris Louis to the geometric designs of Frank Stella, discounts visual depth in favor of flatter, "planar" tensions and interests. Likewise, the best recent literature, from Edward Albee's *Who's Afraid of Virginia Woolf?* to John Berryman's *Dream Songs,* achieves its coherence and makes its points less through sequences of time, as a story in which one thing follows after another, than through space—by repeating images, attitudes, incidents, comments, rituals, fragmented feelings, aspects of character—so that we comprehend the whole by grasping the resonant details spatially, at once. That is, in Kenneth Burke's terms, our developed systems of formal comprehension—of expectations and fulfillments—honed on architectonic structures, must be superseded by response systems that are attuned to formal coherence achieved by repetition—spatial systems of expectation and fulfillment. This change is exemplified in the history of dance —contrast ballet with Merce Cunningham—as well as music, where most advanced contemporary composers de-emphasize the developmental movement of harmony, polyphony, melody and accompaniment for dealing with the possibilities of sound in space, creating complex multi-layered spatial forms built on juxtapositions of events and gestures, often abetted by some form of structural repetition.

This shift towards spatial form generally accompanies, but does not determine, other esthetic trends, such as the tendency towards visionary, non-naturalistic styles which focus upon hidden phenomena and metaphysical themes—the function of the artist is rendering the invisible visible—rather than the rendering of social and factual experience. (Thus, much of the greatest nineteenth-century American art is "modern" before its time.) Precisely because these artists reject any commitment to the realities of external subjects to concentrate on purifying the techniques of their art and using "facts" solely for esthetic purposes, esthetic form in some works, particularly in music, becomes by itself the major "content" and the esthetic line distinguishing form from subject is blurred. Just as Merce Cunningham's dances are primarily about the techniques and possibilities of non-referential dance and *The Brig*'s subject is as much Artaud's theories of the theatre as it is the violence of contemporary life, so *Dr. Strangelove* is more about the resources of irony in film than the absurdity of contemporary nuclear politics. In a rather convincing explanation of this widespread shift, the brilliant American critic Joseph Frank, in drawing historical trends, perceptively relates it to man's changing attitude towards life around him. When mankind confidently understands his universe, he feels able to present it in depth—seeing experience in various planes—and in time. In contrast, two dimensional form arises, Frank believes, "when the relationship between man and the cosmos is one of disharmony and disequilibrium," and, as in our time, man loses "control over the meaning and purpose of life [especially] amidst the continuing triumphs of science and technics." Another theorist, Marshall McLuhan in his *Understanding Media,* attributes the rise of discontinuous spatial form to technological development: as the printing press shaped an area of narrative form, so electronic instruments of communication create the age of spatial form. "Electricity," he writes, "ended sequence by making things instant," adding that "the movie medium [represents] a transition from lineal connections to configurations." The physical sciences, too, in the Quantum theory, insist that traditional concepts of linear causality are undemonstrable and irrelevant. In sum, Frank's and McLuhan's analyses complement each other; for both suggest that, although much recent art may not explicitly describe the contemporary world, it cannot help but reflect it.

At the same time that they embody extensions of the modernist tradition, each of the new American arts has rebelled against entrenched hierarchies dominant, in most cases, in the early and middle fifties; for as the era of Universal Threat replaced that of the Cold War, new artists, keyed to a new sensibility, sought to overthrow their artistic step-fathers, often pursuing to unprecedented lengths the impulse to rebel. In cinema, the enemy was that complex of clichés we call Hollywood; in painting, out of the lull that fell over art about 1955 with the decline of what Clement Greenberg christened Painterly Abstraction, arose the new styles of Jasper Johns, Pop art and others. In theatre, Albee, The Living Theatre's playwrights and others have reacted against the psychology of Tennessee Williams and the sociology of Arthur Miller, while the new novelists conspicuously avoid creating a hero for our time or conducting a search for one. The best contemporary composers, such as Elliott Carter, Stepan Wolpe, Salvatore Martirano and the very young Charles Wuorinen, reject at one extreme the dogmatic chance and formlessness of Cage and his followers and, on the other, European total serialism and American neo-classical developmental styles (of Samuel Barber and the like) for a music that intelligently exploits the entire range of musical possibility, while the new dance discards the conventions of movement and the dependence upon an extrinsic subject for a dance of pure form and total possibility of movement. When Merce Cunningham says he wants "to make a space in which anything can happen," the dancer James Waring echoes him with, "I try to get rid of ideas and the Self. I don't like metaphor, or symbolism."

In the same spirit, some artists have endeavored to dismiss the categories of art (and thus the divisions of this book) as irrelevant by fusing two or more arts into a single whole—Rauschenberg's "combines" link painting and sculpture, "happenings" are theatre, music, dance and sometimes painting, *The Connection* and *The Brig* produce an original synthesis of drama and music. Sometimes, the artist's motives in creating combinations are ironic—Max Kozloff likens some happenings to "the Wagnerian dream of synthesis of the art upon which has been superimposed junk culture." Reflecting, more modestly, the same impulse toward cross-fertilization, some artists have taken the esthetic ideas from other arts and applied them to their own, producing abstract poetry, chance dance, a serially organized novel, and the like.

As the revolutions got underway, in most of the arts there was a moment of conflict as the old challenged the new—when the new was condemned as "anti-art" and, in turn, the old as decadent and irrelevant; but as soon as the issues were drawn, the younger audience championed the new. Indicatively, all the major young American drama critics were enthusiastic about *The Brig* and, in unison, severely criticized Arthur Miller's *After The Fall;* and the new works in other arts received parallel critical responses. Thus, there is good reason to believe that the audience which enthusiastically supports new works today is comprised of a following considerably different from that which admired the new works of, say, fifteen years ago. All too often, one encounters a devotee of Arthur Miller who detests Albee and The Living Theatre, a fan of Martha Graham who walks out on Merce Cunningham, an *aficionado* of Hemingway who "can't read" *The Moviegoer* or *Catch-22,* or, even more tellingly, an admirer of the thirties' and forties' Aaron Copland who is put off by his recent, more complex serial works, *Piano Fantasy* (1957) and *Connotations for Orchestra* (1962); for the new works initiate not only a shift in style but also a change in the audience.

Not only do the young seem to comprehend the formal revolutions embodied in Pynchon's *V.* and *The Connection* with an ease that often baffles their elders, they also appear to have a strong sympathy for the content of new art. For instance, the totally negative sensibility—so thoroughly dissentient it finds nothing but the act of truth-telling worthy of loyalty or admiration—which some older critics and, more typically, parents find objectionable, is precisely the quality that the younger generation finds so attractive in *Who's Afraid of Virginia Woolf?* and *Dr. Strangelove,* in Nathanael West (revived in the late fifties to gain popularity in the sixties), the novels of John Barth and Joseph Heller and even the fad-nihilism of Terry Southern and Mason Hoffenberg's *Candy* and knee-jerk-No literary critics such as Dwight Macdonald. To the young audience, so many of whom since early youth guffawed at the sentimentalities of Hollywood and whose sensibilities were honed on *Mad,* an acute, truly felt nay-saying offers the most immediately satisfactory explanation of their experience.

Coupled to this critical, negative attitude toward life today, contemporary artists express an irreverence toward tradition. Whereas the writers and artists of, say, forty years ago would use the technique of quotation, as T. S. Eliot did in *The Waste Land* and Charles Ives in his Second Symphony, largely to weave resonant motifs into their work, almost all quotations in the best recent work function, often comically, as irony. From John Barth whose references to history in *The Sot-Weed Factor* are inverted or ridiculously distorted, to Stanley Kubrick who juxtaposes the quoted Hollywood cliché of the cripple who learns to walk against a thermonuclear explosion, to Jack Smith who in *Flaming Creatures* has transvestites enact stock cinematic situations, to John Cage who indiscriminately mixes quoted noise (sometimes identifiable music) with nondescript sounds, to Kenneth Koch, Arthur L. Kopit, and the Pop artists, all of whom show an affinity with French 'pataphysics ("The science of imaginary [i.e., parody] solutions."), the art of the past, just like the external scene, is so ludicrously irrelevant that it is used, in the Eliotic sense, largely as fuel for irony.

As they are unable to speak through the past to the present, so the major recent artists (except for some of the film-makers and poets, and William Burroughs in his early works) do not employ art as a vehicle for pure self-expression. They believe that art is a craftsman's product, to be put together consciously and critically, often to employ pre-determined esthetic and thematic ideas, that it reflects more upon itself than upon its author or external reality, evoking symbols rather than images of meaning; therefore, because it resists immediate assimilation, it must be interpreted, often in a multiplicity of ways, before it is truly understood. As the English critic David Sylvester perceptively noted in an essay on Pop art, "Modern artists . . . use art as a form of meditation about art and its relation to reality." In muffling their own voice to speak wholly through the mask of artistic form, often with techniques of irony, these artists do not believe their work can have any extra-esthetic effect upon their audience, repudiating again and perhaps once and for all the heresy that swept over and nearly choked American arts in the 1930's. Quite consistently, then, those recent artists who find artistic examples in the American past, draw from pre-1930's culture—playwrights and poets from Cummings and Eliot, composers from Ives and early Varèse, and painters from Marcel Duchamp (who has lived here nearly fifty years)—thus making themselves heirs to the artistically most fruitful decade in American history, the 1920's.

Most of the revolutions described in these essays started around 1958, and many artists presented their crucial opening or transitional works in the years 1959 and 1960: Elliott Carter's Second String Quartet, Milton Babbitt's *Vision and Prayer,* Barth's *The Sot-Weed Factor,* Albee's *The Zoo Story,* Jack Gelber's *The Connection,* Kenneth Koch's *Ko,* Robert Lowell's *Life Studies* and the first dances of the Judson Church choreographers. Moreover, two of the liveliest and most influential quarterlies of the sixties, *Contact* and *Tulane Drama Review,* published their first issues in 1958. The explanation of this blossoming would seem to lie in two historical changes—one domestic, the other international—in the years just preceding 1959 which probably affected every sensitive American. By the late fifties, the constrictive forces we call McCarthyism had weakened considerably, to reduce the general nervousness over individualized expression and non-conformity that plagued creative Americans in the early fifties. The second event was the rise of Sputnik in October, 1957, which, with a variety of other incidents, influenced the change in our attitudes to world politics from *we-they* (i.e., us and Russia), probably the dominant mode of political understanding since the rise of Hitler and the revelations of Nazi atrocities, to *it-us,* "it" being thermonuclear holocaust and "us" *all* the world's peoples. At this time, most of us became aware that the predicament of contemporary man was universal—since all of us could in a few swipes be erased from the earth, we-they distinctions, even in lesser social affairs, became less relevant. One recognized that in a world cemented to peace by a genuine balance of power—an equal capacity to threaten and retaliate—the two major powers are now ultimately more dependent upon a tacit trust in each other than upon faith in their allies. Just as Khrushchev became in 1959 the first Russian supreme leader to set foot in the United States, so in 1960 appeared Herman Kahn's *On Thermonuclear War* which, more than any other book, clarified the new world situation. In this same vein, much narrative literature of the 1960's, from *Virginia Woolf* though Peter Kass and Ed Emshwiller's movie *Time of the Heathen* to *Catch-22,* refuses to suggest that one person's predicament is less critical than another's. (The exception is that strain of cinema which, in dealing with domestic issues of outsiders and civil rights, finds good reasons for seeing the world as we-they.) These historical forces which produced a shift in moral emphasis, coupled with lack of sympathy for the directions of art in the recent past, led artists, particularly younger ones, to work out new ways of dealing with the formal problems of art and of looking at the reality around them.

Just as world politics seem to be in fast flux in the mid-sixties, with the patterns of authority and loyalty being constantly realigned and an endless series of minor crises continually threatening precarious balances, so the world of American arts is permeated with varied and sprawling activity—energies extending in all directions, numerous schools (with a few members) forming and dissolving, practitioners gaining enthusiastic, but limited and often temporary, followings; so that the scene as a whole resembles, in contrast to the programmed production line around us, a primitive workshop where everyone is off in his own cubbyhole doing his own work. In art, times of flux are times of ferment; and although any final evaluations should be held in abeyance, I would say that the past six years of American art have witnessed an expansion of artistic possibility and of relations within that increased range, as well as numerous works of originality and substance. These years were considerably more fruitful than the preceding half-dozen, and tentatively I would say we are passing through a period of a minor renaissance in our culture.

IV

> It is hard to hear a new voice, as hard as it is to listen to an unknown language.
>
> D. H. Lawrence, *Studies in Classic American Literature* (1924)

What separates the practicing critic from the scholar is that while the scholar is the custodian of the defined tradition, the former, aware of the tradition, yet committed to his own intuition for judgments, focuses upon the present. The mark of the true critic becomes his eagerness to face the multiple problems posed by recent art and to understand them as well as he is able. "A critic worthy of the name," in Henri Peyre's words, "must also venture into the danger zone of new works as yet untried, apply on them his ingenious methods of text analysis, discover their relations with the traditional currents in which they will be inserted, but also perceive them in their newness and originality. To refuse this task or to fulfill it with too glaring inadequacy is, in our eyes, tantamount to confessing that the would-be critic is not equipped with the lucidity and the courage which are the primary requisites of his profession." Here Peyre prefigures the challenge that each of the following critics accepted and indicates the scope of understanding the reader may expect of their essays.

To modify Peyre, nonetheless, I would argue that, for many reasons, the task of dealing critically with new work is best handled by the younger critic who, less committed to certain old styles and ideas of how art should function and more attuned to the *Zeitgeist*, is more likely to recognize and explain perceptively the original form and content the new art takes. In contrast, older critics often exhibit a reluctance to discuss the new. Edmund Wilson, probably the greatest practicing critic we have ever had in America, who so shrewdly placed and illuminated the writing of the 1920's, has rarely written on the imaginative literature of the past twenty years; nor have the other major critics of his generation, or even those ten to fifteen years younger than he, rigorously confronted post-War II writing. Many a younger critic hardly touches upon the very recent scene; for instance, Leslie A. Fiedler, whose essays so brilliantly defined the culture of the fifties, barely mentions the figures of the sixties in a recent book on the "contemporary" scene. And even when they do discuss important recent work, older writers often fail to grasp its distinctive character. Robert Brustein, surely an intelligent critic, in his review of *The Connection* spoke of it as an extension of naturalistic theatre, using an academic label that only slightly fitted and hardly described the work at hand. A discerning newspaper reviewer, Walter Kerr, dismissed *The Brig* for lacking the dramatic form of conventional theatre, and not so long ago an art critic discussed Jackson Pollock's work as primarily "decorative." In other arts, too, one would not need to comb the sandy wastes too deeply to find critics who are unwilling, or unable, to discuss the present except in terms applicable only to the past.

For these reasons, our greatest books and essays on the recent revolutions in arts are written by men under forty, often thirty-five, and even under thirty. What Stanley Edgar Hyman did at twenty-nine in *The Armed Vision* towards defining the uncharted territory of the recent development of sophisticated criticism, Irving Howe did at thirty-two for *William Faulkner* (1952), Edmund Wilson did at thirty-six for the literature of the twenties in *Axel's Castle* (1931) and H. L. Mencken in his thirties did some fifteen years before him for an earlier new literature. Likewise, some twenty years ago, Alfred Kazin, then in his twenties, defined the recent phase of American prose literature in *On Native Grounds* (1942) and Randall Jarrell, recent American poetry in "The End of the Line" (1942); while Joseph Frank, also in his twenties, wrote in "Spatial Form in Modern Literature" (1944) one of the seminal essays on the modern sensibility. In the years following, each of these men did excellent work on pre-contemporary literature, for the coin of critical insight has its other side—the best books on classics and classical problems are written by men over forty.

To accomplish his task, the young critic must first rid himself of constricting prejudices which others, particularly older critics and some contemporary practitioners, will foist on him. These enemies of open-mindedness generally don one of three guises: of the conservative, the revisionist and the saint. The first insists that there are eternal rules for each art and that if an artwork is to be good and to be taken seriously it must conform to these rules. For example, an eminent musicologist, Leonard Meyer, recently complained that chance music is bad because it denies the artist the creative authority he always had in the past and, therefore, that purely empirical criticism, which judges chance music solely by how well it sounds, is also wrongheaded because it fails to deal with what Meyer felt is the true issue, the hand of the author's control. Likewise, John Simon, in reviewing a recent collection of John Ashbery's poetry, ruled that since his lines did not read with the coherence of James Dickey's more conventional verse, then his work was not poetry. Again, Mary McCarthy, presaging her own conservative novel, recently wrote that fiction is defined by the interaction of character, that the good novel contains many full characters, and the best novelist is he who creates a wide variety of characters; in practice, these criteria are hardly applicable to the great literature of the twentieth century. Historically, art continues to change, leaving conservative critics behind, their hands clutching their bags full of rules.

Distinguishing himself from the reactionary, the revisionist critic accepts the modernist revolutions; but he insists that since they lost their energy yesterday or the day before, now is the time for young artists to stop trying to be new and capitalize on the advances already made. "What we need now in literature and in the arts," Cecil Hemley wrote in *New World Writing* in 1957, "is a revolt against revolt." He continued, "Half a century of revolution has brought us to the limits of art, by which I mean the radical, ultimate technical limits," and seven years later, we can say that artists have continued to undermine Mr. Hemley's sense of limits. The point is that there probably are no limits on artistic possibility, just as there are no limits upon the streams of the tradition or combinations of them from which the artist may draw; thus, neither the conservative nor the revisionist positions have any effect upon the working avant-garde artist.

The artists themselves, particularly the avant-garde ones, often propagate the apology of the saint—that holy motives place them above criticism. The creator of art so radically new, so much the vehicle of History, the "saint" claims that no critic for at least ten years, or until the artist's death, could possibly understand his work or, even more foolishly, try to discriminate between his successes and his failures. In suggesting that the final word about the new in art will not be uttered by a critic writing today, the saint has a point. No critic ever has the last word. Nonetheless, his complaint should not discourage first remarks which, one hopes, will induce other critics to set down the second and the third.

In each of the essays here, the critics, all under 35 and eminently qualified, attempt to distinguish and define new trends in their areas of interest and to describe and evaluate the individual artists within these trends, to identify and analyze the intelligible forms and expressed content of the major works (or cry foul, should they not exist or be deficient), to set the new achievements in their historical and esthetic contexts; so as to provide a full, discriminating picture of the most original and significant activity today. The critics attempt to eschew critical and technical jargon, so that a reader interested in, say, painting will see in the essays on music and dance how similar esthetic ideas are used and be able to place the achievement of painting in the larger perspective of American art today. Each critic has discovered works of art whose intrinsic worth, in addition to their newness, merits the attention of the cultured American audience. Each critic endeavors to discern what is characteristically American about the major figures and works in his area, to define how changes in his art reflect esthetic and technological developments and the unprecedented situation of mankind in the post-Sputnik age, and to set the American scene in the context of foreign achievements and directions. Within this framework, each contributor presents his own findings, his choices and judgments; they do not necessarily represent those of the editor or of his colleagues. Nonetheless, in our discussions we discovered that the areas of insoluble disagreement were notably few. Finally, *The New American Arts* has a twofold purpose—to be informative, to describe the important contemporary figures and introduce us to their work; to be critical, to help us comprehend and evaluate the new trends and works in the American arts today.

Richard Kostelanetz
New York, New York
May 14, 1964

P.S. All dates in the text refer to first publication or presentation, not to date of composition. We wish to thank Ben Raeburn and Marcia Cavell of Horizon Press for their generous aid and constant encouragement, the editors of *Contact, Texas Quarterly* and *Stand* for permission to reprint sections of the essay on theatre, Avon Books, the publisher of *On Contemporary Literature,* for permission to reprint paragraphs included in the essays on fiction and poetry, and *The New York Herald Tribune* to reprint fragments in the essay on music; and the many publishers and poets who gave us permission to use quotations from their texts.

R. K.

THE NEW AMERICAN

FILM

HARRIS DIENSTFREY

I

For roughly forty years, the American movie meant Hollywood; and Hollywood, as the River Rouge of mass entertainment, meant the studio system. The only way to make a feature film was to be part of the movie industry, and the industry existed in only one location. Product, process, and place were inseparably joined. All three together seemed as eternal as the stars themselves, until, in the early fifties, things suddenly began to fall apart.

There had been auguries of the coming break-up. After the second world war, it became evident that the genres—Westerns, musicals, gangster and private-eye pictures—which constituted Hollywood's stock-in-trade (at once its great achievement and its severe limitation) were drawing smaller audiences. In response, the industry cast about for new themes, subjects, formats, a search whose main result was a series of relatively new gimmicks: 3-D and a variety of expanded, differently proportioned screens usually outfitted with stereophonic sound system and, in one case, a mechanism that manufactured odors.

Amid all this hardware, the large screen (like sound itself, also originally introduced as a box-office palliative) has turned out to be considerably more than a gimmick. The changed proportions, giving rise to a fundamentally new relationship between figures and background, have intrigued serious and talented directors throughout the world, from Japan's Akira Kurosawa to France's Jean-Luc Godard to America's George Stevens. (An excellent discussion of the large screen is contained in Charles Barr's "Cinemascope: Before and After," *Film Quarterly,* Summer, 1963.)

But Hollywood's audience continued to dwindle, and as if to add insult to injury, the popularity of foreign films gradually began to increase. The two trends did not proceed in a neatly inverse proportion, but their meaning was quite clear. The first successful foreign films were those of the Italian neo-realists who deliberately forsook plot and subtle characterizations to re-create the conditions of life during and immediately after the war. The most popular achievements of neo-realism—Vittorio DeSica's *Shoeshine* and *The Bicycle Thief,* and Roberto Rossellini's *Paisan* and *Open City*— often confused self-pity with compassion and working class sympathies with social analysis, yet their documentary style planted a seed that was to blossom as a new genus some half dozen years later in the work of the independent American movie makers.

The next foreign films to find substantial commercial success on American screens, providing one of those unanticipated 180 degree shifts in popular taste whose causes are always easy to postulate after the fact, were the stylized English comedies which drew much of their humor from a toothless mocking of the English class system—as in *Kind Hearts and Coronets*—and often starred Margaret Rutherford or Alec Guinness, who seemed to play approximately two and a half roles per picture. The success of two such different types of films began the "art house" boom. It was another portent.

In the early fifties, the portents became realities, and the American movie industry was suddenly at bay. The immediate agent was television, which became nationwide in 1951 and during the next few years proceeded to devastate the great duchy of Hollywood as though it had been only the *papier-mâché* fiction of a back studio lot. The average weekly movie audience was cut in half (from 90,000,000 after the war to 45,000,000 some ten years later); the remains of the great Hollywood genres, notably the Western, found a new home in the co-axial cable; and the "B" picture, an essential financial prop of the industry, simply died. The studio system tottered; Hollywood tottered; the American film tottered.

The audience that formerly had responded as a mass, with several small groups on occasion casting protest ballots, now had become a shifting plurality of relatively equal blocs, forming a spectrum of taste that extended from fans of Jerry Lewis to devotees of Ingmar Bergman to lovers of Busby Berkeley musicals. The American film suddenly found itself with viewers who picked and chose much as the book-buying public did. The old assembly line could no longer sustain itself, and collapsed.

Though studios still physically exist in Hollywood, most of them are used for television production—as good a measure as any of how the movies have changed and what television has become. The old companies are now substantially only legal entities: financing and distributing units which contract out for their product with individual suppliers. The factories have become offices, and even the exhibition system that had evolved in response to studio production is slowly changing. Now theatres are beginning to accommodate themselves to their diverse public in much the way that magazines do. Just as there are quality and slick magazines, so there are art houses and neighborhood theatres.

II

Of course not all the old Hollywood of stars and genres has faded away; probably it never will. At the moment, the most obvious of its remnants is the giant blockbusting spectacle that swoopingly relates the rise of a religion or the fall of a nation in some three to four hours. But even stars and genres are no longer quite what they were. The blockbuster's international cast is a sign of the extent to which many contemporary movies are just one more item of the common market.

The most important development to emerge from the changed conditions of movie-making in the United States is the appearance of pictures created not by studios for a mass audience but by individual directors who conceive of them as expressions of their own interests and concerns. American films of this sort certainly have been made before. The work of Chaplin, Stroheim, and Welles spring immediately to mind. But these directors hardly constitute the rule. Nor should such an illustrious list be taken to mean that the current films comparable to them in nature are comparable also in quality or, just as important, necessarily better than their studio predecessors. In terms of verve, cinematic skill, a kind of mythic resonance, and sheer imaginativeness, the achievement of the old Hollywood is among the richest in film history, and stands in and of itself as a remarkable creative accomplishment. The new development essentially means that as a matter of course more and more pictures, their quality another issue entirely, now speak in both their theme and execution with the voice of a single man. In a phrase, the personal vision has supplanted the public one.

Among the younger directors whose work has contributed to this development, four deserve special attention. The first is Arthur Penn, who comes to film-making from a fully developed career as both a television and stage director. Perhaps his non-cinematic experience heightened his sensitivity to the possibilities of the film medium as such, for his films reveal a sensibility fascinated by these possibilities and consciously seeking to exploit them.

His first picture, *The Left-Handed Gun* (1958), was another retelling of the story of Billy the Kid, but this time with the emphasis on the nature of his behavior and its significance. The difficulty with this very impressive film, whose verbal and visual symbols keep reflecting back on the action to reveal the different facets of its meaning, is that its two major themes—Billy as an individual with the impulses of a child but the power of an adult, and the self-delusion of a culture that treats such a figure as a hero—never come together. The picture has no center. Penn finally seems un-

sure as to what it is he wants to say about the issues the film poses
so forcefully.

His second picture, *The Miracle Worker* (1962), is a much
more integral work, though its subject matter, an episode from the
childhood of Helen Keller, is far less interesting. The film has a
carefully studied beauty—Penn has an elegant eye—and it demonstrates his ability to present a story in the round, rather as if it were
displaying a piece of sculpture from all sides, and also to evoke brilliant individual performances within the framework of ensemble
acting. Yet again one has the sense that the director has not drawn
very deeply on his own thoughts and emotions. Perhaps his next
film—*Mickey One,* which Penn describes as dealing with a contemporary man who feels himself psychologically displaced—will
exact the kind of ultimate commitment without which a work of
the imagination can rarely become more than an exercise of craft.

By far the best known of the younger American directors—
and the most brilliant as well as the most complex—is Stanley
Kubrick, whose career has followed a pattern characteristic of
many film makers. His first two pictures he financed with funds he
raised himself, *Fear and Desire* (1953), an avant-garde amalgam
of sex and war, and *Killer's Kiss* (1955), an amalgam of sex and
the underworld, highlighted by a stunning sequence in a warehouse
filled with mannequins, where two men with axes attempt to kill
each other. Those pictures rated him enough attention to gain the
support of a commercial studio, under whose auspices he made
The Killing (1956), the story of a race-track robbery, which in
turn was sufficiently successful to springboard him into the first of
those films which constitute his own choice of subject and treatment and bear that coolness of temperament which is peculiarly his.

All of Kubrick's work after *The Killing* offers a certain aura of
political or social protest. (Though this is true of *Spartacus,* 1960,
Kubrick, hired to direct it, has said he made the film for money.)
Paths of Glory (1957) is in part an anti-war film, *Lolita* (1962)
sympathetically portrays the relationship between Humbert Humbert and his nymphet, and *Dr. Strangelove* (1964) is in a general
way anti-bomb. Yet Kubrick's sensibility seems less held by par-

ticular causes than by the sheer perversity in men and the extremities toward which their beliefs and desires carry them. In *Paths of Glory,* for example, Kubrick is much more comfortable dealing with the "sadistic" general who likes to enjoy himself and sees no reason to rock the boat than with the idealistic captain who seeks justice. The meticulous exactitude that marked this film, moreover, has been superseded in the ones to follow by a usually amused but always detached exploration of the genuinely idiosyncratic. Thus, *Lolita,* as Kubrick quite properly filmed it, is a love story in which the lovers are a spectacle so weirdly painful, simultaneously sad, cruel and witty, that one does not know whether to laugh or cry; and the bomb and its advocates in *Strangelove,* that black paean to integrity and personal commitment, are not so much an evil that must be eradicated for the good of humanity as the most contemporary metaphor for the madness of life in general.

Less known than either Kubrick or Penn is Irvin Kershner, who currently is in the process of passing from the direction of standard genre material to more personal films. In the late fifties, Kershner directed several exciting, skillfully constructed crime pictures (*Stake Out on Dope Street, The Young Captives*), and then in *The Hoodlum Priest* (1961) made a film clearly closer to his own interests. Based on fact, the picture describes the efforts of a Catholic priest to establish a halfway house where delinquents can live for a while after leaving jail. Like Truffaut, Kershner can give a scene life through the movement of a camera. By virtue of his cinematic inventiveness and vitality, he avoided most of the special pleading and social-work categorizing common to a film like *The Hoodlum Priest,* revealing his characters whole and as individual personalities.

The fourth of the young directors now working in the industry who calls for special note is Denis Sanders. With his brother (Terry) as producer, he has made two pictures each concerned with a young man reaching his way toward a moral commitment. If the first, *Crime and Punishment, U.S.A.* (1959), never succeeded in transplanting the fever of Dostoevsky to sunny California, it nonetheless was a serious attempt to portray the confusions and moral bewilderment of a contemporary. The second picture, *War Hunt* (1962), set in Korea, uncertainly aligned two situations that never properly connected. One concerned the introduction of a young soldier to war, the other the behavior of a psychopathic fellow soldier who blacks his face and goes out each night to kill the enemy. (After the cease fire, the psychopath runs away. To the Captain's statement that "the war is over," he replies, "There'll be another.") Yet the picture has a quiet respect for the details of both people and places, and at its best renders the experiences of its characters with a crystalline objectivity.

This list does not exhaust the group of younger directors currently seeking to develop their own voices, and all that this implies, within the world of commercial film-making. But it is large enough to indicate that the process has now become a natural and viable one in a setting where previously it had been allowed only a most marginal existence. Nothing else reflects so well the changes in organizational structure and audience that have overtaken the American film.

III

It is against this background that one must place the appearance since approximately 1958 of a scattered but populous community of "non-commercial" independent movie makers—several hundred at least—who have turned to film as naturally as earlier generations turned to novels or poetry. Mostly young, these filmmakers are "non-commercial" in the sense that they work entirely outside the regular system of finance and distribution. Arranging for regular commercial screenings of their films is usually as difficult for them as financing the films in the first place. They somewhat resemble the prototypical poet who lives and writes in a garret, then publishes his efforts in his own mimeographed broadside.

In so far as one can speak of these independent films as having a common esthetic, it is an esthetic of informality and spontaneity and naturalism run rampant. It is an esthetic that opposes the staged, the planned, the theatrical. But this really overformalizes a situation that at base is more anarchic.

Essentially, the independents are out to overturn the existing rules that constitute standard movie technique, in much the way that Jean-Luc Godard was when he shot most of *Breathless* with a hand-held camera. It is not revolution for the sake of revolution, a matter of simply thumbing one's nose at the cinematic establishment, but rather a serious attempt to extend the "grammar" of film. Most of the rules now in effect in the United States are those imposed by the conditions of studio production, a style of mechanical perfection and professionalism that has always been a hallmark of Hollywood and currently is most evident in the cycle of technicolor fantasies about high life on the Madison Avenue-suburbia circuit. These films (inevitably starring Doris Day or a reasonable facsimile thereof) look as if their decor, lighting, and actors have all gone through identical processes of beautification. The influence on the independents of the Italian neo-realists arose precisely because these directors took their cameras out of the studios and put them in the streets, thereby demonstrating the superfluity of the giant organizational complexity that was straightjacketing American movies. Through much the same logic, a large number of independents will hail virtually any homemade movie, no matter how clumsy or unconscious, as a work of historical importance because it represents another blow at the existing rules, another demonstration of film's variousness and individual accessibility.

But the impulse behind the independents is not just a formal one. They are also moved by their genuine love of the movies. Their predecessors—among them Maya Deren and Robert J. Flaherty (the latter's naturalistic techniques are another important influence)—tended to love Art or Man, but they themselves, whatever their other affections, affectations, or beliefs, love movies. In seeking to extend the formal and technical range of film, then, they are trying at the same time to imbue movies with their particular sense of the world, to take a mode of the imagination that has given them enormous pleasure and use it to serve their own imaginations. For many, it makes no difference where such a course leads; probably the further out the better. Thus, at one extreme, the independent film movement is simply a conglomeration of people who like to make movies about things they like, the cinematic equivalent, however bohemian its form, of Sunday painting. But at the other, it constitutes an attempt to open the movies directly onto contemporary experience and to express through them the life and world their makers know at first hand.

It is in the blending of documentary and fictional reality that many of the independents have found a style particularly congenial to their interests. One of the first such couplings was Sidney Meyers' *The Quiet One* (1952). Regarded as a documentary because it was built around a core of fact, it might better be considered a "reconstruction." Considerably aided by a delicate and compassionate script by James Agee, which gives to the film its overall tone and attitudes, it sensitively re-enacts the history and emotional rehabilitation of an introverted Negro boy.

The most important figure among the initial practitioners of this style of "fictional documentary," because he began with a fabrication, is Morris Engels, who has been making films in New York since the early fifties, and at present, reportedly is preparing an episode for an omnibus picture with the theme "children of the world." Engels is a plain-style poet of the urban neighborhood. All of his pictures are set in those small areas of New York City where the inhabitants know each other's names and problems and all shop at the same corner grocery. Engels treats New York as if it were filled with clusters of two- or three-block-long neighborhood communities. Mixing professional with non-professional actors, he tells his almost plotless stories about people of everyday familiarity (who, though they have become the staple of television drama, very rarely have been the subjects of films) against the daily life of the city. His first film, *The Little Fugitive* (1953), typically "stars" both Coney Island and a neighborhood of residential brownstones, as well as a small boy who runs away from home, which is to say, an apartment in one of the brownstones. Engels' succeeding films are similarly wrapped around other New York leisure-time amusements—in *Lovers and Lollipops* (1957), a trip to the Statue of

Liberty; in *Weddings and Babies* (1960), an Italian street festival. There is a sprightly charm to these pictures, and they always afford a constant visual pleasure, their physical setting is so solid and prosaically real. But a kind of emotional emaciation gradually lays them waste. Sentimentality takes the place of perception, and any orneriness or indecision in a character is labelled a childish, neurotic twitch. The characters thus become straw people, smoothly bland, set against a captivating background of concrete and mortar.

Engels represents an intriguing transition point in contemporary film. His low-budget, homely street movies have influenced the much more stylistically dazzling and inventive French "new wave," one of whose creators, François Truffaut, himself a skillful director of children, even went so far as to dub the American the "father" of the new wave. On the other hand, Engels himself learned a good deal from the Italian neo-realists, whose ideal was a film with no story at all. Politics aside, the highest aspiration of Italian neo-realism was a picture about average people experiencing the routine events of their daily lives, clearly Engels' objective as well.

It is precisely this emphasis on the average and routine that distinguishes Engels from most of the independents who followed him. Where he accepted society as given, they disdained it. Where he emphasized the typical and the modest, they focused on the marginal and the rebellious. When the cinematic "underground" burst into view at the end of the fifties, an entirely new phenomenon on the American scene, it spoke with the voice of the dissatisfied young.

IV

The film that did the most to herald the new coming was John Cassavetes' *Shadows,* made in 1958 but not distributed commercially until two years later. To film-makers and audiences, it was evidence that an integral movie with dramatic force could be made for the phenomenally small sum of $15,000 (part of it collected from the listeners of a New York "underground" radio program, a typical example of the unorthodox methods by which the independents manage to finance themselves). Particularly striking in view of *Shadows'* unity was Cassavetes' use of loose improvisation. No less of an achievement was the purely commercial fact that the picture got itself exhibited. The procedure has become a standard one for the independent film-makers—a screening at an international film festival that hopefully will evoke enough affirmative response to attract a commercial distributor. (Indeed, the comparative success of *Shadows* catapulted Cassavetes into Hollywood, where he formerly had been an actor, and where now he has directed two features, *Too Late Blues,* 1962, and *A Child Is Waiting,* 1963, both uneven attempts to weave various kinds of spontaneous and documentary-like reality into extremely theatrical plots.)

The New York of *Shadows* exists in an entirely different world from the New York of Engels' films. Here the setting is a raucous, slightly sinister 42nd street, jazz joints, bars. Mostly it is a nightmare world, but even in the day, the light has a heavy overcast. The camera's flat, grey images are those of a slightly abstracted city dweller who no longer consciously registers the streets and sights around him. One of the best things about *Shadows* is this natural matter-of-factness, and the wary ease with which its characters make their way through the urban landscape, careful but still very much at home.

Along with the change in setting has come a comparable change in tone and focus. The atmosphere is tinged with hostility and dissatisfaction, and the characters are all outsiders looking in —Negroes, beats, young people passing between adolescence and adulthood. They have love affairs, wander about the city, get into fights, try to earn a living. Everyone seems to be caught in a psychological no man's land between respectability and bohemianism, not sure which direction they want to take.

Much of *Shadows* is awkward and unconvincing. Its largely improvised dialogue often sounds like high school theatrics, and its dramatic climaxes usually manage to be both naïve and pretentious. But the film has a good feel for the indecisive, unhappy aimlessness of young people who find they do not quite fit the going society, a quality it transmits with particular keenness through the playing of Ben Carruthers as a young beat with lots of time and little notion of how to fill it. Carruthers, an intense actor who gives the impression of teetering on a thin edge between rage and laughter, is a perfect agent for the film's mixture of dissatisfaction and vitality.

The work of the independents offers only one major exception to the sympathetic concern with people on the margins of respectable society shown by *Shadows*. This is the journalistic documentary usually produced for television. Film-makers working in this area include Richard Leacock, Robert Drew, Don Pennebacker, and the Maysles brothers. The general approach of their documentaries (whose style has been given the name *cinéma vérité*) is to fix upon an individual whose activities have some topical interest and then follow him around with a hand-held camera. Such newsreel-like ventures aim at getting only the objective facts. They avoid all conscious interpretations and judgments. One of the best of these films—and like most, concerned with figures who could not be more "in"—is *Primary* (1960), which features Humphrey and Kennedy going through their paces in the Wisconsin presidential primary. A precise, absolutely non-partisan, noncommittal record of a politician's daily grind when running for office, the picture gains its fascination through its cornucopia of details and its off-stage glimpses of the candidates.

But except for these films, it is always the outsider who stands stagefront in the work of the independents, from the alienated American Indians of Kent MacKenzie's overly long, inadequately thought out labor of love, *The Exiles* (1958–61), to the burlesque dancer of Michael Putnam's *The Hard Swing* (1962), a careful piece of naturalism that neither sentimentalizes nor sensationalizes its subject nor moralizes about her audiences. It is characteristic that one of the few independent films concerned with politics should take as its subject people in conflict with the House Committee for Un-American Activities, Michael and Philip Burton's polemically unconvincing but alertly photographed *Wasn't That a Time* (1961).

The social attitudes that underlie most of these films get their most forceful and direct expression in *Sunday* (1961), an angry

and energetic fifteen-minute short by Dan Drasin. Shot entirely on
the spot during an afternoon rally protesting a municipal decision
to close off a park in New York City to Sunday folk singers, the
picture leaves no doubt about its sympathies. Under its opening
images of folk singers gathering for the rally, the sound track plays
"This Land Is My Land" (probably recorded sometime later in
the protest).

Drasin has explained that at times he marched and sang along
with the protestors, photographing as he went. For all his enthu-
siasm, he was still alive to the humor of the situation. The examples
of youthful earnestness caught on *Sunday's* sound track speak for
themselves: "They just want to kill the Village." "It's all a plot of
the real estate interests." When the demonstrators form a singing
march around the park (the tension between them and the police
clearly rising), a voice notes as if in defiant explanation of such a
non-violent maneuver: "Gandhi always was a big influence."

The rally finally explodes, and in the melee that follows—the
riot squad that has been pouring into the park manhandles several
demonstrators and haul a few off to jail—*Sunday* makes its point
unmistakably clear. Drasin, who was only eighteen when he made
the short, transforms the crowd into a collective hero, the police
and city officials into the Enemy. For a few moments, one sees a
minor pitched battle in the Great War between the Bureaucrats
and the People, the State and the Citizen—between them and us.

In a number of the new pictures, the stance is much more
militant, the tone considerably shriller. One such film is Edward
Bland's *The Cry of Jazz* (1958), a racist documentary turned backwards, with Negroes alive and vibrant, whites decadent and
doomed. Another is Sidney Meyers' *The Savage Eye* (1959), a film
able to find in anything at all, gambling, weight-reducing, or watching a strip-tease, a sign of the virulent corruption presumably at
the core of American society. Finally, there are Shirley Clarke's
two features, *The Connection* (1961) and *The Cool World* (1964),
both of which tend to reach their highest emotional peaks when
belittling strawman symbols of the middle class. The thesis in all
of these pictures is a procrustean bed to which everything else is

trimmed, including members of the audience, who are put in the position of either agreeing with the thesis or finding themselves stamped moral idiots.

But the best among the independent films bear witness rather than hurl imprecations, and two of the most impressive must still be mentioned. The first is Peter Kass and Ed Emshwiller's *Time of the Heathen* (1960), a film that despite its shortcomings (not content with examining the horrors of atomic violence it takes on those of racial prejudice as well) achieves in sequences of remarkable intensity a rare union of idea and visual form. The picture also contains a brilliant performance by the young actor, John Heffernan, who plays its emotionally crippled protagonist, a former air force pilot connected with the dropping of the A-bomb.

The second film, probably the only new work to take its subject from outside the United States, is Lionel Rogosin's *Come Back, Africa* (1959), whose mere existence is something of an achievement. The South African government gave Rogosin permission to film a documentary about native music. His actual intent was a picture "concerned essentially with human conditions as they exist in the Union of South Africa under the ruthless policy of the present regime." Ironically, the sequences of native music that he did film, among them penny whistlers on the streets of Johannesburg and a wedding procession winding through the native quarters, provide a leitmotif showing the one way the natives achieve a freedom denied to them in every other area of life.

Come Back, Africa is a vividly successful demonstration of the whole panoply of improvisational, documentary-like techniques which have become the staple of the independent film-makers. The cast was almost entirely non-professional, the story was "neither purely factual nor really fictional," the dialogue was devised largely by the cast itself. Rogosin discusses his reasons for using these methods in "Interpreting Reality" (*Film Culture*, No. 21, 1960), the most intelligent analysis of the "improvisational style" yet to appear. Particularly revealing are his comments on how he filled the leading role, that of a Zulu who comes to Johannesburg looking for work. Rogosin first tried professional actors, but they were

all unsatisfactory—too "American," he writes. He then decided
the film needed a tribal African whose biography more or less
duplicated that of the imagined hero. The man he chose was so
new to city life that making a film "bewildered and frightened" him.
Rogosin finally decided just to watch faces.

> I was convinced I had to cast the hero by concentrating on faces,
> letting them pass before me by the hundreds until the single "per-
> fect" one would somehow turn up and I would somehow rec-
> ognize him. . . . I went on a search of Africans lined up at the bus
> queues. . . . I went . . . to the railroad stations. Then suddenly,
> as if out of nowhere, I saw the face of the man I wanted. . . . The
> man we later got to know as Zachariah . . . was certain we were
> the police.

Rather magically, it turned out that "Zachariah's character and
background fit perfectly into my image of the film's protagonist."
In a sense, then, *Come Back, Africa* is the story of Zachariah
himself.

Unlike many of the new films, the ultimate emotional effect
of *Come Back, Africa* is close to pity and terror. Rogosin shows a
society moving toward a convulsion that seems destined to tear it
apart. Several times in the picture, one sees thousands of natives
pouring out of the subway into Johannesburg. One observes the
bland, reserved faces (and notes the occasional startled look of
someone who suddenly spies the camera watching him) and the
obedient, automaton-like men heading for their work, and it is clear
one is seeing an army whose uniform is the pigment of its skin.

At the end of the picture, Zachariah, who has spent the night
in jail for having been discovered asleep with his wife in the serv-
ant quarters of her white employers (against South African law),
returns home to find her dead. She has been strangled, the audience
knows, by a "renegade" African. But the immediate cause of her
death is relatively unimportant, a meaningless contingency in a
sense. It, or something equally terrible, was inevitable, regardless
of the hands that actually brought it about. The stark last scene of
the picture is unforgettable: Zachariah wailing in blind anguish,
pounding the rickety table in his single room shack. Then, under

the sound of his rage comes the sound of an army of people pouring from the subway station. This scene contains the future, and its character is terrible to imagine.

v

With the fantasies of the new film-makers, one moves to a different realm, where the air is headier and scenes of contemporary life give way to filigree imaginings. The general mode is the same, improvisational and plotless, but the texture is quite different. Where the "documentaries" are kin to the daily newspaper, the "fantasies" belong to the world of the private diary, most often those invented out of whole cloth.

The best of the "fantasies" is *Pull My Daisy* (1959), a half-hour short by Robert Frank and Alfred Leslie. Narrated more or less spontaneously by Jack Kerouac, the film is a boozy, boisterous, good-humored homage to the natural man, beat variety—and entirely lovely. Few pictures have rendered light with such frothy delicacy (Jacques Demy's *Lola* is another) or discovered beauty in everyday objects so unselfconsciously.

Set in "this loft that's in the bowery in the lower east side, new york" (Kerouac's commentary has been published in an Evergreen paperback), *Pull My Daisy* belongs to the grand tradition of *épater les bourgeois,* though, in this instance, "bourgeois" should be read as "women." Two beats—Allen Ginsberg and Gregory Corso, charter members of the beat pantheon—drop in to visit their friend Milo (played by the artist, Larry Rivers). He is still away at work, so they spend their time smoking marihuana, composing wacky poems, and engaging in maniacal Socratic conversations. Milo's wife, meanwhile, persists in preparing for a visit from a street-corner bishop. When Milo comes home, he unconcernedly brings another beat. By the time the bishop arrives, bearing in tow a feminine entourage of heavily corseted mother and spinster-cold sister, the beats are higher than ever, giggling, happy, friendly as pets. The camera is much the same.

The beats ask the bishop some "really serious questions." "Is ignorance rippling up above the silver ladder of sherifian doves?

. . . Is alligators holy, bishop? . . . Is all the white moonlight holy? . . . Is holy holy?" The bishop comes up with what might be considered a felicitously Zen-like reply—"I think it's best that I go now and make my holy offices"—and leaves. The wife, boiling angry, throws everyone out. But what does it matter to Milo and his friends? They bounce down the loft stairs, instinctive enemies of female commissars and the middle-class way of anti-life. "Let's go," Kerouac exclaims, " 'sgo. 'sgo. . . . Off they go."

In recent years, the devotion to fantasy among the independents has become more and more pronounced. With the establishment around 1962 of the Film-Maker's Cooperative in New York City, those working in this mode have acquired an extremely vocal and active organization to distribute and publicize their films. The turn from hyper-naturalism to fantasy might be pinpointed within a single film, Jonas Mekas' *Guns of the Trees* (1961), which almost programmatically alternates one with the other. (Mekas is a founder of the Film-Maker's Cooperative, and through his magazine *Film Culture* and his column in *The Village Voice,* is the independent film movement's foremost publicist.) *Guns of the Trees* indulges in some sophomoric film symbolism and "poetry," but the intensity of its rebellious social anger is nearly enough to make up for its weaknesses. Two years after *Guns of the Trees,* Mekas' brother, Adolfas, made *Hallelujah the Hills,* an airy (sometimes too thinly so), anarchistic fantasy, happily devoted to the proposition that life is joy.

In the most extreme of the new fantasies, the private world of the movie maker is the only one visible, and the viewer must translate it back into his own as if he were dealing with a kind of hieroglyphic. A *cause célèbre* among such "pure fantasies" is Jack Smith's *Flaming Creatures* (1963), a picture refused various public showings (in Brussels and New York) because it devotes a sizable portion of its approximately fifty minutes running time to regaling the audience with a large assortment of waving penises and testicles and now and then a bouncing balloon-like breast or two.

Flaming Creatures is inventive, often lovely, and alternately funny and boring. There is no adequate way to describe it without implying that it has more form than it actually has—that is, very little. In general design, it is a collection of stock situations from Hollywood "B" films—the vampire rising from its coffin; the castanet-clicking, mascara-dripping Spanish dancer in a sailor's port; the near rape of the defenseless heroine apparently cut off from rescue by an avalanche (here, help never does get through)—all enacted by transvestites and a single woman. Mocking neither its subject nor its players, *Flaming Creatures* is something like a musical comedy view of the blissful lunacy of sexual perversity, as well as an homage to a neighborhood circuit movie queen like Maria Montez (whom Smith has apotheosized in an insightfully wacky article called "The Perfect Filmic Appositeness of Maria Montez," *Film Culture,* No. 27, Winter 1962–3).

One trait of the "pure fantasy" is its attempt to subordinate action to emotion, defining the character of the former, in so far as it exists, by the latter. The rape-orgy sequence in *Flaming Creatures* is one of the few instances where the attempt is completely successful. A girl, flat on her back, is being mauled in about a half dozen ways by as many transvestites. Horrific screams, slightly muted, fill the sound track. One of the girl's breasts is bare, and is jounced up and down throughout the sequence. The camera moves nonchalantly from bird's eye views of the assault to head-on closeups of a hand shaking a penis to shots of a chandelier trembling over the whole shattering event. It all manages to be quite childlike in spirit and tone. Like the beats in *Pull My Daisy,* the transvestites (and the protagonists of other fantasies, such as Vernon Zimmerman's *Lemon Hearts* and Ron Rice's *The Flower Thief*) are exemplars of innocence and true feeling.

But for every such sequence in one film that succeeds, one can point to a half dozen in an equal number of pictures that do not. The pure fantasies, by far the least successful development of the independents, usually wind up being exercises in low-grade solipsism. Products of a contemporary romanticism, they assume that the expression of a sincere emotion automatically induces in viewers a convincing and valuable emotional experience. To the maker of the pure fantasy, one need only express one's "true" feelings, and everything else will take care of itself. In *Flaming Creatures,* for example, it is obvious that everyone connected with making the picture had enormous fun. This delight is meant to play a prominent part in the film's enjoyment. But to see people having a marvelous time is hardly the same thing as having a marvelous time oneself or, indeed, as even finding theirs worth watching.

VI

There is little point in trying to guess where the independent film movement will go from here. The issue contains too many imponderables. How many of the new film-makers, having found they really can make movies, have anything meaningful to say and the long-range devotion and talent to say it? To what extent might the independents stifle themselves by coterie snobbishness, or uninformed, unexamined social anger? When will both the "underground" and the "commercial" independents become more aware of the different burdens and freedoms placed on each by their separate types of audiences?

The only certain fact is that the independents outside the commercial orbit are now a permanent part of the cultural landscape. The forces that produced the "new wave" in France, the "free cinema" group in England and comparable constellations, as yet without the benefit of journalistic tags, in Italy and Japan, also produced the new movie makers in America. So far as the young are concerned, one might almost speak of a world-wide shift in cultural commitment from the printed word to the visual image.

But in the United States so far, the artistic achievements produced by this shift have been scattered and uncertain. The American film is caught in a long transition that is also a tantalizing moment of promise. And there is no saying when the promise will mature—this year, or next, or not for another decade.

THE NEW AMERICAN

THEATRE

RICHARD KOSTELANETZ

> *Drama should present not new stories but new relationships.*
>
> Friedrich Hebbel

Historically, the movement here named the New American Theatre was born with the opening of Jack Gelber's *The Connection* at The Living Theatre in New York City, July, 1959. Two months later, at the Schiller Theatre Werkstatt in Berlin, opened another first play by a young American writer, Edward Albee's one-act *The Zoo Story* (written in 1958) in a double-bill with an equally puzzling example of the new European theatre, Samuel Beckett's *Krapp's Last Tape.* By January, 1960, in our age of jetted culture, both plays arrived in New York. Since then, Gelber and Albee have each produced full-length plays, becoming the major figures in a movement which includes Arthur L. Kopit, Kenneth H. Brown, Lorees Yerby, Robert Hivnor, Kenneth Koch, James Purdy (all of whom have had their works produced in New York), other young playwrights whose plays have appeared in numerous regional and university theatres around the country, and even others whose work has yet to get beyond the printed page.

In retrospect, we can identify the three historical developments that made the New American Theatre possible. The first was the postwar emergence of a new European theatre led by Samuel Beckett, Eugene Ionesco, and Jean Genet, which overthrew many of the theatrical canons of the previous generation and, thus, provided the freedom that made experiment possible. In the eyes of the budding young American playwrights, the Europeans demonstrated that revolt could succeed both in creating brilliant art and in vitally communicating it to receptive audiences. The second force was the emergence of the off-Broadway theatre. True, in the first few years of its success, it failed to discover any significant young native playwrights. However, once everything but new American plays found an eager audience—European classics, contemporary European works and Broadway-botched plays by major American writers—John Unterecker could accurately forecast, in the spring of 1959, "For the first time since the early O'Neill days conditions are ripe for the emergence of a new set of young American dramatists with the courage and the talent to experiment."

What finally made the new theatre possible was a wide-spread dissatisfaction with what the older playwrights were doing. Since *A View from the Bridge* appeared in 1955, Arthur Miller has offered only one new play, *After the Fall* (1964), which, though considerably better than the novel-turned-into-movie, *The Misfits* (1961), still suffers from grave failures in language and moral stance. Despite Miller's experiment in the play's form—to depict events taking place in the narrator's mind—*After the Fall* runs a course of fairly conventional, undream-like naturalism without achieving the social pertinence that made Miller's most significant work, *Death of a Salesman* (1948), so influential. Indicatively, while the older American critics generally appraised *After the Fall* as one of Miller's lesser works, the major younger critics, to the last man, hurled their fury at it.

Tennessee Williams, in contrast, has continued writing plays, or rather the same play over and over again, drawing from his closet-full of Williams-types the same old skeletons outfitted with new clothes and new names. A more irritating force in the fifties was the troop of imitators whose portraits of "sensitive" people could barely pass for Tennessee Williams' first drafts, and a small army of punching liberals who could make easy moral distinctions with the air of Gospel Truth. It was against these playwrights, too —and, as we shall see, against these sorts of mentality—that the New American Theatre rebelled.

What defines the New American Theatre is not merely these new names, but also the new theatrical styles which they have created. The critic's first temptation—to follow Martin Esslin and hurl the catchphrase "theatre of the absurd" to lasso them all—is really a mistake, for not all these playwrights see metaphysical absurdity at the center of our existence. Even then, Albee, for example, flickers overtones of the absurd in one play only to omit it completely from another. Nor is the formula of "metatheatre," coined by the theorist-playwright Lionel Abel, helpful in defining the New American Theatre. In fact, there is little common artistic ground in the new playwrights' work. Where they do unite, however, is in shouting a vociferous No to the two kinds of theatrical currency of the postwar years—the sexual-psychological dramas of Tennessee Williams and the social-realism-(semi-) tragedies of Arthur Miller.

I

The most promising of the new playwrights, Edward Albee, produced by 1964 two one-act plays of varying quality, two sketches of little consequence, an unsuccessful adaptation, and one brilliant full-length work; and nothing, except the perils of success and a somewhat weak critical faculty, can seemingly hinder future growth. Though it is difficult at first to summarize Albee's key interests in a single sentence—his themes are as diverse as his subjects—he has clearly defined both his attitudes and his theatrical style.

His *The Zoo Story* is an excellent play, deserving all the praise it has received; but it is also a misunderstood one. The scene opens with Peter, a tweedily dressed, graying father in his middle forties, sitting on a bench in Central Park. From the side comes Jerry, a disheveled man several years younger, announcing in a loud disturbed voice, "Mister, I've been to the zoo." Peter responds perfunctorily, returning to his book; but Jerry, feigning politeness, continues to solicit his reluctant attention, offering to tell Peter what he did at the zoo. Though he never relates this story, he does tell of his vain attempt to establish communication with his landlady's mangy dog. After this long monologue, Jerry starts to tickle Peter and forces him off the bench. Once Peter prepares to fight, Jerry, drawing a knife, flips it at him to make the battle "more evenly matched." Peter picks up the knife and holds it out with a stiff arm as a defense. Jerry impales himself on it—quite deliberately, it seems—and once he feels death coming, he says, "Thank you, Peter. I mean that now," adding, "You have comforted me. Dear Peter."

With only the slightest sensitivity toward the suggested and the symbolic, one can see that below the surface lies a homosexual undercurrent. Jerry never explicitly announces his desire to entice Peter, but his passions are implicit in nearly every speech he makes. Early in the play, Jerry addresses Peter as "boy" and then alleges that Peter can sire no more children, a charge which Peter reluctantly acknowledges. Jerry goes on to announce that he lives next door to a "colored queen" and that he often tells strangers, "Keep your hands to yourself, buddy." Peter's stock reply is an indignant, "I must say I don't . . ." and throughout the play, he is truly unaware of Jerry's real intention.

Albee, like Tennessee Williams, has the gift of transforming a physical object into a dramatic symbol; so that every time the object is mentioned we become aware of its ulterior meaning. Here Albee has several sets of symbols, including dogs and cats, animals and vegetables. Dogs are surrogate males, and cats become females. Thus, when Jerry says he wants companionship with a dog, he symbolically announces his homosexual designs. Secondly, an "animal" is a male who will not respond to a homosexual pass, while a "vegetable" is more acquiescent. Around the directions North and South Albee weaves another stream of symbolic suggestions. Early in the play, Jerry makes sure that he has been moving northward, but "not due north" through Central Park; later he describes how he brought his mother's body north; and just before he dies, he tells Peter, "I decided that I would walk north." In the north, of course, is death.

Once we recognize these symbols, much of the play's "mystery" becomes clear. We can easily grasp the significance of Jerry's attempt to befriend a dog and, moreover, appreciate it as one of the most moving speeches in recent American theatre. When he notices Peter's inability to respond to the suggestions in the story, Jerry sorrowfully says, "I suppose you don't know quite what to make of me," and Peter does not. Becoming more aggressive, Jerry makes physical advances on Peter, first tickling him until his voice becomes falsetto and then nudging and lightly punching him off the bench. Since Peter's responses carry feminine suggestions, Jerry says, "You're a vegetable! Go lie down on the ground." (Translated: You're a passive male, so be a female with your back on the ground.) Again Peter misses the point; so Jerry condemns his lack of empathy: "Don't you have any idea, not even the slightest, what other people need?" Peter, thinking Jerry wants the bench, challenges Jerry. He, in turn, draws his knife, giving it to Peter who takes it, holding it out in front of him like an erected phallus. Culminating the surrogate seduction, Jerry impales himself upon its blade, has the equivalent of an orgasm (the published script reads: "Tableau, for just a moment complete silence"); and, in his dying speech, tells Peter that because, "You've defended your honor . . . you're not really a vegetable; you're an animal." In his desperate action, Jerry has solved his predicament—he has found sexual contact to assuage his desire and death to end it.

This underlying action is, I think, the real content of *The Zoo Story;* for when an interviewer suggested to Albee that the play was "surrealistic," Albee replied, with characteristic bluntness, "It's all realism." On one level, then, Albee is writing about the predicament of the lonely homosexual who is never quite sure if the man he tries to pick up is "gay" and whose possible contacts are limited. On another level, he depicts one man's terrible isolation and his desperate need to break out of his shell. Because the play is realized on both levels, *The Zoo Story* is the most fluently wrought and tightly executed of all Albee's plays; it is, too, one of the great one-act plays in American literature.

Soon after its success, Albee released two other short plays, *The Death of Bessie Smith* (1959) and *The American Dream* (1960), and two sketches, *The Sandbox* (1959) and *Fam and Yam* (1960). All but the last have brilliant moments, but none has the impeccable coherence and emotional intensity of his first one-act. They suffer from a similar major defect—each time Albee piles two dramatic actions into a single framework. *The Sandbox,* perhaps the best of the four, opens with a satire on the ideal American family; but Albee, unable to continue, introduces a clumsy transition and ends with a somewhat mysterious and corny sequence about Grandma's death. In *Bessie Smith* Albee tries to tell the two stories at once. The first, a tale of social injustice announced in the title, remembers a historical travesty—because the injured Bessie Smith was not admitted to a white hospital, she died. The second, more interesting story describes the neuroses and social tensions of Southern white folk. Only occasionally do the two plots intersect. *The American Dream* is a more disheartening failure, for here Albee takes on a larger problem—that of American ideals— only to sink into cheap comedy and contrived pathos. *Fam and Yam* is a trivial joke about a young playwright's attempt to get an older, successful dramatist to admit that dolts and money-grubbers control the American theatre; there must be a million more propitious ways to dramatize this theme. Too often in these early plays, Albee lets his dramatic talents overcome his good sense, creating a surface of theatrical interest on weak foundations.

II

In *Who's Afraid of Virginia Woolf?* the two streams of Albee's talent converge, and the result is explosive. From *The Zoo Story* and *Bessie Smith* came his ability to depict tense human relationships and from *The American Dream* and *The Sandbox* came a comic talent, now greatly matured. In *Virginia Woolf* Albee creates a play that is not just sometimes funny and sometimes terrifying;

he successfully fuses terror and comedy into a single current and sustains it as the tone of the play, accomplishing an artistic feat unprecedented in American theatre. Then, for two of its three acts, it is one of the most dramatically sharp, witty, and moving plays ever written in America.

In outline, the story is bare. Its setting is a conservative living room (in this respect, the play is a savage satire on the traditional living room play). George and Martha, a middle-aged college professor and his slightly older, more sensual wife, have just returned from a Saturday night faculty party at the home of her father, the president of the college, satirically named New Carthage. Soon afterwards enter Nick and Honey, a handsome young biology instructor and his simple, giggly, slim-hipped wife. The time is 1:30 in the morning, and for the following three hours—both on the stage and off—the couples engage in drink and conversation. It is a tribute to Albee's genius that he can turn such unpromising materials and so little action into theatrical fireworks.

In its basic structure, *Virginia Woolf* is a four-way game of what might be called strip-polka. In this ritual dance, each character bares himself to the others, revealing that the appearance each presents is merely a facade to mask the hideous truth, the ugly wolf (of the title) that each of us tries to hide. In the first act, a drunk Martha exposes a not-so-drunk George by announcing that he married her in hopes of getting the presidency of the college; in fact, despite the best of connections, he has always been a failure. Martha also reveals that as a college sophomore she eloped with the campus gardener, only to have her marriage annulled, though, she adds, "there was entrance." George informs Nick, a newcomer to the school, that "musical beds" is the faculty sport and that, if he wants to gain professorial support for his ambition, "The way to a man's heart is through his wife's belly."

The guests, too, enter into the spirit of the evening; and we discover that Nick married Honey because her father had money, that her father earned his fortune as an unscrupulous "Man of God," that Honey's "hysterical pregnancy" rushed Nick into marriage before he could reconsider, that slim-hipped Honey has inordinate fears of sex and of having children and, consequently, has spells of vomiting and thumb-sucking. To retaliate against her husband Martha encourages Nick to seduce her, but the conceited and muscled Nick is too drunk to complete the act and is henceforth known as "the houseboy." The final revelation is that the son that Martha continually mentions is merely a fantasy she and George created to compensate for their inability to have children. In this peeling away of artifice is all the dramatic tension of a whodunit, but here the interest is "what's-he-hiding."

The stripping down is finally not only the play's central action but also Albee's way of evoking its central meaning. Each of us creates masks to hide the terrible underneath we are unwilling to unveil, to assuage psychological insecurities, to make us socially presentable, to enable us to go on with life. Thus, what we as the audience should feel for the scene before us is not pity, which is an emotion of sympathy for people who have problems that, by good fortune, do not plague us. Rather, for the characters we should feel the compassion that comes from an honest recognition that all of us face a similar predicament, that the need to create a pleasant surface to mask the ugliness of our selves is intrinsic in the human condition.

What sustains our interest in *Virginia Woolf,* then, is first an awareness of personal complicity and, then, Albee's brilliant and masterful theatrical technique. His sense of timing is breathtakingly deft, particularly in the dialogues—a steady stream of sharp, punching speeches, full of memorable epithets. Many of Albee's inventive invectives have since secured such a firm place in the ears and conversation of many American couples that, from time to time, one hears reports of people who "play Virginia Woolf."

Early in the play, just before the guests have arrived, Albee writes a dialogue that evokes that peculiar love-hate George and Martha have for each other:

MARTHA: Hey, put some more ice in my drink, will you? You never put any ice in my drink. Why is that, huh?
GEORGE: (*Takes her drink.*) I always put ice in your drink. You

> eat it, that's all. It's a habit you have . . . chewing your ice
> cubes like a cocker spaniel. You'll crack your big teeth.
> MARTHA: THEY'RE MY BIG TEETH.
> GEORGE: Some of them . . . some of them.
> MARTHA: I've got more teeth than you've got.
> GEORGE: Two more.
> MARTHA: Well, two more's a lot more.
> GEORGE: I suppose it is. I suppose it's pretty remarkable . . .
> considering how old you are.

Though *Virginia Woolf* contains no single speech of such sustained
passion and tortured lyricism as Jerry's story of the dog in *The Zoo
Story,* Albee in this later play brilliantly employs language, not as
poetry or lush prose, but for stunning dialogues that ignite the key
moments of the play. Likewise, he has mastered the Shakespearean
trick of switching the pronoun reference; so that George and Nick
are always on the verge, in their language, of swapping wives.

Not only do Albee's characters sustain the burning tempo of
this dialogue for most of the play, but they also interact with each
other with an appropriateness that is rare in today's theatre. All
four figures are realized creations; because Albee convinces us that
their neuroses are terrifyingly real, their attitudes and impulses
assume a consistency that makes them all imaginatively credible
and the actions and conflicts of each are seen as the natural results
of his particular passions. To condemn Albee for not capturing the
academic mind or the quality of faculty life, as many critics have
justifiably done, is also to miss the real point. These characters are
first of all human beings; and like all of the great dramatic creations, they embody aspects, not the totality, of the universal condition.

All this is not to say the play is flawless. The third act is a real
problem. What is supposed to sustain the audience's interest is the
son who is said to be returning from college, and the final surprise
should be the revelation that there is no son. But since there is no
sign of him in the program and since we know how Martha lies,
most of us already doubt his existence, thus escaping Albee's
crowning blow. Moreover, in contrast to the conciseness and speed
with which he uncovers the other gory details, he drags this one

out to excessive lengths, interspersing a dull debate between George and Martha over whether the moon is up or down. The reason is that the child's exorcism, he has admitted, was the root idea of the play (an image perhaps taken from Ionesco's *The Chairs* of 1952), and then all other exorcisms were, to Albee's symphonic mind, variations on the theme. Also, in *Virginia Woolf,* Albee still hangs on to a few bad habits left over from *The American Dream,* such as his penchant for the cheaply funny line (Nick tells Martha that his being a biology instructor gives him special qualifications), his readiness to let important problems disintegrate into light jokes, and his inadequate sense of social, in this case campus, reality. (For example, the details of Nick's biography—star quarterback at eighteen, M. A. at nineteen—should earn him a place in Ripley's book of improbabilities. Also, George, with his worries about promotion, seems more an executive than a scholar, while Honey, with her obsession for correcting everyone else's grammar, is more the teacher.) Then too, the play is filled with overtones that George and Martha represent the decline of America—he makes speeches with a Spenglerian ring and refers to the evening as a "dry run for the wave of the future," while their first names echo the original Washingtons—but this portentous dimension remains just a faint shadow.

On the other hand, to accuse Albee of creating a happy-ever-after ending to please his Broadway audience, as several critics have done, reveals a failure to perceive that the play has an underlying structure of a group psychoanalysis. In the course of the evening, all the characters recognize their illusions and false fears— the reality of their psychic weaknesses; and thus each achieves a stronger strategic position from which to conquer them. George and Martha appear to have regained their tenuous—for lack of a better word—love; and Honey vows to overcome her fear of pregnancy. At the end of *Virginia Woolf,* they exhibit a mental attitude that could well lead to a less neurotic life; we do not see that they have suddenly become normal. In psychoanalysis, developing the right attitude is a first step; life's greater obstacles remain to be conquered.

Albee has refused to create heroes or anti-heroes, for essentially he deals in group predicaments. All his characters, no matter how different in outward appearance, suffer from similar failings. In *The Zoo Story* Jerry bears as much responsibility for the failure of communication as Peter; and in *Virginia Woolf* each character has some sort of sexual problem. Here, I think, is the key to understanding Albee's ultimate intentions. He wants to describe not the world we see but the human condition he knows. As the playwright Kenneth H. Brown put it, "Albee writes out of his own mind, [while] I write [about] what I see outside of my mind." To say it differently, Albee is a visionary or expressive writer, rather than an empirical or objective one. At the center of his vision is human failure, the inability of all of us to fulfill the images we cut out for ourselves, or even to satisfy our basic human needs. Thus, in Albee's world, parents have no respect for children, nor children for parents; the attempt of one stranger to make contact with another always fails; sexual intercourse never takes place and sensual desire exists only to be frustrated; and all relationships that should be founded on love are cemented by either hate or habit, insecurity or greed. It is easy to claim that Albee has a warped and/or a narrow view of human possibility, but to praise or dispraise him only as a social critic is to miss the point. His vision is important because it is his uncompromising and deeply felt view and relates to what each of us sees. However, not his vision but his ability to realize it dramatically and coherently is the major sign of his achievement as a playwright.

Albee's place in theatre tradition has been somewhat misunderstood. In his otherwise brilliant *The Theatre of the Absurd* Martin Esslin identifies him as an absurd dramatist; but Albee's style is quite different. "Absurd" plays contain absurd (i.e., ridiculous, nonsensical) events which depicts man's predicament before metaphysical absurdity (i.e., unfathomable mysteries of ultimate truth). In Beckett's masterpiece, *Waiting for Godot,* two men totally devote their lives to waiting for a Godot who obviously is not coming (the absurd situation); and because Godot, the equivalent of God (or the bearer of ultimate truth), is not here now and shows little promise of coming, the world is metaphysically absurd. In contrast, Albee is concerned with man's physical predicament— the need to mask deficiency and to seek human contact, the causes of human motivation. Indeed, what is new about Albee is less the form of his plays than a sensibility whose intense and thorough negation is unprecedented in American theatre. In this respect, of all European playwrights, Albee is the closest to Genet, and Genet, Esslin notwithstanding, is not an absurd dramatist either. Of major recent plays, *Virginia Woolf* is the closest to Genet's *The Balcony;* in both works the playwrights rip through the artifice of costume, stripping each character down to his essential lubricity; and Albee's work resembles Genet's in structure—a series of similar rituals on a single theme, rather than a more traditional arc-like plot. (*The Zoo Story,* in contrast, has the distinct turning point—Jerry's monologue—of conventional structure.) To trace another tradi- tion, we could also place Albee in the similarly blasphemous cur- rent in American fiction that runs from Nathanael West's *The Day of the Locust* through Terry Southern's *Flash and Filigree* and Leslie A. Fiedler's novelette, "Nude Croquet." In lieu of a better alternate term, I call this style the Art of Total No.

Albee's adaptation of Carson McCullers' superb short novel, *The Ballad of the Sad Cafe* (1963), is on all counts a disappoint- ment; for although Albee recognized the pitfalls of adaptation, he was unable to avoid them. Not only did he fail to engage the mood of the book, or reproduce authentic Southern speech or exhibit a felt sympathy with its theme, he also failed to add anything to the original script. McCullers' play version of her own novel, *The Member of the Wedding* (1950), is considerably more successful.

Still, there is little reason to interpret Albee's failure here as evidence of his declining powers as a dramatist. Rumor has it that Albee wrote his adaptation some years before its staging and that his deep admiration for McCullers, her work and her personal mis- fortunes prompted him to do the production. The fears for Albee's future arise from a scrutiny of his past. His development has been conspicuously uneven—the first one-act was surely his best, while his fifth play, the first full-length, is the second best—for he is, as we noted before, all too liable to let his dramatic talent and self-confidence smother his intelligence, and he has displayed signs of the weakness that has so stalled Tennessee Williams' artistic career, the self-indulgent impulse to repeat himself. On the whole, though, Albee is maturing as a dramatist, and it is best to think of *Sad Cafe* as Albee's wasted pitch—he is resting his arm for a dramatic fast ball even more blazing, dazzling and tricky than *Virginia Woolf.*

III

While Edward Albee is the major young playwright, The Living Theatre is the most important theatrical enterprise. Through its productions, two young playwrights, Jack Gelber and Kenneth H. Brown, have contributed significant work, respectively in *The Connection* and *The Brig;* but it is because Judith Malina and Julian Beck, the directors of The Living Theatre, infuse so much of their own passion and ideas into everything they do, often transforming amorphous manuscripts into stunning productions and thus making it difficult for the critic to discern whether the playwright or The Living Theatre is most responsible for the work's success, that one must discuss Gelber's and Brown's plays in their original contexts, as Living Theatre performances.

The Connection, Gelber's first work, is more theatrically original, more pertinent to the problems of our time, and, to some, more profound than anything Albee has done. Although Gelber lacks the sheer dramatic genius that sustains Albee through the most slender materials, Gelber bases his play on the more interesting foundation of the predicament of contemporary man. One sign of his seriousness is his apparent choice of influences. Whereas Albee draws largely on Williams, Strindberg, Genet and sometimes Ionesco, Gelber reflects Gorky, O'Neill, Pirandello and Beckett. At once we notice how much more deeply concerned with man both in history and in essence Gelber's mentors are. From Gorky, it seems, comes the idea that extreme poverty forces one to face the basic questions of existence, from O'Neill, an ambivalent attitude toward man's desire to escape through alcohol and heroin into fantasy; from Pirandello, the desire to knock down the barrier between audience and stage; and from Beckett, the theme of contemporary man's awareness of ultimate absurdity and the image of his waiting for salvation. But once Gelber assimilates these influences and casts them in an American scene, they become facets of his own style. Ostensibly, *The Connection* depicts narcotics addicts. Although the director of the original production, Miss Malina, dedicated her work to "Thelma Gadsden, who died of an overdose of heroin," the life of the junkie is neither sentimentalized nor damned. He is neither the hero in a corrupt world nor a doomed and worthless being. Gelber depicts addicts as human beings, each suffering from his own problems; hence, he transcends a concern with addiction *per se* to make it only one possibility in a larger debate about the quality of contemporary life.

As theatre, *The Connection* is extremely effective. To shatter the distance between the stage and the audience—that glass wall so rigidly maintained by classic theatre, by Albee's and most absurd theatre—Gelber presents not a *show* but a *specimen* of life. Rather than a clear beginning and a definite end, *The Connection* presents a situation which existed before we entered the theatre and will continue to exist after we leave. To achieve this effect, Gelber opens with Jim Dunn, the fictional producer, stepping off the stage and presenting himself to the audience. He, in turn, introduces "Jaybird, the author" and explains that on the stage are addicts he has recruited to "improvise on Jaybird's themes" for a documentary motion picture. Two cameramen come through the audience onto the stage. Jaybird starts to explain his play. Jim Dunn interrupts him and calls up to the addicts; they in turn talk back to Jim. By this time, the audience is participating emotionally in the life on the stage.

Only by identifying with the "photographers" and accepting the reality of the scene can the audience appreciate *The Connection*. The play's key devices aim to engage us in the scene, until, at least in The Living Theatre production, we believe that we are there, that Leach, Ernie, Solly and Sam are not actors but real junkies. Only if the play completely captures one's attention will the question implicit in the action become apparent; this question is the play's theme: "You there in the audience. Now that you have seen life as it really is, do you want to be turned on?" Here is how the play poses the question. Through the first act, the men on stage anxiously wait for a character named Cowboy to return from picking up some "horse" at his "connection." Rubber-band nervous from waiting longer than they expected, the addicts take out their frustrations upon each other, and in his animosities each one reveals his particular human problem—unfulfilled career, intellectual disillusion, unemployment, and sexual ambivalence.

At the opening of the second act, Cowboy, dressed in the white of an angel of mercy, returns to make the connections. (The play's title has, of course, a twofold meaning, referring both to the man who sells heroin to the addict and to the act of plunging a heroin-filled needle into an arm.) In an off-stage bathroom, Cowboy gives each man a shot, a "baptism," as he calls it. From the audience comes the voice of one of the two "photographers" of the "improvisations." He too wants a shot. Jaybird tries to dissuade him but becomes convinced that he, as the author, must also undergo the authentic experience. Both follow Cowboy into the off-stage bathroom.

The question is posed. You have little reason to believe that the world has any order, meaning or purpose; it is to you, in short, absurd. You recognize that, like everyone else in your society, you ultimately want the happiness of self-contentment. You are offered heroin, a quick, painless, easy way to achieve the out-of-this-world ecstasy of euphoria. True, it may be illegal, but why does that matter? Is the morality of heroin really much different from that of other pleasurable stimulants such as alcohol, benzedrine or marijuana? Sam, the big Negro, voices the moral center of the play: "People who worry so much about the next dollar, the next new coat, the chlorophyll addicts, the aspirin addicts, the vitamin addicts, those people are hooked worse than me. Worse than me." They are "hooked worse" to Sam's thinking because they must go through so many more steps to achieve the happiness Sam gets in one shot. Sam has other advantages—his life is less anxious, less complex, and less enslaved to social needs. If the great aim of life is irresponsible sensuality, as it seems to be for so much of America, why not achieve it quickly and directly?

But, never letting the argument become one-sided, Gelber has another addict, the intellectual Solly, admit that dope is self-annihilating. "The seeking of death is at once fascinating and repellent. The overdose of heroin is where that frail line of life and death swings in a silent breeze of ecstatic summer. The concept of this limbo you can hold in your palsied hand. Who else can make so much of passing out?" In this key question of to connect or not to connect is a complex play of values. In offering us not a clear resolution but a suspension of moral judgment and an impasse of choice, Gelber is distinctly true to our predicament.

Not until the text of *The Connection* was published did theatre critics realize how much The Living Theatre's actors and director, again Miss Malina, had transformed Gelber's lines. The script itself is not very distinguished, and I suspect that many an experienced eye would not find it promising. Hung around the play is some noose-like repartee between the producer and the playwright about the possibilities of improvised theatre. It makes the opening minutes dull and fortunately disappears before it can strangle the show. For another thing, the addicts' language is colorless. Gelber's few figures of speech, such as "turn me on," are institutional passwords—no longer metaphors reflecting the wit of the author but the addict's shoptalk for familiar experiences. To give these lines significance, the actor must emphasize tone and rhythm, inflecting like a jazzman to make a note imply much more than it is. The following line on the printed page is too undistinguished to halt the reader's attention. "That's the way it really is. That's the way it really is." But once the actor uses certain facial expressions and body movements and controls the tone and pace of his voice, he can multiply the phrase's connotative suggestions. Through the play, seemingly dull lines become intense, moving speeches. Moreover, Miss Malina successfully integrates the jazz interludes played by Jackie McLean, Freddie Redd and their group into the narrative; for unlike O'Neill, who created characters who talked coherently while supposedly in total stupor, Gelber lets jazz replace speech whenever his characters are too stoned to talk. Just as Gelber depends upon the actors to make his lines resonant, he expects the director to define the characters more clearly than the manuscript presents them. Thus, much of the credit for the brilliance of The Living Theatre's production belongs to Miss Malina, who shaped the actors, lines and sound into a dramatically electrifying and significant whole.

For his second play, Gelber moved outside of seemingly personal experience to create in *The Apple,* produced at The Living Theatre in December, 1961, a play whose only apparent purpose, as far as I can tell, is to violate purposely every rule in the dramatist's handbook. (In practice, "new" theatre does not disregard all the rules; rather, it is a synthesis of contemporary feeling and appropriately selected old rules.) His characters are hackneyed and overdrawn. The figure listed in the published script as Tom (though in the production, all actors are supposed to use their *own* names) is an incredible composite of the worst traits of the ten biggest bigots anyone knows. He is given to hurling such a gross deluge of derogatory epithets at any minority or eccentricity that nearly every line he utters is embarrassing. The other roles are equally exaggerated. Secondly, what seems to be the theme of the play is not dramatized but announced—at both the opening and the end of the play to make sure no one misses it. The message is pontificated by Ace (listed as "a Negro"): "Now, did everyone take a breath of air?" he asks the audience. "Breath creates. Yes sir and madam, I'll say it again: breath creates. If you don't believe me, try not breathing. When you breathe your muscles move and when your body is moving you get to feel good and warm all over. You keep moving, baby, because that's being alive. Alive." In short, stay loose to live—the old hipster refrain. But the play is neither an aid nor an inducement to attaining such salvation. Gelber seemingly raises the great modern problems—alienation, loss of identity, failure of human communication, etc.—but every time he approaches one of them it disappears into a fog of nonsense. Another idea, perhaps the real theme of the play, emerges by default—the anarchy of human behavior. The apple of the title is taken every which way by everybody until it loses whatever traditional symbolic value it once had without gaining any new meaning, except, of course, irrationality and possibility. But whereas the absurd playwrights, especially Ionesco, develop a *form* to depict anarchy, Gelber does away with form completely and creates anarchy in the flesh. In the end, *The Apple* offers us human life caught between two opposite mirrors, reflecting merely itself again and again. Whether Gelber will write another excellent play is still problematic; his latest work, a novel *On Ice* (1964), was artistically ambitious, but unsuccessful. But, in any case, he has left behind him *The Connection,* a script which can be the core of a most remarkable and deeply challenging theatrical experience.

Just less than four years after the opening of *The Connection,* The Living Theatre presented Kenneth H. Brown's *The Brig,* repudiating once and for all the swelling opinion that for important new American theatre it was merely a one-shot house. *The Brig* moved even further away from the conventional drama of language towards a theatre primarily of noise, movement and ritual. The result was a theatrical performance of extreme originality and inescapable terror.

Behind the barbed wire that separates audience and stage is a playground-wire cage; in it are the double-deck bunks of ten imprisoned marines. Outside the cage are four sadistic guards who speak paternally of "my house" or "my hotel" and force the prisoners to do menial tasks, to obey stupid rules, to stand up straight while being punched in the solar plexus; and who arbitrarily assign degrading punishments, such as apologizing to the toilet bowl or crouching in an inverted garbage can whose top is being pounded. The prisoners are known only by their numbers or the common address of "maggot" or "worm"; they may read nothing but the Marine Corps Manual; they may not talk to each other or receive messages from outside; and each time they intend to cross any of the white lines scattered around the stage, they must address the guards, "Sir, prisoner number . . . requests permission to cross the white line, sir." The result is a vivid picture of dehumanization. Judith Malina's direction is, once again, thoroughly brilliant—the movements are carefully choreographed and the sounds well-organized so that the stage is continually alive. However, seeing *The Brig* is an excruciating experience, for the stage noise of feet stamping, unison-shouting in response to military commands, the endless repetition of requests for permission is incessant and stupefying. But only by making the audience feel all but the physical pain can the director get us to identify with the plight of the prisoners.

After several minutes of racket, we feel the urge to leave. The show is simply too hard to take. At times, the noise takes on the rhythmic and tonal order of music in much the same way as, say, the percussive effects of Edgard Varèse's *Ionisation* become music. When the men thoroughly scrub the barracks, surely the most extraordinary scene in the play, two men march in the right corner of the stage; others ask for permission to cross the white lines in a staggered order until the effect is that of a fugue, while others just make miscellaneous noises. Against the sounds of house-cleaning implements a soldier sings "The Halls of Montezuma" with a result that is somewhat musical and, as music, somewhat beautiful. But these moments are rare, for most of the time the noise remains noise and quite unbearable and repelling at that. I think, to pursue the logic of The Living Theatre, we *should* feel the desire to leave. We identify so completely with the crew-cut American men that when one soldier breaks down screaming, "My name's not six— it's James Turner," our sympathies quickly rush out to him. Only by cracking can he preserve his human integrity. As he is straitjacketed and carried off the stage, we in the audience, if we have any sense in our heads, should see the point has already been made and take off for the back door and fresh air. But we don't. Another prisoner is released a few days early for good behavior, while a new man enters to take his place. (Since neither his nor anyone else's crime is disclosed, there is a sense of arbitrary authority.) Prison life returns to "normal"; after the immates bed down for the night, the Warden asks, "Are my children asleep?," the prisoners scream, "Yes sir," and the exhibit ends.

In form, *The Brig* is thoroughly original. It is not an absurd play, for Brown does not expand his concern with the nonsense of military rituals to suggest that the universe is meaningless; but it is a play completely without plot and all that it requires—conflict, character development, dramatic interest and denouement. (A scene of peaceful Japanese life, which was in the original manuscript as a bald contrast to life in the brig, was wisely cut from both the final production and the published version.) Except for the momentary break of Number Six's fit, nothing upsets the sustained and monotonous noise and movement. As the repetition of rituals of dehumanization is the play's central action, its form is spatial rather than narrative; and for this reason we remember *The Brig* not as a story but as a sound-image of brutality. In this respect, the evening's moving force is not the play, which is static, but the individual playgoer in his developing reaction to the events on the stage. "It can't be so," is our first response. "The brutality is exaggerated. Someone will come forward and announce it is all a joke." But no one does. So we exist in unresolved conflict with the play, until each of us recognizes that he must take an attitude to the "real life" before him. The *New York Times* critic Howard Taubman, for one, asked for a Congressional investigation of Marine brigs, while Walter Kerr expressed sympathy for the audience; and the more sensitive Robert Brustein of the *New Republic* came away with the urge to "start a jailbreak of (his) own." To each man, then, his own denouement.

The overarching influence on *The Brig,* guiding surely its director and perhaps its author too, is Antonin Artaud's collection of polemical pieces, *The Theatre and Its Double,* first published in Paris in 1938 and in New York twenty years later. Artaud's main idea is that theatre in its highest and truest form "consists of everything that occupies the stage, everything that can be manifested and expressed materially on the stage and that is addressed first of all to the senses instead of being addressed to the mind as is the language of words." He believed, developing ideas implicit in August Strindberg's later works, that a true theatre poetry would exploit the physical resources of the stage, emphasizing "gestures and postures, dance and music" to create a *purely theatrical language,* while bad theatre (quality, for Artaud, became synonymous with style) subordinates the demands of production to the play's text. Following these precepts, Artaud as a practicing critic preferred the Balinese dance theatre to all European work. Only if theatre uses all its resources, Artaud concluded, can it achieve its traditional function of moving the spectator, to use his own favorite metaphor, with the force of a plague. Finally, in asserting that there is "an element of cruelty at the root of every spectacle," Artaud aptly summarizes the effect of *The Brig*. Like Brechtian theatre, Artaud's theatre stimulates feeling rather than evokes it; and just as Brown's characters, like Genet's, are primarily motivated by the will to power, so Brown's theatrical technique, again like Genet's, strives to have a powerful effect upon its audience. Martin Esslin sees that much European theatre today embodies Artaud's theories; but only in *The Brig* are they for the first time fully realized.

In another aphorism, Artaud raises a key problem in critically discussing the production of The Living Theatre. "In my view," he wrote, "no one has the right to call himself author . . . except the person who controls the direct handling of the stage." To pursue this point, I can see good reasons for saying that Beck and Malina, not Gelber and Brown, are the "authors" of these plays. First, they tend to take manuscripts which no other director would know how to direct and mold them to their own purposes. Secondly, by adding so much to a script and by realizing things which are merely amorphous in it, they have more authority over the final production than a conventional director has. However, there is, in the end, one all-inclusive reason for discussing these plays primarily as the works of their official authors: The manuscripts of both *The Brig* and *The Connection* do contain the major components of the final play. Beck-Malina should be thought of as strong directors who, more than most in their trade, infuse their own ideas and sensibilities into every work they produce. Since 1947, Julian Beck and Judith Malina have fought for their independent, experimental theatre; and now since *The Connection*'s world-wide success they have, despite recurring financial and legal troubles, become an established institution; they will exist as long as Malina and Beck have feet to stand on and voices to use and surely continue to produce plays which challenge the limits of theatrical possibility.

Just before the Internal Revenue Service closed The Living Theatre in the fall of 1963 for failure to pay taxes, they started to rehearse two one-act plays. The one I have read, *Potsy, or the Human Condition: An Epilogue* by Lee Baxandall, is an original, inspired comic work that at once parodies and reaffirms the absurd tradition. Everyman Potsy finds retreat from life in a privy, only to discover "society" wants to electrify the hole and convert it into a bomb shelter. Before its agents can destroy his refuge, Potsy gives a multi-lingual incoherent speech (which echoes and mocks Ionesco) and jumps in. The truest sign of Baxandall's comic talent and integrity is that he avoids the cheap gags the situation would have offered a lesser writer. As for Brown, his second play, *Three Dreams from Dell's Couch* (1964), which I read in manuscript, reveals some conventional dramatic virtues, particularly in evoking normal human beings; but its original dimension—that of presenting the characters' dreams on a raised stage—seemingly has little effect upon the play's final direction.

IV

Like all artistic movements, the New American Theatre includes several playwrights, nearly all one-work men who at the moment remain lesser lights, and a host of budding playwrights soon to be turned on. The most substantial of the former group is Arthur L. Kopit, like Brown still in his twenties, whose *Oh Dad, Poor Dad, Mamma's Hung You in the Closet and I'm Feelin' So Sad* received in 1962 one of the most expensive (and successful) productions in off-Broadway history. Unfortunately, whatever personal talent Kopit had to exhibit was nearly smothered by lavish costuming, *prima donna* actresses, and over-emphatic, yo-yo-tempoed directing. The published script offers a better idea of Kopit's strengths. Of all the young American playwrights, he is the best absurdist in the Ionesco tradition, capable of creating Marx Brothers-like belly-laugh jokes which, at their best, expose the absurdities of a certain type of life. The wealthy young son, for instance, travels with a billion stamps, three coin collections, a live piranha, cases of books, etc. Kopit also has an enormous gift for parody, giving his dowager marvelous exaggerations of Tennessee Williams' monologues, while the line that climaxes the nonsense, "What is the meaning of all this?" echoes the portentous lines about life's meaning at the end of Chekhov's *The Three Sisters*.

The major failing of *Oh Dad* stems from Kopit's inability to propel his wild jokes into the metaphysical absurd. The great comic absurdists, Beckett and Ionesco, are older men who have developed an ironic stance in face of their disillusionment. Young Kopit (B. A. Harvard, in engineering; fellowship winner) simply has not had the kind of disillusioning, isolating experience that produces an authentically absurd view of life. In the spring of 1963, Kopit announced a new play, *Asylum,* only to cancel the production. The title suggests he may pursue the life-as-madhouse theme of *Oh Dad;* and in it, or perhaps one or two plays after, he could well develop that profound awareness of absurdity that should underlie his marvelous comic sense.

In the spring of 1963 opened another play by a promising young dramatist, *Save Me a Place at Forest Lawn,* the first of two one-acts by Lorees Yerby. Two octogenarians contemplate the future. One is ebullient but neurotically insecure; the other is dull but resilient. Over lunch in a cafeteria, the latter, for the first time in their long friendship, reveals that she knows her late husband was deeply in love, not sexually but just emotionally, with her friend. After a brief flurry, an exchange of damning accusations, the two, out of fear of subsequent loneliness, re-establish their bond over the ridiculous vow to be buried in the same mausoleum. With keen senses for creating sprightly dialogue and evoking the comic absurd, Miss Yerby shows how people take trivial things too seriously by dramatizing long debates over whether or not to tell the waiter that the gravy has spilled into the beans or to induce the male octogenarian to come over to their table. Her second one-act play, *The Last Minstrel,* was distinctly less satisfactory—a few obvious reversals seemingly taken and watered down from Genet's

The Blacks are applied to the American scene—but Miss Yerby remains a talented playwright.

George Dennison's *A Service for Joseph Axminster,* which the Judson Church Poet's Theatre in New York presented in the winter of 1963, contains elements similar to those in Yerby's better play. Like her, Dennison has a fairly firm sense of character, a true ear for dialogue, an excellent sense of humor, a feeling for absurdity, and a fair ability to create a dramatic encounter. In too many respects, however, this play excessively echoes Samuel Beckett's best work; for like his master, Dennison sees hobos, alienated from false ideals and the passion for possessions, as the most appropriate characters for a metaphysical play about the absurdity of existence; and in structure, action and tempo, the piece continually recalls Beckett. At times, a personal voice emerges, capable of creating its own effects, as in his characters' echoing of phrases from the Book of Ecclesiastes. In this, and in a less successful short piece, *Vaudeville Skit* (1963), which the composer of its music, Al Carmines, imaginatively produced with the Judson group in the summer of 1964, Dennison displays a sure dramatic sense and a decisive taste that he has yet to cast in an individual style.

Also part of the New American Theatre, though more difficult to classify and analyze, is Jean Erdman's *The Coach with the Six Insides* (1962). Miss Erdman, an eminent dancer, adapted James Joyce's *Finnegans Wake* (presumably with the help of her husband, Joseph Campbell, co-author of *The Skeleton Key to Finnegans Wake*). Though the production was of necessity a bowdlerization and reorganization of the original—only a few of the scenes in the play, she admits, exist in the book—she did manage to convey the spirit of the original as well as successfully integrate song, dance, and a few of Joyce's more comprehensible lines into a fairly neat whole. She retained the book's basic myth of Fall and Redemption and its plot of the conflict between Charwoman Kate, mother, daughter and two sons (though inexplicably omitting completely H. C. Earwicker and the archetypal Old Man) as well as the basic narrative principle of *Finnegans Wake*—one scene or action tells many stories simultaneously. Remaining loyal to Joyce's language, Miss Erdman freely improvises within this framework. Unless one is familiar with the book, the action is inordinately difficult to follow; occasionally, the scene will focus, usually around a developed relationship or an Ionesco-like series of nonsense dialogues.

Still, what is brilliant in the performance is largely Miss Erdman's work. She found four co-actors who can sing, dance and deliver Joyce's puns so that as few as possible get lost, and Teijo Ito has added a lively and original musical score. By a deft control over this wealth of materials, she can, for instance, tell jokes or suggest emotion through language, body action and music, or any combination of the three. Thus, though the audience may not comprehend all of Joyce's prose, it still cannot help but be aware, often subliminally, of the spirit, structure, and perhaps the themes of the original book. In the end, Miss Erdman makes us very much aware both of what can be done with Joyce and with the possibilities of the stage. The result here is a kind of Total Theatre, in the Artaud sense, that gives the senses responsive to music, movement, and speech, a most unprecedented, pleasurable, if perhaps exhausting, experience.

The nonsense absurd tradition has also seemingly influenced two young women playwrights of promise, Maria Irene Fornes and Rosalyn Drexler, whose works, curiously, are quite similar. Both create a woolly comedy, compounded largely of nonsense, sexual suggestion, preposterous situation and incongruous juxtaposition, that sustains our interest but fails in the end to transcend itself. Whereas the best absurd playwrights—Beckett is the model—devise jokes to express and embellish their theme (as do Kopit and Albee to a lesser extent), the humor in Fornes' and Drexler's plays is thin and distracting, because it assumes no ulterior, either thematic or symbolic, dimensions; nor does it rise to the thoroughly sophisticated literary nonsense of French 'Pataphysics. For them, to paraphrase Gertrude Stein, a joke is a joke is a joke. In Drexler's *Home Movies* (1964), the buxom dowager has an affair first with an extremely effeminate male and then with a huffy Englishman dressed in boxing shorts (this encounter climaxes with an hysterically funny wrestling match on the trysting bed), her daughter grows daisies on the tips of her bra, and so forth.

The Successful Life of 3, Miss Fornes' best play, traces in ten scenes an inconclusive ten-year pursuit of an affair. Each of her three characters has a single stylized expression which, in the course of the play, often takes the place of a punch line. But in this and in her other work the joking, while often quite clever, remains unfocused.

The same sort of wild comic spirit animates the work of two male playwrights, both in their mid-twenties, Robert Head and Ely Stock. In Head's supremely imaginative *Sancticity* (1963), three characters—Blackout, Maraschino and Zero—perform a series of short playlets. What at first seems to be a parody of Pirandello turns into a wild farce in which stock situations are undercut by the slow infusion not of parody, but of nonsense; but this tone, too, is undercut by the real terror of the final sketch, an Afro-American ring-shout. The play, which I read in manuscript, would require enormously quick and versatile actors, as well as a director who might be able to uncover a solid underpinning to what in print seems just extremely inspired nonsense.

Less imaginative than Head, but with a more profound grasp of human emotion, Stock creates in *A Mouse for Haggie* (1960) a play which constantly suggests, yet finally evades, allegorical interpretations. A nightclub owner, her janitor, and a professional mouse-catcher stake their existence on catching a mouse that disturbs the nightclub. With his Malamud-like ability to evoke the essences of people at the pitch of passion, Stock gives his characters the rich Yiddish-English speech that permeates much of our best recent fiction. Finally, just as Head, Stock and most of the young playwrights capitalize on the theatre's capacity to present themes *visually,* so R. L. Sassoon and D. H. Elliott cleverly devised in *Up* (1963) a truly absurd mime that creates two distinct characters, has them interact and, then, illustrates a certain statement about human existence.

Of the many playwrights whose work so far has regrettably seen more of the printed page than the stage, the two most substantial are Kenneth Koch and Robert Hivnor. Koch in his two books of poetry—his mock epic *Ko, or a Season on Earth* (1959) and a collection called *Thank You* (1962)—displays a free-spirited, absurd imagination capable of the most imaginative flights of fancy and wit; and unlike most "witty" poets, he is thoroughly funny. His work suggests he is unable to take anything seriously, except his general thesis that life is absurdity, lunacy and possibility. In his short-short play *Bertha,* Koch in ten short-short scenes of mock blank verse establishes that Queen Bertha, a stand-in for Queen Elizabeth I, arbitrarily used her power to satisfy her madness, that her closest aids thought her crazy, and that, for the perfect final touch, despite all these failings she inspired confidence in both her armies and their captives. In *George Washington Crossing the Delaware* Koch cuts into both sides, British and American, with a fierce satirical destructiveness—platitudes are ridiculed, intentions undercut, and achievements attributed to chance or the opponent's incompetence—to show that accident rules history. Koch's other plays include *The Election* (1960), which simultaneously mocks the 1960 Presidential campaign and The Living Theatre's *The Connection; Easter,* a brief collection of incongruous scenes, such as children rolling Easter eggs to the accompaniment of Wagner's *Parsifal; Guinevere, or the Death of the Kangaroo* (1954) which is as incomprehensible as his early long poem, *When the Sun Tries to Go On;* the much gossiped-about *The Construction of Boston* whose humor disintegrates into in-group silliness; and *Angelica,* a mildly amusing, modestly imaginative opera libretto about nineteenth century French poetry that does not, in the form in which I read it, measure up to Koch's original intentions. Though Koch has not yet been able to cast his vision of life into a single work as fully fleshed and complex as *Ko,* he is capable of writing a play as zany, sharp and destructive as anything any neo-Ionesco playwright has done.

Robert Hivnor is one of the most imaginative playwrights writing today, and his uncompromising originality is probably the major reason why his works have not received the attention they merit. In his first work *Too Many Thumbs* (1947), for instance,

Hivnor tells of a very talented chimpanzee, possessed of a large body and a small head, who in the course of the play moves up the evolutionary ladder to become a normal man and ultimately a god-like creature with an immense head and a shriveled body. (I have never seen it performed; but I have been told that the visual effect can be achieved through the use of masks and costumes.) The lines are often very witty and the ironically linear structure (later used by Ionesco in *The New Tenant*) quite original; by pursuing the notion of human development to its inevitable conclusion, Hivnor quite swiftly demolishes mankind's pride in having achieved a higher state of existence. His second play, *The Ticklish Acrobat* (1951), which I do not admire as much as others do, exhibits again some true originality and a light satirical flair, but the difficulty of constructing a set whose period recedes in time several hundred years with each act has probably discouraged more than a few producers. His most recent work, *The Assault on Charles Sumner,* yet unfinished, is an immensely sophisticated history play, regrettably requiring more actors and scenes than an unsubsidized off-Broadway production can afford and containing more blasphemy than Broadway can tolerate. Hivnor scrutinizes the supreme example of the liberal intellectual in American politics, nineteenth-century Senator Sumner from Massachusetts, to find that though he had been ineffectual politically he was the first American saint. The play opens with a savage prologue, already published, describing the funeral of the last living Negro slave, Gullah, and his subsequent entry into the other world. Here Hivnor goes straight to the center of our major historical conflict—white man and Negro—only to damn both, or, more precisely, to criticize those failings that have nothing to do with race: stupidity, hypocrisy, indolence, platitudinousness. In the tradition of Total No he places the blame for our predicament on all, rather than just an evil few, of us. Once Gullah is in the other world, the pompous Sumner, who insists in vain that surely the black man must remember him, tells Gullah, "Sir, no American has yet been let into heaven." "Not old Abe Lincoln?" the Negro asks. "Mr. Lincoln," Sumner replies, "sits over there revising the Gettysburg Address." Unfortunately, in the first public reading, March, 1964, the play's later sections did not fulfill the expectations of the prologue, for Hivnor did not sustain the attractively intense negation, satirical leanness, or thematic coherence of the opening scene. Like George Buchner's *Danton's Death* and D. W. Griffith's *Intolerance,* Hivnor's *Charles Sumner* attempts to define a large historical experience, and it embodies the kind of daring originality one has always found in his works.

Of all the important novelists and poets who have in the last few years written plays, only two, Koch and James Purdy, have done particularly impressive work. The latter's *Cracks* (1962), in its published version, is a Beckettesque play about the unfathomable mysteries of existence—the "cracks" that people from time to time become aware of, though they cannot identify their source—all rendered in some of Purdy's best lilting dialogue; however, when the work was performed in New York in 1963, along with an adaptation of several Purdy stories, Eleanor Phelps as the old woman stole the show from the director and the playwright, transforming it into a homey sketch about a quaint old woman. Nonetheless, Purdy's plays are inferior; indeed, as the successful adaptation of his "You Reach for Your Hat" showed, some of his stories are more dramatically viable than his plays. Of the established poets, a less accomplished dramatist is Robert Lowell, whose trilogy of plays *The Old Glory* (1964), which I have seen only in manuscript, is an adaptation and revision of three classic American stories—Hawthorne's "Endicott and the Red Cross," his "My Kinsman Major Molineaux," and Melville's "Benito Cereno"—all of which employ a fictional-historical incident to present a universal theme, the successful revolt of the son-like underdog against father-like authority. Though each of the plays embodies an achieved structure and, especially *Benito Cereno,* a compelling situation, I could not decide just from the manuscript whether the tough, heavily metaphoric poetic language would, on one hand, muffle itself or, on the other, insufficiently distinguish the characters or, indeed, realize Lowell's dramatic intentions.

Just before his presumed suicide in 1955, the poet Weldon

Kees finished *The Waiting Room,* a one-act play; and just as his Robinson poems are among the most totally depressing verse ever written in America, his play realizes a despair that is overbearing in its intensity. Three women gather in a bus station waiting room to wait for a bus that seems destined never to arrive. In their conversation, each reveals her own pressing problems, remains oblivious to the confessions of the others, and thus fails completely to be each other's comforter. The telling symbols are neatly evoked— the central one being a depleted balloon—and the outpourings of despair take on an unfaked reality. Still, in the last moments Kees inexplicably suggests there are exits out of this hell (a taxicab, no less!), reversing the course of the play and destroying much of its earlier effect. Like so many plays by American poets, from Wallace Stevens' *Three Travelers Watch a Sunrise* (1916) to the present, Kees' play suffers from one glaring failure—his characters do not sufficiently differentiate themselves or interact.

The poet Bruce Woodford, in his symbolist play *The Prisoner* (1958), gets around this problem by having only one major character. The cell into which the prisoner is thrown becomes his own isolated mind; and his aged cell-mate, we discover, is both an alter-ego and an image of himself fifty years later. In language, structure and theme, the play attains a certain realized excellence and hard finish that, for the New American Theatre, is quite atypical.

On the other hand, nearly all plays by noted American poets are disappointing. Koch's compatriot in the New York school of American poetry, Frank O'Hara, has written several plays very much like Koch's in style but considerably less successful. *Love's Labor: An Ecologue* (1964), for instance, is a parody of a romantic pastoral—the role of Venus is played by a man dressed in a lush gown, the shepherd's sheep are unsightly dancers of both sexes, the "gorgeous girl" is too chubby to attract anyone's whistle; but because neither a particular vision or defined attitude to life emerges from all this, the jokes seem contrived—a general criticism which applies to O'Hara's other plays. Likewise, John Ashbery, a third associate, has in *The Compromise* (1956) and *The*

Heroes (1953) written plays which fluctuate between the preposterous and the commonplace.

Our novelists are hardly more successful at playwrighting. The published sections from Saul Bellow's forthcoming play suggest that *Humanitis—A Farce* * would be considerably less important than his excellent fiction, if not rather trivial, while both James Baldwin's *Blues for Mr. Charlie* (1964) and Henry Miller's *Just Wild About Harry* (1962) disintegrate into didacticism. Indeed, too many other recent plays by non-playwrights that I have come across, usually in their published versions, from W. S. Merwin's *Favor Island* (1957) and J. P. Donleavy's *The Ginger Man* (1963) and his *Fairy Tales of New York* (1961) through Reuel Denney's *September Lemonade* (1955) and Howard Nemerov's *Cain* (1959) and *Endor* (1961) to Elder Olson's and Richard Eberhart's verse plays and Lawrence Ferlinghetti's unperformable experiments, have been uncontestably dreadful, suffering from didacticism or an absence of theatrical focus or of over-all dramatic sense. Nonetheless, the Ford Foundation, in an unfathomable decision, has started to assign established novelists and poets, some of whom have little interest in theatre, to the regional repertory groups. The money could, I think, be more advantageously spent on prizes to functioning young playwrights.

v

Ever since the critics who feel obligated to find the Good, Here and Now, discovered that the old pros were no longer up to snuff, they have boosted a troop of false messiahs. The most pernicious is the playwright who uses devices to appear advanced but who actually represents a theatrical retrenchment of old styles. New York's most intelligent and consistent newspaper critic, Walter Kerr of the *Herald Tribune,* regularly deposits glowing words on this sort of play; so that, as soon as Kerr mentions a young playwright "who is original enough and witty enough to make even the avant-garde seem faintly old fashioned," one can be sure the play is at base rather conventional. That phrase of praise he gave

* Produced under the title *The Last Analysis.*

to Murray Schisgal whose two one-acts *The Typists* and *The Tiger* (1962) seemed descendents of the schmaltzy pathos of Paddy Chayevsky.

The regulars also pushed Jack Richardson. His plays, while moderately witty and revealing more promise than Schisgal's, are disturbingly derivative, often ineffective, and paralyzingly mechanical. His *The Prodigal* (1960), which Kerr called "a permanent contribution to the contemporary theatre," and *Gallows Humor* (1961), whose first part is his most imaginative work, were both off-Broadway successes, while his Broadway effort, *Lorenzo* (1962), was a rapid flop. This failure will perhaps prompt Richardson to re-examine his style; for while he has a good theatrical sense and a sophistication beyond his years, he has yet to transcend easily identifiable influences and find an individual voice. With William Snyder's *The Days and Nights of BeeBee Fenstermaker* (1962) the problem is different, for Snyder does have a good ear for the American idiom, as does William Hanley whose short plays opened in the same year; and an accurate sense of human motivation. Nonetheless, the theatrical style in all these works is undiluted American "realism" which, in the 1960's, smells more of the musty textbook than of contemporary theatre. Likewise, the several plays of LeRoi Jones, effective more as topical polemic than as drama, are at base theatrically too conventional or imitative to be part of the New American Theatre.

Several false messiahs emerging from the discernible left are just as unpromising. In 1960, The Living Theatre produced Jackson MacLow's *The Marrying Maiden,* an experiment in theatre of chance. MacLow took Richard Wilhelm's translation of the Chinese classic *I Ching,* cut out phrases and let the lines fall where they may into a fixed script. Thus, the actors, entirely dependent upon the result of the roll of dice, would execute one of the pre-arranged patterns of action and speech. With its characteristic courage, The Living Theatre gave it a full-dress production; but the result was uniformly soporific. A less extreme work in this direction, essentially a compendium of literary aphorisms, is Diane DiPrima's *Murder Cake* (1959), which never climbs out of the muck of incoherence. Pursuing the directions suggested by Samuel Beckett's brilliant *Krapp's Last Tape,* several young American playwrights have attempted works which are largely monologue. The best of these, Shimon Wincelberg's well-written *Kataki* (1958), presented briefly on Broadway and then revived off, is so much stronger in character development than theme that it hardly becomes more than just a tour de force. For this reason, it was probably a more successful work of art in its original form as a TV play. Adrienne Kennedy's *The Funnyhouse of a Negro* (1963), the story of a lonely, light-skinned Negro girl's journey from madness to suicide, is more interesting in the playwright's attempts to dramatize the stages of her fantasy life. Though Miss Kennedy handles her materials with a promising originality and sensitivity, the subject of the play would find a more suitable form in first-person narrative fiction. Occasionally touted as a potentially great playwright of Total No, Arnold Weinstein presented in *The Red Eye of Love* (1961) a satire of a money-oriented world which, to my mind, is extremely uneven, often embarrassingly unfunny, only rarely biting, and painfully obvious. His sketch, *The History of America* (1963), fails to find an appropriate symbol for its pretentious title or even sustain itself as a three-minute dramatic piece.

Sometimes billed as a savior of the American theatre, the spontaneous revue is really a peripheral activity. In New York, the groups adopt catch-titles such as "The Second City," "The Premise," "The Living Premise," "The Noble Path," and so on; and, in the performances I have seen, these shows tended to be moderately satirical, usually slapstick, and more fluent when prepared while clumsy when spontaneous. Their basic failure stems from human inadequacy—it is simply impossible for anybody, even Lenny Bruce, to be spontaneously funny every night of the week. What is remediable, and thus more disturbing, is the impulse to let the satirical bite sink into toothless slapstick. What, in contrast, was most impressive about the similar, pre-written and well-rehearsed British group that did *Beyond the Fringe* (1962) was the way they could sustain high levels of both sophistication and satire through nearly every sketch. Nonetheless, vaudeville is still vaudeville, no matter what the brow of the comedians; and as such it seems to have negligible influence on the New American Theatre.

VI

The New American Theatre is still a movement of individual talents; and although I can identify strains of sensibility such as Absurd or Total No, I would refrain from using either of these terms as a collective label or even sticking them with other banners, such as Atomic Age or Post-Expressionist. What makes them new, first of all, is their revolt against the two once-dominant, now-moribund theatrical styles of the postwar years, Williams' psychologese and Miller's socialese. Moreover, though Albee's plays may not be theatrically as thoroughly radical as The Living Theatre's productions or, to a lesser extent, Kopit's single work, the intensity and impatience of his negativism are still strikingly original qualities in American theatre.

The new playwrights are remarkably different from each other, and the simplest way to illustrate this is to list the influences echoed, in varying degrees of faintness, in each one's work. In Albee, we noted, are murmurs of Genet and West; in Gelber, we find Beckett, Pirandello, Gorky and O'Neill; in Kopit and Koch, Ionesco and the nonsense playwrights; in Brown, epic theatre and documentary films; in Lorees Yerby, Beckett and Genet; in Jean Erdman, Ionesco and Japanese Noh Theatre; and in Hivnor, Giraudoux and perhaps Genet.

Of course, the New American Theatre has not as a whole achieved the broad excellence and sophistication of recent European theatre, and not one of our playwrights is yet as indisputably significant as Beckett, Ionesco, Genet or, perhaps, even Pinter, while the New York scene seems a little brother, albeit aberrant, to the Parisian. Nonetheless, in these American plays are certain qualities which the Europeans have not realized. As the success of The Living Theatre's European tour would indicate, *The Connection* embodies, like William Faulkner, Jackson Pollock and other advanced American art, an imaginative originality and force that

Europeans find lacking in their own work. *The Brig,* in its European tour, will, one expects, elicit a similar response.

In the history of modern drama, the New American Theatre continues the tradition of revolt against what has become hackneyed and meretricious in favor of forms and ideas more deeply in touch with contemporary life. In form, the best new theatre discards both naturalism (or, as in *The Connection,* uses it for non-naturalistic ends) and the frothy comedy of manners—the two dominant traditions of American theatre—for more fluid and metaphysical, rather than prescribed and detailed, conceptions of dramatic reality. In this respect, it continues the best modern, largely European tradition of a theatre that offends rather than assuages, that undercuts easy explanations, whether they be Freudian, Marxist, Christian or Darwinist, to affirm what we in the sixties more and more realize, that life escapes our attempts to define it in final terms. (Perhaps this explains why the full-length plays have weak or non-existent third acts.) Except for The Living Theatre's pieces, the new plays all present a scene that remains alien to us—we cannot enter their worlds, so we disinterestedly observe the dramatic action develop a thematic point. In being so standoffish, the new American playwright separates himself from the American mainstream, swamped with protagonists, meliorism, contemporary idioms and soft wit, to seek his links with the counter, perhaps underground, tradition of American theatre—one that deals unsentimentally with life's essences rather than its events, that is ontological rather than realistic. The high-points in this tradition are E. E. Cummings' *Him* (1927), T. S. Eliot's *Murder in the Cathedral* (1935) and Louis O. Coxe and Robert Chapman's *Billy Budd* (1949).

The playwrights of the New American Theatre, in contrast to the Broadway regulars, create symbols and interpretations of reality, rather than present it directly; and they have abolished the hero with whom the audience can easily identify—the detective, the "sensitive" young man, the general, the lover—and the traces of sentimentality that unfailingly prompt heart-warming admiration. If we are induced to identify at all, as in the plays of Gelber and

Brown, it is with the victim and his unheroic predicament. Abolishing the hero is intrinsic to the larger purpose of most of the new theatre—to abolish facile ethical distinctions. What it presents, finally, is the universe of moral ambiguity and ultimate absurdity that is ours today; and in this respect it is, I believe, distinctly more true to the experience we know than is the theatre of the fifties.

Though I doubt if the New American Theatre will ever dislodge tripe from its entrenched hold on Broadway or if our theatre will ever be as substantial as the Parisian, its future is still extremely promising. Both Albee and Gelber regularly conduct playwrighting workshops, spreading the spirit of revolt to the brighter, budding playwrights. On the other side, one of the two best plays succeeded on Broadway, while the other had a long run off-Broadway as well as a European tour; and both have gained the loyal following of a young, intelligent audience. More than ever before, producers, both on-Broadway and off-, are willing to sponsor plays by young American writers. Numerous workshops have formed, thanks to charitable sponsors and energetic young organizers, which present plays not able to secure a commercial production; and from time to time, these plays, such as Drexler's *Home Movies* or LeRoi Jones' *Dutchman,* will induce regular producers to offer a professional staging. Largely because of the firm determination of their producing directors and the generosity of the Ford Foundation, theatres outside New York City are becoming increasingly important. Though, aside from the Arena in Washington, the Alley in Houston and the Actor's Workshop in San Francisco, they have generally shied away from producing untried American works, they will probably, under Ford encouragement, contribute more toward creating a significant native theatre. Perhaps in the next few years more theatre groups, both in and out of New York City, will develop the repertory systems that make theatre more interesting and varied for actor, director and audience alike. Unquestionably, the American theatre has emerged from the doldrums that swallowed it in the mid-fifties, and at the mid-point of the sixties it is still evolving, with barreling energy, in many directions. This could well be the crucial decade in American theatre, the one in which it will once and for all overcome the nearly total mediocrity that in the past has been its dominant fate, to become, as our fiction and poetry are, a significant force in American and world culture.

PUBLISHED VERSIONS OF THE PLAYS

Albee, Edward. *The American Dream* and *The Zoo Story* (Signet Books, 1963).

———. *The Death of Bessie Smith, Fam and Yam,* and *The Sandbox* (Signet Books, 1963).

———. *Who's Afraid of Virginia Woolf?* (Pocket Books, 1963; Columbia Records—DOL 287, 1963).

———; and McCullers, Carson. *The Ballad of the Sad Cafe* (Atheneum —Houghton-Mifflin, 1963).

Baldwin, James. *Blues for Mr. Charlie* (Dial, 1964).

Bellow, Saul. *Humanitis—A Farce,* in *Partisan Review* (Summer, 1962).

Brown, Kenneth H. *The Brig,* in *Tulane Drama Review* (Spring, 1964).

Denney, Reuel. *September Lemonade,* in *New World Writing #7* (1955).

Ferlinghetti, Lawrence. *Unfair Arguments with Existence* (New Directions, 1963).

Gelber, Jack. *The Apple* (Grove, 1961).

———. *The Connection* (Grove, 1960).

Hanley, William. *Mrs. Dolly Has a Lover and Other Plays* (Apollo, 1963).

———. *Slow Dance on the Killing Ground* (Random House, 1964).

Head, Robert. *Sancticity,* in *Tulane Drama Review* (Winter, 1963).

Hivnor, Robert. *The Ticklish Acrobat,* in *Playbook* (New Directions, 1956).

———. *Too Many Thumbs* (University of Minnesota, 1949).

———. Prologue to *The Assault on Charles Sumner,* in *Noble Savage #3* (Meridian, 1960).

Jones, LeRoi. *Dutchman* and *The Slave* (Morrow, 1964).

Koch, Kenneth. Collected plays, to be published by Grove Press.

Kopit, Arthur L. *Oh Dad, Poor Dad, Mamma's Hung You in the Closet and I'm Feelin' So Sad* (Hill and Wang, 1960).

Lowell, Robert. *The Old Glory* (Farrar, Straus, 1965).

Merwin, W. S. *Favor Island,* in *New World Writing #12* (1957).

Nemerov, Howard. *The Next Room of the Dream* (University of Chicago, 1962).

Richardson, Jack. *Gallows Humor* (Dutton, 1961) .

———. *The Prodigal* (Dutton, 1960).

Sassoon, R. L.; and Elliott, D. H. *Up—A Mime,* in *First Stage* (Fall, 1963).

Schisgal, Murray. *The Typists* and *The Tiger* (Coward-McCann, 1963).
Stock, Ely. *A Mouse for Haggie,* in *Brown Review* (Winter, 1960).
Weinstein, Arnold. *The History of America,* in *Kulchur #9* (Spring, 1963).
————. *The Red Eye of Love* (Grove, 1962) .
Wincelberg, Shimon. *Kataki,* in *Best Plays 1958–9* (Dodd, Mead, 1959).
Woodford, Bruce P. *Twenty-One Poems and a Play* (Alan Swallow, 1958).

THE NEW AMERICAN

PAINTING

POST-ABSTRACT-EXPRESSIONISM: MASK AND REALITY

MAX KOZLOFF

> *Man is least himself when he talks*
> *in his own person. Give him a mask,*
> *and he will tell you the truth.*
>
> Oscar Wilde

The impetus of art in the 1960's belongs to an American generation still under forty, aware of its origins in Abstract-Expressionism, but committed to a dynamic that has profoundly altered the look of pictorial and three-dimensional activity. More important, the psychological environment, the creation and apprehension of art, has been practically reversed from what it was only a few years ago. The humanistic context within which visual art has been most frequently experienced and judged has somehow failed in relevance. Such notions of a painting as the expression of its author's vision or emotion, or of paintstrokes as perhaps the last uniquely individual handiwork in man-made objects, are coming more and more to be discredited. Equivocation of form and content is now the principle of an art which strangely begins to evoke our condition and our times. Even when one is dealing, for instance, with painting that is decidedly allusive, if not literal in the objects and images it depicts, one cannot respond as one does to representational art.

How and why this metamorphosis has come about, and what are its implications for the future, is the story of New York avant-garde of the last seven years.

One has to speak initially of an esthetic backlash against Abstract-Expressionism, distinguished by a stylistic disorganization where there had once been a considerable idiomatic unity. If the present continuing pluralism of styles becomes centrifugal rather than centripetal, it serves to convince the artist that his own sensibility no longer has the endorsement of a group or an overarching idea—a situation that discourages more blatant forms of pretension. Younger artists no longer speak in the moral imperatives of their elders. Being relatively more on their own, they are seeking to align themselves with others in ways that can only emphasize the abruptness and calculation of their own development. Nothing in the careers of artists now in their fifties compares with the suddenness of the youngest generation's accelerated broken-field running, in which precocity and technical brilliance (hitherto rare qualities) mingle with promiscuous switches of approach (also rather uncommon in the past). Much of this suggests a re-evaluation of the relationship between conception and performance—two activities which are growing further apart from each other in new painting. Ideas intrude upon, and finally oppose, an organic process of vision. Partly involuntarily then, and partly consciously, recent art attacks not merely the coherence, but the "sincerity" of its mentor. Characteristically, such an attitude is anti-romantic.

One would be very hard put, however, to call the present phase "classic." Quite aside from there being no traditionally "classic" qualities such as decorum, consonance, and stability in painting of the early sixties, the traditional term itself no longer has any meaning. Even as defined by Irving Babbit, who said of the classic imagination that "it is seeking to disengage what is normal and representative from the welter of the actual," nothing in Pop art, assemblage, and abstraction, the strongest tendencies today, applies. What we have, rather, is the continuation of an earlier aggressiveness and flamboyance, which generates more power than ever, because it is no longer specifically personal. And as for disengagement from the actual, this is exactly the reverse of what has happened.

In point of fact, there has been a relative collapse of the idea that paint can allude to a sensation or a presence outside itself. Actuality is defined as the intrinsic quality of the medium. Reacting against the feeling of one naturalistic artist, who maintained that "most abstract pictures are really representations of some other, make-believe world," young abstractionists manipulate paint as if it were a thing merely, with the results that their paintings begin to look like objects (when one is not, as so frequently, dealing with objects themselves). In turn, this accent on the concrete (as distinct from a circumstance such as the textural) is a foil for the withdrawal of any emotional demonstrativeness. When previously a built-up paint surface ostensibly testified to the state of an artist's feelings, the later eradication of such surfaces indicates, not necessarily a coldness of the author, but a deliberate removal of feeling to a schematic level.

In postwar American painting, there was an inevitable contradiction in the hope that a unique transient physical performance could be literally embodied in a static, immobile medium such as paint, a medium which would freeze, not that performance, but only its traces. By the late fifties, artists realized that emotion could not be reliably externalized in such a manner, and that the self-defeating contradiction could not be resolved. They therefore tended to pry performance loose from any implication of uniqueness and spontaneity, and escape from the dilemma of Abstract-Expressionism, by baldly acknowledging it.

Indeed, even physical dissatisfaction with the appearance of "Action" Painting (the term coined by Harold Rosenberg) has brought into existence an elaborate critique which sweeps across many levels of meaning. There has been a waning interest in deep space, complex form, gesture, impasto—all those self-proclaiming signposts of New York painting in the 1950's. Recent work is visually much flatter and simpler. Above all, one finds it insisting upon optical clarity, and "closed" as contrasted with "open" form. But these formal preferences imply a great expressive change. Flatness, uniformity, and brightness are never ends in themselves. Speaking in 1957 of the elder New York Abstract-Expressionists, Meyer Schapiro said:

> The consciousness of the personal and spontaneous in the painting and sculpture stimulates the artist to invent devices of handling, processing, surfacing, which confer to the utmost degree the aspect of the freely made. Hence the great importance of the mark, the stroke, the brush, the drip, the quality of the substance of the paint itself, and the surface of the canvas as a texture and field of operation—all signs of the artist's active presence.

In ironing these things out, the young artist de-emphasizes that presence, perhaps, but only in order to shift focus radically upon the intellectual premises and devices of his work.

If, too, the painting no longer looks "freely made" it is because the artist is defining freedom, not in the way something is made, but in the naked assertion of his will, even if that assertion takes the form of self-effacement. In recent abstract art, no less than Pop art more obviously, the artist puts great restraints upon his will, in order to materialize, say, certain industrial processes, or formal rhetorics—(the two sometimes combining)—all the more clearly. Appearances re-enter the work of art with increasing directness, and compositional relations are frozen in such a manner that newly limited possibilities of interpretation paradoxically commence a subject of inquiry. It is mysterious not to have alternatives. The very frankness of the treatment becomes introverted.

Technically, the similarities between such otherwise contradictory painters as Nicholas Krushenick, and the abstractionist, Ellsworth Kelly, lie in their common concern with the element of artisanship. The sharpening of contours, the uniform smoothing of areas is accomplished in both men by an attentiveness to paint application which veers towards the mechanical, and indeed, with a related pop artist Roy Lichtenstein, has largely been achieved by mechanical means. Taken to an extreme, this tendency is exemplified in the practice of certain geometrically oriented abstractionists who prescribe the execution of their pictures to commercial sign painters. The hand, in effect, laboriously counterfeits what the machine does effortlessly. Reacting even against this human element, the influential Josef Albers, of the Yale art department, published his "Interaction of Color" (1963), in which he promulgates the use of silkscreened colored papers in chromatic exercises, because they eliminate the possibility of accident and inconsistency in choice and juxtaposition of hues. If this comes out of the German Bauhaus, then the current predilection for the mechanical was also preceded by 1920's Purism, in Ozenfant and Le Corbusier, with their attendant beliefs in the beauty of the machine and the virtue of standardizing forms. But American art of forty years later exists in a different dimension. By regularizing chance features of the work of art, that is, by numbing the hand, the artist stakes all on the cunning of his eye, and the display of his mind. The machine is really invoked only to contradict it. In a recent manifesto (of the "Anonima group"), this development is characterized as showing "Man as the machine's rival. Through it, man says to the machine: 'I *am* precise and accurate. But I can turn logic to my own uses as you can not; I can even take logic to its extreme where it becomes conflict and contradiction. I can give a kind of information which *surprises.*'" It is debatable as to how objective and impersonal such "information" is.

Actually, the appearance of new media and mechanical devices in American art has accelerated rapidly since the war. One thinks initially of Pollock's duco paint and dripping, and de Kooning's ripping and repasting, as well as the introduction of the sign painter's liner brush for oil drawing (delightedly employed by Gorky.) More lately, one sees tipping or tilting of the canvas (Jenkins, Morris Louis), the development of plastic and acrylic pigments (Noland, Louis, Olitzki, Held), metallic pigments (Stella), signboard painting (Rosenquist), stenciling of all kinds (Johns, Rauschenberg, Rivers), wax encaustic, (Johns), belloptican machines and metal screens (Lichtenstein), and silk screen-transferred photographs (Warhol, Rauschenberg). Naturally, this is not to speak of the unprecedented media in sculpture, from styrafoam and sculpmetal to fiberglass, nor of assemblage, whose recent efflorescence has not only provided the greatest esthetic sanction of new materials, but is their *raison d'être*.

Assemblage, in many ways, typifies the climate of post-Abstract-Expressionist art. The reason why collage should have become as intrusive as it did in this mode is partially explained by physical and associative limitations of paint handling (which none of the new media or techniques ever quite seems to reduce), and also by the frequently unconscious longing for tangible forms and substance experienced by the younger generation. Unquestionably too, assemblage is a reflection of American technology—its insatiable appetite for change, its planned obsolescence, and its grotesque excessiveness. The artist can scavenge all this acutely and sarcastically for its resale value. In assemblage, as in Pop art and abstraction, all three of which gradually tend to include or overlap each other (e.g. Marisol, Sven Lukin and George Ortman), are stressed the same processes of manipulation and recombining of materials as opposed to execution *with them*. The word "execution," in fact, no longer describes accurately the activity of the artist. On the contrary, he rearranges elements or puts them into different contexts, rather than alters the physical shape (of paint or clay), as in conventional production.

But where assemblage differs from the other approaches, however, (quite aside from its radically different physical format), is in its taunting attitude toward the outer world, and that very industrialization off which it feeds. The mechanistic here is a form of self-mockery and provocation. (Richard Stankewicz, Lucas Samaras and Bruce Conner.) Finally, the tone of assemblage carries hints of nostalgia, impurity, and pathos, because it forever contrasts the novelty and inventiveness of its ideas with the age and delapidation of its materials—or at least their banality.

To a considerable degree, the reverse is true of some recent abstract painting, in which the conventionalized ideas are banal (i.e., chevrons), or simplistic, but the material, say the brilliant plastic paint in Louis, is both new and freshly used. This is the classic confrontation between the abstract and literary imaginations. And yet, though "purist" color field or "hard edge" painting looks optimistically and materialistically (I do not necessarily say hedonistically) upon the world, and assemblage's viewpoint is often pessimistic and disquieted, both movements are again akin in certain fundamentals.

Certainly both depend upon a refunctioning of means into ends, so that in assemblage, the very objects employed are the "originals" (a basic distinction from sculpture) and in abstraction, the mere processing of forms itself takes over the expressive burden. Unquestionably, this elimination of the allusive conventions of art, and the gained directness of presence, operates with an unprecedented fierceness upon the spectator's sensibility. These are the poetics of shock, and it is to the credit of young American painting to have exploited them so systematically. In one stroke, illusion gives way to reality, and method becomes matter.

If, however, such choices suggest the return of subject matter, they at the same time cloud the issue of abstraction-versus-representation. Brutally simplified, a dilemma of American painting in the fifties revolved around the problem of recurring imagery, and the tension occasioned by incorporating it into a predominantly abstract, non-figurative vision. Here the human presences in de Kooning (1953), and Pollock (1950), were not nearly so prophetic as the symbols and ciphers of Bradley Walker Tomlin and Adolph Gottlieb, exactly because such recognizable entities could remain perfectly abstract and yet signify concrete things of the world. From here it was a relatively short jump to the superimposition of such reproducible motifs upon the picture field—a development which reached an early culmination in the targets of Jasper Johns (1954–5), in which sign and picture field became the same thing. In Johns, the painting itself ceased to "contain" any specific event, but rather wholly substituted for an object, thereby neatly bypassing the representational element of art entirely. Put differently, the convention that a painting and the thing it depicts are separate is destroyed, and that aspect of art as integral artifact cancels its traditional function of alluding to something outside itself. Instead of some reperceived and refleshed image, one sees altered or "assisted" dummies, effigies, facsimiles, reincarnations of that image, now grossly physical in that it is both object and presence indivisibly. As a result, one has *presentation* rather than *representation,* and the dilemma of the figurative is short-circuited. It is a turn of events that favors sculpture, and the three-dimensional arts exceedingly.

An artifact, say a comb, cannot have subject matter, but it may not be insignificant that it is a comb. Semantically, for all that there is no subject matter in recent art, one finds plenty of iconography. The repertoire of substances and things which are annexed bodily into the work had to come from someplace, and none was more natural than the urban American environment. It is one of the great ironies of recent art history, that after establishing a real cosmopolitanism in the early fifties, our painting should have reverted to the most blatant regionalism in the sixties. Jukeboxes, signboards, television, movies, magazines, mail-order catalogues, food displays and other Americana proliferate in the galleries. Not since the depression has there been anything so unashamedly local as motif in American art, and, in fact, a nostalgic flavor of the thirties and forties (that is, the childhood of most of the present artists) permeates recent work. (At various moments, Keinholz, Wesselman, Thiebaud, Lichtenstein, Saul, Marisol.) Larry Rivers was perhaps the initiator here. In some measure, this is attributable to a normal defensiveness against topical journalism, salted by a real sympathy for a simpler and less affluent America (in which popular culture too, was purer and more "innocent"). But not to be overlooked also, are the outright sources of a continuing regional iconography in Stuart Davis, on one hand, and de Kooning on the other. Nor is it even far-fetched to see an influence of Demuth on Robert Indiana, and Sheeler on James Rosenquist. From these outputs have come echoes at once more literal, and inevitably more kitsch-like.

What remains far more interestingly problematical and thoroughly original, is not the theme, but the *attitude* toward the motif. In this respect, oddly, one discovers the sources of comment are not so much things in themselves, but methods and techniques of communication. Into the typical American ambiance of the communication industry, of the transmission of prepared and complete messages, the artist intrudes and displaces with his own message. He then suddenly engineers an interference, creating a kind of ventriloquism in which a personal statement comes forth in the guise of a totally impersonal framework. The commercial idiom is subverted even as it is made to perform extra-curricular esthetic work. As to the message itself, one is likely to remain even now in fundamental doubt. One of the most difficult chores for the intellectual has been to accept the Pop theme with any seriousness whatever, and this is precisely a mental limitation which the painters themselves attack with exemplary zeal. It is disconcerting to realize that the real philistines are the cognoscenti who distrust any art such as this—which they think is more acceptable to mass taste than their own. Highbrow artists have simply delved into lowbrow culture in order to shock whatever of the middlebrow is in all of us. This, at least, is a comprehensible phenomenon.

Nevertheless, there emerge disquieting implications. Not in the least improbable, for instance (in fact much insisted upon by the artists themselves), is a generalized empathy with commercial art, its forms and the goals. Another more obvious alternative points towards parody. Even when, as most recently, the means chosen are extremely illusionistic, and the area between the automatically reproduced and the individual imagination diminishes so much as practically to uphold the machine-made as art, the possibility of satire still exists. A third interpretation which comes no less legitimately to mind concerns an intellectual interest in the process of having and converting sensations in such a manner as to focus attention on the creative act. That is, the accent shifts from *what* one sees to *how* one sees. Here the iconography is no more than a mask of neutral material behind which the artist speaks mediumistically, urging one to make formal discriminations among his pictorial activities. In this view, Pop art merely adopts a scheme which detains awareness of its basic formal propensities. The new picture embodies a dry ice variant of the self-involvement in the Abstract-Expressionist picture.

None of these possibilities, contradictory as they are, can confidently be ruled out or altogether accepted. This is proof of a basic ambiguity which keeps open the range of consciousness, even if it is too soon to tell how much it has enlarged the accomplishment of American art. Everywhere one is presented with the spectacle of artists pushing their work to its furthest consequences, and yet remaining ambivalent in purpose. Their impulses are clarifying, and their results elusive.

New York art is at bottom dualistic—vaguely impotent before the deluge of events and appearances around it, but at the same time raging to give them some kind of communicable order and persuasiveness that will speak inalienably for the individual personality. All the schemata and conventions—targets, stripes, and signs which have been appropriated by the young American artist are in one sense exasperated attempts to create a style which perpetually eludes him. (The deficiency of his European colleagues, generally, is that they possess precious little but style.) The closest he has come is to impersonate and mimic other people's styles or even civic emblems (emphatically enough shaped forms), which gives him at least a crypto-identity, but still leaves him short of that mastery of the outer world which is his goal. Much the same applies to contemporary highly reductive abstract painting which irately "normalizes" all elements within its field, but no matter how authoritarian in appearance cannot make them look definitive. Their absence of tradition and a chronic self-doubt are finally compensated by the artists with that sting of belligerence which we are coming to accept as characteristically American. One only needs to add further, a sense of irresolution elicited by the suddenly perceived awkwardness of the artist's own presence, which he must neither stamp out nor indulge, in order to achieve his expressive aims. Perhaps it is not so surprising after all that recent art speaks in the falsetto, and moves with the spasmodic cadences, of a puppet.

The *eminence grise* of post-Abstract-Expressionist art is Jasper Johns. In 1958 he first showed his celebrated "targets" (target forms on canvas, above which were horizontal compartments containing plaster casts of parts of the human body), and thereby materialized a predicament in criticism as well as put American art on its present path. No one could have imagined then how illustrative of the future were his schemata which figuratively seemed to be making a target of the fragmentation of the whole man and the disintegration of a continuous, organic process of vision and construction. That Johns himself explained the invention of his flags as the outcome of a dream in which he had seen that motif clarioned, hardly helps clarification. No Abstract-Expressionist, after all, ever claimed to have gotten his ideas from dreams, least of all ideas as irritatingly commonplace as these. The suggestion of imagery that was received automatically and unconsciously had an implausibility that contrasted with the actual product; in essence, nothing could be more ordinary. With his first public showing at the Castelli Gallery, 1958, the critical term Neo-Dada came into existence.

If one examines this idea in the light of Johns' work since then, the Dada element becomes, I think, only half applicable. But this is already fifty percent more than is acceptable for the many who eventually came to reject the entire label. The single, continuing, undeniable principle of Johns is his practice of "displacement" —meaning the transposition of an idea, motif, or object from one context to another. Johns does not undertake a single work without operating by displacement and attempting to widen its possibilities. Furthermore, it is necessary that the one context "art," or at least recently past art, be fixed, while the other context varies. Therefore, by selecting flags, targets, numbers, letters, coat hangers, maps, shadow outlines, the artist elevates the function of *choice* as the decisive imaginative act, in that it circumvents the original usage of the motif and opens it up to a completely different form of consumption. Johns himself has said, "I am concerned with a thing's not being what it was, with its becoming something other than what it is, with any moment in which one identifies a thing precisely and with the slipping away of that moment. . . ." The more this aim brings him to emphasize displacement as the transforming agent (as opposed to execution), the more a Dadaist he is, the more, in fact, he becomes the single most important inheritor of Marcel Duchamp. Indeed, Johns is responsible for reintroducing Duchamp as the most potent, overarching influence on the younger generation of American artists.

Still, he is singularly unfaithful to his mentor. Not only because his themes are different and his outlook more public, but because he conceives his work primarily in the guise of a painter (which he can't help being), does he part ways with Duchamp, particularly the Duchamp who had striven successfully to repudiate his own painterly gifts. In Johns there is an involvement with paint handling that comes overtly out of de Kooning and Philip Guston. Thus, even though one of his primary accomplishments has been to formulate predictable and reproducible structures for the picture, he contradicts their nature by implementing them unpredictably, and more, with a freedom gained by Action Painting. Further, when Johns displays patinaed bronze casts of flashbulbs and light-bulbs, he joins and yet opposes the things in themselves with a way they might be represented, not merely produced. This, too, relates to Dada, except that Johns' pictorial activity still pumps its own spontaneity into the construct, and thus affirms the art against which he would otherwise seem to be reacting.

Doubtless Johns is questioning the nature of reality by juxtaposing the concrete paint strokes with the tangible artifact, and this suggests that neither of them is enough to complete the statement which is for him the goal of the created work. Rather it is the viewer who is left with the task of completion, but unfortunately without sufficient visual clues to discharge it. Or perhaps, with too many. Thus Johns will paint a map of the United States as if it were a landscape, stencil the names of the states as if they were on packing cases, and color the stencil in hues that "jump" or recede uncontrasted in their separate areas. A Johns painting is a series of cancellations as much as it is a sequence of additions. One of his typical procedures introduces a system which is perfectly understandable, and then rules out whatever legibility it had by adding some kind of limitation or excess in its operation. As an example, he will superimpose the numbers from 0 to 9 over each other, arriving at a kind of planned confusion. *With Johns, object presented, visual effect, and final content by no means coincide.*

However he may pry apart relationships which are usually laminated by esthetic causality, Johns does not present the spectator with a disunified painting. On the contrary, one is made to understand that the work is deliberately open to interpretations, that it *wants* to be viewed in as many ways as possible. Such is his concentration on alternative readings that subjects and handling are not so much subordinate in importance, but relatively stabilized and neutralized conventions which hold physically in place the mental polarities which compose the experience. Unlike Duchamp's, the appearances which we recognize in Johns have no private or special character, nor do they contain any sociological commentary. Johns invents or sometimes evokes connections, he never "pictures" them. In this, he oddly agrees with the rationale of, say, an Abstract-Expressionist like Hans Hofmann, when the latter says that "it is not what a form is, but what a form does, which is important." With Johns, however, displacements, mirror effects, identity changes, and physical compressions are substitutes for forms. Except that his relationships are not compositional and that his paint gestures reject the emotive, Johns echoes the concern of Abstract-Expressionism to articulate the internal dynamics of vision . . . not merely how paintings are put together. The intimate, sentient, frequently grey-toned pictures of Johns welcome critical analysis but remain wonderfully enigmatic.

Just the same, their historical importance has been immense. From Johns, and Rauschenberg, with an equal but considerably different form of brilliance, have issued the basic esthetic of much recent assemblage and Pop art. And Johns in particular has cast influence upon certain forms of abstraction which could never have developed without the spectacle of his contrariness. I am thinking now of the very young Frank Stella, (b. 1936) of whom one cannot speak as the leader of a group, but who has nevertheless crystallized a sensibility very germane to the aspirations of a number of colleagues. Represented in the "Abstract Expressionist and Imagist" show of the Guggenheim Museum in 1961, the "Geometric

Abstraction in America" exhibition (Whitney Museum, 1962), and "Toward a New Abstraction" (Jewish Museum, 1963), Stella stood out in perverse relief, as if he were the conscience of his peers. That conscience manifested itself, apparently, in nothing more than parallel alignments of stripes, executed most often in metallic colors, separated by the tiniest channels of unprimed canvas, and contained within frames that varied from U forms to polygons, the centers most recently holed out. That Stella is a perfectly non-objective artist there can be no doubt; and that he makes of each of his pictures a solid object is equally obvious. For his accents—on the oddness of the shape, which destroys the picture convention of rectangularity; on the "thingness" of the paint, which suggests a substance, metal; and on the width of the stretcher, three inches— all point to a view of painting as artifact.

Thus, Stella, like Johns, quite aside from simulating manu- facture and seemingly abdicating a great deal of personal respon- sibility, operates by the principle of displacement. What is odd here is that he has been able to displace completely within the realm of abstraction. He accepts each form as it is, as unalterably real— annihilating one of the basic premises of abstraction—but does not trespass into anything in the least observed or associated. After establishing this essential paradox, Stella, now unlike Johns, per- sists in keeping his still point, and diminishes all possibilities of "relationships." In fact, his art concerns itself with such problems as boredom, monotony, even hypnosis (as hinted at by concen- tricity). By eliminating any kind of connectedness between any two areas other than what his initial choice of system predicates, Stella totally thwarts visual probing. The befuddled spectator perhaps then tries for conceptual significance, only to be warded off by the painter's purposeful blankness of mind.

Johns operates to allow as many possible interpretations of his work; Stella, neatly and diabolically, aims to invalidate all in- terpretations. If one responds to his paintings visually or formally, one is being perverse. If one rejects them on the basis of their "principle," one is being obtuse. In the end, they will not counte- nance being used in any way, so that our liking or disliking them is irrelevant. They are perhaps the closest that paintings have yet come to being mere objects. More importantly, because of this arrogant uselessness (purchased, however, with the most humble, artisanal devotion), Stella, in my opinion, may be the first to attain an Abstract-Dadaist position.

Apart from Johns, there have been considerable precedents for this whole situation, precedents that go back right into the 1940's, and to a much older generation. In the work of three important artists who stood apart from Action Painting, artists who are termed color-field painters (Rothko, Still, and Newman), lay a pictorial region—anti-Cubist, as well as gestural, but overtly chromatic—which opened up several questions to be explored. Their pictures generally consist of huge monolithic walls of color, punctuated or contained by minimal, highly generalized structures —vertical lines, horizontal layers, or agitated flaked-off edges. But although still highly respected, Clyfford Still, because of his overwrought emotionalism, and Mark Rothko, owing to a hyper-individual poeticism, have both receded to historical, and somewhat less than vital status for young painters. Far and away, the unpainterly Barnett Newman continues to be the old master and the most pertinent influence upon the present abstractionists.

If one asks the question, why Newman?, a number of answers suggest themselves. To begin, he is the only one of the three whose handling is fairly even, unstressed by manual irregularity. Even the flat, smooth surfaces of Ad Reinhardt are more inflected with feeling, if not human imperfection, than Newman's. To be sure, there was a time when Newman was considered a purveyor of grand sensuous effects, an interpretation which the sheer impact of, say, sixty square feet of cobalt blue might well reinforce. Yet the color is not used to overwhelm the senses, so much as in its curious muteness and dumbness, to shock the mind. Newman habitually gives the impression of being out of control without being in the least bit passionate. During the early fifties, it was incorrect to think of Newman's work, though not of Rothko's and Still's, as morally activated—concerned with pruning art down to its essential flatness but still to make it count more than ever in this rarified air. What the color-field artists had in common with Abstract-Expressionism, after all, was this emphasis on a kind of heroic rhetoric. Newman's stance I think, can now be seen as considerably isolated from Rothko's and Still's, as an attack against rather than affirmation, of abstract art's potentialities. To give an example, one needn't go further than the way he composes. Frequently the artist will place, far out or down towards a margin, a thin band or trimming; on a vast field, he might be said to split a hair. Pleasureless concentration on pure color, supremely illogical assymetries of composition rendered on a scale which the artist has allowed to be called "sublime," these are trademarks of Newman's which have become extremely prophetic. If he is so useful to young artists, it may be because his work is so absolutist and yet so incomplete.

How Newman actually came to posit an art on such paradoxes is not particularly clear. Ad Reinhardt's origins, in contrast, are quite obvious. So, too, is his relevance to contemporary abstraction. Now in his early fifties, Reinhardt has long been speaking in the accents of mainline European purism (deriving most saliently from the Bauhaus), which he has nevertheless managed to clothe in the austere guise of a pioneer American vanguardist. As a polemicist, Reinhardt persistently inveighs against practically every quality that promotes distinction and can lend interest to the bringing together of visual forms: value contrast, tactile change, spatial dynamics, and so on. But all this negativism has merely been a screen for the far less vocal protection of Reinhardt's own sense of art—manifested most typically in picture facades that seem to purvey one unitary sensation, such as of black. Only upon the most minute scrutiny, then, does one discover that his darkness yields segmental surface sheens of copper blue, green or purple. Disturbing in Reinhardt, whether conscious on his part or not, is the dissolution of an already most faintly perceived grid-like stability into the invisible. Insistently provoking the spectator to discover almost indecipherable changes (not even so much of hue, as of light refraction or mineral content), he dilutes the nascent discovery in such a way that one is always finding a relationship only to be on the verge of losing it. Furthermore, it is not possible to tell whether Reinhardt is motivated by some pristine conservation-ism or a hostility whose overtones are by no means "pure." Certainly whatever visual play emitted from the penumbral regions of one of his canvases comes to have an explicitly optical, rather than sensuous value. And it is here, I think, in the implicitly mechanistic ambiance of Reinhardt, and in the specific discomfort and incredulity which he provokes, that many younger abstractionists have assigned themselves a territory in which to move.

Somewhere along these lines, indeed, several tendencies can be seen to converge even as they overlap. A strictly optical shock in which the eye responds exclusively, or at least is held to, the way a combination of two colors will "jump" in a kind of electric vibration or give off resonating after-images of a third hue—is an attack which typifies the work of various quite young artists such as Larry Poons, Tom Downing (a Washington, D.C. painter), Richard Anuszkiewics, and at times, Ellsworth Kelly. Most often in these men, compositional schemata, from meshes to polka dots, are regularized in order to focus on the strictly physiological repeating activity of the color choices (say, purple against orange), *so that one is not allowed to contemplate an area or passage in itself*. Even so, the possibility of running visual charges along edges, or stringing them by lines, let alone playing them off larger forms of every conceivable shape, demonstrates the curious future and variable range of this mode of painting. It is at once more pugnacious than any previous idiom—in its jangling discords, and in the way it compels strict responses from the eye—and more passive—in its radical suppression of human will. One's very difficulty of bridging the gap between these two extremes—now far removed from the innocent pedagogy from which they derive—is an indication of the content to which optical painting aspires.

It is in fact impossible to overlook a deliberately aberrated quality, a stunning emptiness, injected into American abstract painting of the last few years. One of the ways in which a spectator becomes conscious of it is his perpetually violated sense of proportion. By this I refer not so much to the mammoth physical scale of the present work (to which most spectators have become accustomed through Abstract-Expressionism), but the fact that generally one element within the picture confines has been permitted to get more or less cancerously out of hand.

Once again, much of this has its own history. Aside from the pioneer color-field artists who equated pretty much the whole pictorial zone with the artistic statement, the direction of much American painting has tended towards the enlargement of a characteristic image which then fills out or leaves mere slivers of the original ground showing. Between 1956 and 1959, among the older Action Painters this applied to de Kooning, Kline, Motherwell, and Gottlieb, as well as to somewhat younger painters such as Frankenthaler, Jenkins, Dzubas, and Parker. Quite a good deal of this development can be interpreted as a reaction against a vestigial appearance of drawing in a painting that had otherwise rejected the tenets of drawing in favor of a totally paint-conceived form of expression. An objection of equal force, incidentally, held for brushiness which focussed, rather than diffused, energy, and tied down the field of attention by the sprinkling of narcissistic "incidents." Works which attempted technical resolution of this problem by bringing the whole picture facade into homogeneous play were to be seen in the Guggenheim Museum's 1961 "Abstract Expressionists and Imagists" show. Only vaguely was it understood that there had appeared a monolithic form, although it was very hard to interpret it as "event, symbol, or abstract interior" (H. H. Arnason).

No one has remarked, or at least remarked with enough clarity, how notably antagonistic are many current forms of abstraction. Whatever outright incident or visual behavior they present seems always at the point of vanishing or slipping off a perimeter, and consequently flustering the spectator in the manner of an askew picture on a wall. Their few contrasts, delineated forthrightly enough, are also in their placement made to seem unreasonable. But such unreason is in turn contradicted by the calm, laboriously executed uniformity of the surface. What is at stake is not merely an anti-symmetrical position (which can be perfectly well comprehended) but figurations which suggest systems, which are in the end completely alien to system. Anticipations are set up as to how to read a picture, only to be denied. Kelly, the earliest proponent of such tactics, will introduce a meandering color mass (originating in Arp) in such a way from the side, that it appears to be merely the furthest excrescence of an area extending beyond the rectangle. And even when, as in Stella, the perimeters are respected, they are repeated with such a monotonous concentricity by stripes within the picture shape, that the edges once again cease to have any meaning whatsoever. Untoward pressure against the margins, strongly presented forms in unstable situations, heavily saturated opaque color which remains generally inert: such are the characteristics of an abstraction which builds up considerable energy of contrast and hue with no apparent purpose other than to ignore it. One has the presentation of brilliant, emphatic, magnified, obsessing images, squeezed dry of all violence or moral fervor. Paintings by Feitelson, Liberman, and Kelly, shown in the most recent section of the Whitney's 1962 retrospective "Geometric Abstraction in America," evidenced a whole break in feeling, while not greatly modifying the vocabulary of the geometrically based tradition from which they stem. The terms "hard-edge" or "Abstract-Imagist," like so many labels, fail to define a painting such as this, of lurid formal magnifications, and atrophied consistency. (How inadequate would be "soft-edge" as a definition of Rothko!) With increasing distinctness, such quasi-negative aims (prophesied by de Kooning's statement that "a geometric form is not necessarily clear") attract echelons of American artists.

A third area of abstract art at the present moment is the only one which can claim some interest in delectation and sensuous pleasure. The genealogy of Morris Louis and Kenneth Noland conjoins in Rothko—from whence comes their essentially chromatic way of seeing things—and Helen Frankenthaler—to whom they owe their initiating techniques of splatter and transparent paint-weaving. During the mid-1950's, Louis, in Washington, D.C., produced a number of enormous color abstractions by laying transparent rivers of acrylic paint over unprimed canvas, upon which it soaked in to give a dyed effect. This latter is the typifying embodiment of a painting which came to look substanceless, and had a distinctly orphic or lyric potentiality (in Louis particularly splendid), before emblematic conventions, in the shape of chevrons and stripes took it over. In its iconic clarity, such work as Louis' and Noland's was, by 1961, fully abreast of the geometrically derived abstraction which was its contemporary—though much more locked in compositionally, through necessity to emphasize the dynamics of color. A certain algid brilliance, at once refined and rigid, was the result. It remained to Jules Olitski, finally, to consummate the incestuous marriage between color-field painting and the aberrant branch of abstraction by employing one or two color dots or lopsided globules against a chromatic field. If his work is any indication, however, the union only incidentally escapes being detrimental to both forms. The attempt to reformulate pictorial quality strictly in terms of color has a tinge of high ambition to it, deliberately compromised here by gratuitous eccentricity. Prismatic authority and great chromatic vibration are somehow embedded in a construct that is mechanistic, without being rationalistic. Without denying the special flavor of such a blend, I find it at the moment unconvincing as a visual experience and too obtrusively esoteric as a concept.

All in all, present abstraction has worked a very definite change on spectator responses in the last six years. With all their cards on the table, so to speak, the varieties of this new work nevertheless resist any kind of emotional assimilation, even as they offer a practically instantaneous visual experience. Total optical apprehension and knowledge of the instrumenting process occur at about the same quick rate. As the critic Hilton Kramer put it:

> "The rhetoric of this painting [is to be found] in those optical inflections which do not invite the spectator's attention so much as stun it. The duration of one's aesthetic experience with painting of this school is not an exploratory nature; one does not probe these paintings, one recovers from their optical audacity and literal brilliance. They resemble musical compositions that consist of one piercing note followed by a silence in which the ear recovers its normal balance while still filled with the echo, memory and shock of the aural assault."

The questions simply remain: What motivates the assault? Or why this moratorium on nuance? Rejecting virtuosity while maintaining competence, this percussive painting exerts a kind of bright revenge on the critical schools of formal analysis and rhapsodic evocation. More and more in recent abstraction, it is becoming impossible to ignore the disconcerting and rather odious presence of Dadaism.

It is therefore extremely interesting to note that the co-existence of the "new abstraction" (as it was fatuously called at the Jewish Museum), and Pop art, has not been without mutual benefit, nor has it been coincidental. Pending a detailed study into their exact relations, (which at the moment resembles an armaments race), the connections between the two are apparent enough to suppose a fluid interchange of sensibility. Thus, abstraction has a specific pungency about it, and Pop art, in its compositional predilections, exhibits much of the intractable waywardness of abstraction. The two are actually combined with wonderful temerity by Nicholas Krushenick. Robert Indiana, James Rosenquist, and Roy Lichtenstein, who form the hard core of Pop art, have an obvious affinity with the flat brilliance of a Kelly or a Held. In one sense, it is not too far-fetched to consider the former as abstract artists into whose work a gaggle of allusion and quotations have wandered.

About two years ago, such a statement would have done considerable violence to one's responses precisely by its reasonableness. The immediate impact of Pop art, on the contrary, was to overwhelm the spectator with the presence of "subjects" so monumentally banal, that no escape into detached viewing of abstractly composed pictures was possible. But this blatancy was a position which still, theoretically, could hold a personal choice in solution. As Leo Steinberg remarked of Lichtenstein's concern with comic books and display ads, his iconography "was sufficiently ugly so that no one would steal it." And yet the evidence is that Lichtenstein was drawn to the comics because he felt them neither ugly nor beautiful, but merely the repository of forms and sensations which interested him. The spectrum of the artists' opinion on this subject varies, of course. Andy Warhol's is the most extreme, claiming not only great beauty in commercial culture, but eschewing any necessity to gain distance from it whatsoever. His repeating sequences of Campbell soup cans or Marilyn Monroe, however, function in their browbeating monotony in ways not dissimilar from Stella's stripes—that is to say, as the most literal repeated affirmations of unappropriated materials. Because the motifs remain relatively untampered with and their inclusion mystifying, the results evince a curious abstractness of feeling. For the grating together of the two circumstances does not produce, finally, any associative or even explicitly Dadaistic presence. In doing nothing whatsoever to disguise his procedure, Warhol underlines one of the peculiarly self-defeating values of Pop art, its absurdity. Underneath the great hoax of his reputation, he remains the unabashed commercial artist.

It may have been in an effort, then, to escape this debilitating still-point, that artists like Oldenburg, and more recently Rosenquist and Wesselman, have launched themselves into assemblage, and even further, into a quasi-environmental form of expression. Leaving aside for the moment the lineage of this whole tendency, one can nevertheless see here a striving for meaning that utilizes real objects and actual space as rhetorical agents. Oldenburg's soft vinyl telephone or french fries happens to be a case in point, as well as of a quite comic transformation of material. And Rosenquist's billboard images, to which have been added various domestic appointments (with uneven success, I might add), are other, more hybrid attempts at the same kind of breakthrough. Both examples nevertheless simultaneously depend on classic Surrealist devices (such as Magritte's naturalistic form and chiaroscuro but arbitrary coloration, or his representation of representations), and insights from the current abstraction such as its economy of means, or its still-life character. Even more, in the work of Jim Dine, there are outright allusions to Abstract-Expressionism (drips, impasto, etc.) in addition to the two other currents, so that the range of processes and the alterations of vision in Pop art seem almost endless.

In view of this accent on process, it is becoming increasingly difficult to speak of Pop art as popular. For one thing, some of its "subjects," such as Lichtenstein's transcriptions of Cezanne or Picasso, have nothing to do with kitsch culture. Then, too, there has been a recent drift away from commercially charged motifs to neutral, if everyday impedimenta, which make various esthetic discontinuities more visible (i.e. Oldenburg's telephone, Robert Watts' bread). Both Johns and Rauschenberg work so emphatically within this mode that they were even excluded from the "New Realists" exhibition at the Janis Gallery in 1962. But it is questionable now whether this word "realism," semantically so dubious, even applies to the painting under discussion. What unites works, in other respects extremely far ranging in their choice of directions, is a kind of agreement to generalize the motif so as to provide an extra-schematic dimension to an already highly schematized point of departure.

No matter which artist is considered—Indiana, Wesselman, Lichtenstein—one notes a certain flattening of planes, a coarsening of contour, and an absence of focus (though not necessarily of sharpening) which cannot possibly deceive a spectator into thinking he is seeing a facsimile of the actual object. Complementing this undeception are readily apparent changes of scale and medium. (That photographs of these works are so libelous is the best argument for them as unique objects.)

The play of allusions here becomes rather ironic. If there is a streak of heightened or caricatured, and hence fraudulent, naturalism in his original source, the artist intensifies it, not to speak of subdividing and transplanting it. His response to the conventions of the commercial artist, designer or illustrator, is to make them still more conventionalized. In the added falseness of tone he rehabilitates a sometimes enormously unpromising area for esthetic goals. The very primitivism wreaked upon the initial themes treats them as the outright fiction which their authors are only too anxious to fob off as a glamorous reality. Traditionally enough, the artists oppose whatever truth of the outer world (in this case certain elaborate lies) with the superior truth of their own work. However varied their achievement—indeed, it varies considerably—the validity of their premise is perfectly clear.

So closely as at times to be indistinguishable, assemblage parallels the explorations of Pop art. Its parentage, however, is different, and its ramifications are even more far-reaching. Springing initially from Marcel Duchamp, and engendered once again in the late fifties by Johns and Rauschenberg, assemblage gained momentum on a number of fronts. It is the catch-all phrase for such things as collage with delusions of grandeur, sculpture which announces its origins in artifact, and object-sullied paintings. Added to this, one finds a gradually more selfconscious development that began with agglomerates of objects, spread into environments composed of them, and then turned into quasi-theatrical presentations called "happenings," the creators of which unhesitatingly revert to one form or the other. Thus the poetics of the movement are now, as at their inception, continually open to reformulation.

Perhaps its most systematic theorist has been Alan Kaprow, who spoke in 1960 of happenings as "acts of acceptance of the phenomena of the outer world"—where "the field is created as one goes along . . . (and) are simply another degree of extension within a mode whose very principle . . . is precisely extension." Red Grooms, Jim Dine, Kaprow, and Oldenburg have been practitioners of happenings, but it is perhaps the last who has best characterized, not so much the principle, as the content of the medium, when he said:

> I am for an art that a kid licks, after peeling away the wrapper.
> I am for an art that is smoked, like a cigarette, smells like a pair
> of shoes. I am for an art that flaps like a flag, or helps blow noses.
> . . . I am for art that unfolds like a map, that you can squeeze,
> like your sweetie's arm, or kiss, like a pet dog. . . .

In one sense, this whole phase of sensory exploration is an outgrowth of Abstract-Expressionism, especially in its cult of immediacy and improvisation, but now pushed out into the realm of the social, the animal, and the ephemeral. It is like the Wagnerian dream of synthesis of the arts upon which has been superimposed junk culture. There have been Futurist and Dada antecedents for this too, but none with such a curious dualism of optimism and anarchy that seems to embrace real life most literally, but also so restlessly as only to backfire into inadvertent ridicule—of the motifs, and the productions in which they figure.

After gaining notice in the two "New Forms-New Media" shows at the Martha Jackson Gallery in 1960, assemblage achieved international renown in the exhibition of that name at the Museum of Modern Art in 1962. As Pollock to Abstract-Expressionism, the man who stands as progenitor to the whole mode of assemblage, whether in its static or mobile forms, is Robert Rauschenberg. In fact, the suggestion of motion, of mind as well as of things, is actuated by his "combine paintings," in which the idea of the spectator's participation in the activity of the picture is solicited, not by emotive brush strokes, but rather more bluntly by a chair or a ladder. Fans that "blow" gusts of paint and radios that blare from behind the canvas are examples of extra-pictorial activation that surprise as much by their literalness as baffle by their final recession before the claims of paint. As for the latter itself, it is difficult not to be aware that it has been demoted from the quite exalted status it once had in, say, de Kooning, Rauschenberg's mentor. The highly sensuous impact of Rauschenberg contrasts with the meanness of his materials so that one becomes conscious of a kind of bright nihilism in this painter, a continual reconstitution and loss of energy in a matrix whose most salient note is an elegance of concept that holds all its disparate materials in balance. Any emotional coloration, any evaluation of subject, is withheld—this is precisely Rauschenberg's special accent.

Several elements in this remarkable artist are worth attention. One is his totally open-ended view of chance. In "Factum," 1957, for instance, he duplicates his own paint-bespattered composition, thus demonstrating that chance lacks individuality and that the freely wrought is not necessarily spontaneous. It is the quintessential criticism of Abstract-Expressionism. On the other hand, as his friend John Cage once related when Rauschenberg's paintings were being transported, any damage "wouldn't concern him at all—it would be part of the painting's natural life." (As contrasted with Johns, for whom damage "would reopen the aesthetic problem.") Another consideration is Rauschenberg's multiple montage-like inclusion of objects which do not commit him to a specific view of the American urban environment, yet physically allows him to document it with a breathtaking range and justness. Just the same, his themes are often merely disquisitions on vicarious communication, expressed quite characteristically in his rubbings and transferred silkscreens of photographs, where one is always at some and possibly several points of remove from the actual events or objects. And even when one has the latter in hand, so to speak, their very tangibility is questioned by their inclusion in a predominantly pictorial field. It was from Rauschenberg's example that Jim Dine (as Oyfind Fahlstrom said), could imagine the juxtaposition of an electric light and painted, caricatured light beams—which forces one to ask but prevents resolution of the problem: which is more "real," the immaterial light from the lamp, or the thingness of the paint?

Illuminated by Rauschenberg, this questioning of the existential status of things is at the root of the marvelously fruitful esthetics of assemblage. Taken out of the context of painting itself, the valence of assemblage diminishes. But enough remains to inform the sibling work of people as diverse as H. C. Westerman, Robert Morris, Bruce Conner, and Edward Keinholz, to name only a few. Their great pitfall is to allow acceptance of the created presence to become an absolute in itself. For the more a shock value becomes the artistic aim, the less the work stands independently as form, and the less, even, is its applicability to experience. In the best pieces of the artists mentioned, the rampant literary associations—and they might jump from nineteenth century Americana to Skid Row dereliction—work hand in hand with the basically indefinable and mysterious effect of assemblage as a mode of existence. That is to say, one is put into great doubt once again as to the identity of the object. Unabashedly concrete, the created image yet yields its qualities reluctantly to the mind. Especially is this obvious when the assemblage approaches in its behavior some of the particularities of sculpture. In fact, the nature of sculpture is inter-rogated by assemblage. For all that they are shaped uniquely by the individual hand, three-dimensional sculptures are coming to appear like artifacts, just as artifacts, eventually pushed back into the natural world, are salvaged to be reincarnated in a new life. Far from being solely a matter of categories or semantics, these shifts are of the essence of much non-pictorial activity today. On one hand is stated the proposition that nothing is esthetic merely, and on the other, the counterproposition that the useful or the ruined can always be made esthetic.

After discovering this basic principle for himself, a spectator realizes that it is only a question of accent or emphasis which de-cides whether his experience is essentially that of assemblage or sculpture. The career of the brilliant Richard Stankiewicz is illus-trative of an oscillating sensibility within this whole region. Com-posed of rusted boilers, abandoned plumbing parts, pipes and metallic fittings of every kind, his work first had an assemblage character, by turns wryly witty or primitivistic. But of recent years, his vision has become more abstract and spatially convincing even though the materials he uses have remained basically the same. Much of this can also be said for the metal armatured canvas con-struction of Lee Bontecou. Similarly, with John Chamberlain and David Weinrib, both of whom employ either tatters of mangled automobiles or snipped enameled metal poles and plastic, three-dimensional accomplishment is memorable. Weinrib, who is the oldest of a group of sculptors which includes Tom Doyle and Mark di Suvero, has notably explored the possibilities of an en-vironmental configuration. One can become physically entangled in their work. And this is not to overlook an overall tendency which they exemplify, along with George Sugarman, and the young San Franciscan, Robert Hudson, towards polychrome sculpture, the most remarkable since the end of the last century. It is therefore not at all surprising that these sculptors have direct affinities with painting, Chamberlain with de Kooning, Sugarman with Stuart Davis, Hudson with Frank Lobdell, Weinrib and his friends vari-ously with Franz Kline and Al Held. In general, conventions which painting had long ago exhausted have been engaging the attention of serious sculptors in their infinitely more resistant medium. In turn, too, the initial obtrusiveness of unusual materials fades as spatial dynamics make themselves felt.

Whatever it is that may typify American art of the last seven years, it is neither a single stylistic idiom, nor an ideological consonance, but at the most a mental outlook that expresses itself by obliqueness and indirection, almost cancelling what it apparently sets out to do. In such work initial appearances are invariably never to be trusted. Largely this is what modifies their treatment of ugliness, otherwise a problematic preoccupation in many camps. To be concerned with what is literally the most tawdry and repellent appearances in American civilization is not an activity that would have succeeded, I think, without a correspondingly intellectual interest in redefining the nature of the work and our perception in its own terms. It is this endeavor, finally, for all that its origins might be traced back into Abstract-Expressionism, which maintains a note of discomfort for spectator and artist alike, and by implication keeps the avant-garde spirit alive.

In recent art, intellectual current has been switched from physical performance and emotional continuity—the failure of which produces a most immediate kind of anxiety—to doubt about the distinctions between media and styles, artifact and art—which in turn discharges a less intense, but far more pervasive anxiety. For nourishment, the whole of the European and American twentieth century past is being recapitulated, to be churned up by the kind of inner challenge of this program. If the Dada and Surrealist elements of our tradition were the first to be reappraised, the Constructivists and Bauhaus were the next to fall under a scrutiny of American artists, whose sense of the contemporary makes them fundamentally disrespectful, and whose local experience becomes more and more vicarious and irrational.

More positively expressed, however, the discoveries of contemporary art have to do with the nature of the contained emotional complexes in a pictorial or three-dimensional work. It has been by no means proved that an agitated brush mark connotes emotion, or that a flat, uniformly applied paint surface signifies detachment. These are only the crudest psychological notations, or rather prejudices about the content of a work of art. Most important, the insight is already upon us that our intuitions of spontaneity or calculation may have nothing to do with the emotional state evoked within us—for neither takes into account the artist's own separation of conception and execution, consequences of which are becoming ever more apparent in the galleries. Time and again he disproves that intention equals result, an erroneous belief which was at the core of many theories about Abstract-Expressionism. Cued by a wealth of infinitely subtle contexts, an "hysterical" square is altogether possible. What one sees at the present time are manipulations of such contexts—mutations of anaesthetized passion. Behind such masks, the ambivalences of contemporary civilization are finding perturbing expression.

THE NEW AMERICAN

POETRY

JONATHAN COTT

I

What is "new" in the best contempoary American poetry is hardly what we usually think of as new. A "revolution" has occurred, but it is one that returns us to the poetic worlds of four culturally and chronologically disparate writers: Tu Fu, Catullus, François Villon, and Charles Baudelaire. They are the seminal poetic models for our time, not only in the most obvious sense that they have influenced poets as diverse as Robert Lowell, Kenneth Rexroth, Louis Zukofsky, and Carolyn Kizer, for example, but more importantly because they assume the stances and gestures which almost all contemporary poets accept as the basis of literary creation. That is to say, their poems are the projections of exacerbated sensibilities; and in their poems we see how the Self—constituting the starting point for the poets' explorations of their own psyches and of others'—enables them to write, although with different techniques, of those feelings with which poets have always been concerned: longing, loss, grief, joy, wonder.

It is fair to say, I believe, that in contemporary poetry, if not in astronomy, the Ptolemaic system—where the poet stands for the earth—is more suitable to creation of important poetry than the Copernican system—where types and myths stand for the sun. One should not take this somewhat heady statement as prescriptive; it is descriptive in the most particular way. Almost all recent American poetry from the most "conservative" to the most exploratory— whether by J. V. Cunningham, James Wright, or John Ashbery— supports this point. It is inconceivable, for example, for a contemporary American poet to write a dream allegory like *The Faerie Queene* or design a gigantic typological structure like *The Divine Comedy*. The two great long American poems of the century— Pound's *Cantos* and William Carlos Williams' *Paterson*—are, for all their disguises, personal in the extreme. Pound does nothing less than incorporate in himself the personae of Master Kung, Odysseus, Malatesta, John Adams, et al.; while Williams discovers man himself to be a city, "beginning, seeking, achieving and concluding his life in ways which the various aspects of a city may embody."

We should realize, however, that we too often value Tu Fu, Catullus, Villon, and Baudelaire for their sensibilities alone without recognizing that these poets' greatness derives in part from their responding passionately to and embodying in unique ways their demoralized ages. Contemporary American poets do so, as well, whether by exploring their "alienated" selves or by fragmenting their syntax and working with confusion in order to reflect truthfully on their positions in disjointed times.

The question finally is not whether widely admired poets like James Dickey, Anthony Hecht, W. S. Merwin—I choose these three at random—are "new," but rather whether they explore their selves, their world, and their language in particularly intense or imaginative ways. I do not think that they do; and we might best concentrate on the most important contemporary American poetry by introducing three types of sensibility and the poets of each "type." These poets have at least one thing in common: they have discarded the exploded mythology and the half-truthful "revelation" and assume the Self as starting point in making issue with themselves and the world.

II

My secrets cry aloud.
I have no need for tongue.
My heart keeps open house.
My doors are widely swung.
An epic of the eyes
My love, with no disguise.

My truths are all foreknown,
This anguish self-revealed.
I'm naked to the bone,
With nakedness my shield.
Myself is what I wear:
I keep the spirit spare.

These two stanzas from Theodore Roethke's early poem "Open House" (1941) suggest the tone and method of our first group of poets—poets who expose themselves and by doing so paradoxically make sense of their predicaments; nakedness becomes their shield. Four poets of recent years have most successfully assumed the stances of the four classic poets talked about above, and together they have produced our most forcible body of poetry: Theodore Roethke, John Berryman, Sylvia Plath, and Robert Lowell.*

The poems of Theodore Roethke, who died at fifty-five in the summer of 1963, explore the world of the "minimal"—a world in

---

* Owing to necessary space limitations, one can only mention as belonging to our first group fine poets like Stanley Kunitz, Delmore Schwartz (in earlier poems like "The Heavy Bear," "Starlight Like Intuition," and "A Dog Named Ego, the Snowflakes as Kisses"), Karl Shapiro, Randall Jarrell, John Logan, Theodore Weiss, J. V. Cunningham, David Ignatow, Josephine Miles, and Elizabeth Bishop. Here also belong three of our best young poets—W. D. Snodgrass, Robert Creeley, and Thom Gunn (born in England and now residing in California)—and the two most talented "Beat" poets, Gregory Corso and Allen Ginsberg.

which even the dirt breathes "a small breath," a world in which external and internal realities exist on the same psychic terrain and become identical. Roethke searches below the external surface of his self in order to arrive at the inner soul; the "delineation of the ideal" becomes apparent through the poet's scrutiny. With *The Far Field* (1964), a collection of Roethke's last poems, and the earlier collected verse, *Words for the Wind* (1958), we have Roethke's full testament of this search.

The poet consistently presents himself to us, naked and rampaging his Self. "A man's a beast prowling in his own house," he writes in a later poem, "The Pure Fury." And only in an induced dream-state can the poet arrive at what in "Otto" he calls his "lost world." To reach this world, Roethke must make a poetic journey from "exhaustion to exhaustion" (a phrase he takes from Yeats) during which he dives down in his dream state through all layers of his psyche. Re-integration often occurs in the greenhouse, Roethke's lost world, his personal "symbol for the whole of life, a womb, a heaven-on-earth" ("Open Letter," in *Mid-Century American Poets,* edited by John Ciardi). For Roethke, Father is the Great Gardener. After having "returned" to his "heaven-on-earth" in "The Lost Son," the poet cries out: "Ordnung! Ordnung! Papa is coming."

It is almost embarrassing for a critic to interpret Roethke's work in terms of Freud and Jung. Roethke's series of fourteen child-like, dream-like monologues in *Praise to the End* succeeds so beautifully in communicating "the spring and rush of the child —and Gammer Gurton's concision" ("Open Letter") and in revealing secondary elaboration of subconscious roots of thought and feeling that one would rather think that psychologists obtained their perceptions of dreams and childhood fantasies from Roethke. Conceptions such as "Dreams as a Form of Ideation" and "Nightmares as Objectifications of Organic Sensations," etc., seem foolish when applied to Roethke's work. To say that the line "I have left the body of the whale, but the mouth of the night is still wide" ("The Longing") has "Freudian overtones" is quite idiotic. The bedrock reality and radically "regressive" images of Roethke's poems are so striking and essential that Freud is superfluous. Roethke's work is the discovery of himself; and his poems need no symbolic correlatives to explain them.

The manifest dream content in Roethke's poems consists of objects existing in the world of the "minimal." "The small! The small! I hear them singing clear/On the long banks, in the soft summer air," Roethke writes in "A Walk in Late Summer." And this is a world of sweet-peas, weeds, stones, meadow mice, little girls. But as we can see from almost any quotation from Roethke's poems, the poetic materials spring up from the greenhouse where the poet spent much of his childhood, from the soil of the garden, from the marsh. "Weeds, too, he favoured as most men don't favour men," Berryman wrote about him. And although in "The Abyss" Roethke writes that "too much reality can be a dazzle," he wants only to tell of his intense love for the objects and events of the natural world. In "Night Journey" he writes how on a cross-country train he "stays up half the night/To see the land I love."

Roethke employs images of the world of the "minimal" in all his love poems (hardly equalled for their passion in our time) or meditations or songs: "Love, love, a lily's my care"; "I remember the neckcurls, limp and damp as tendrils." But this world also includes "A kingdom of stinks and sighs,/Fetor of cockroaches, dead fish, petroleum,/Worse than castoreum of mink or weasels,/Saliva dripping from warm microphones,/Agony of crucifixion on barstools" ("The Longing"). For Roethke's world is his mind; his mind, the world; "A ghost comes out of the unconscious mind/To grope my sill. It moans to be reborn!" And it is reborn. Roethke's poems are the means by which he connects the everyday world with his unconscious ghost. We see, for example, how a creature of the world and the creature of the poet's mind in "Night Crow" become one—because they are one:

> When I saw that clumsy crow
> Flap from a wasted tree,
> A shape in the mind rose up:
> Over the gulfs of dream
> Flew a tremendous bird

Further and further away
Into a moonless black,
Deep in the brain, far back.

Ghosts are made real, animals made human; for in Roethke's dream-world there is little distinction between the two. Plants, too, take on human properties. In "Orchids" the flowers have "soft luminescent fingers . . . loose ghostly mouths." In one of Roethke's last great poems, "The Geranium," the poet's relationship with a flower is as human as his love for Jane in his often-anthologized "Elegy for Jane." "The Geranium" resembles this poem in its beautifully cadenced lines and tone of loneliness and grief:

When I put her out, once by the garbage pail
She looked so limp and bedraggled,
So foolish and trusting, like a sick poodle,
Or a wizened aster in later September,
I brought her back in again
For a new routine—
Vitamins, water, and whatever
Sustenance seemed sensible
At the time: she'd lived
So long on gin, bobbie pins, half-smoked cigars, dead beer,
Her shrivelled petals falling
On the faded carpet, the stale
Steak grease stuck to her fuzzy leaves.
(Dried-out, she creaked like a tulip.)

The things she endured!—
The dumb dames shrieking half the night
Or the two of us, alone, both seedy,
Me breathing booze at her,
She leaning out of her pot toward the window.

Near the end, she seemed almost to hear me—
And that was scary—
So when that snuffling cretin of a maid
Threw her, pot and all, into the trash-can,
I said nothing.

But I sacked the presumptuous hag the next week,
I was that lonely.

Roethke writes of such extremes of emotion that one wishes to judge his poems on their power and his imagination alone. Roethke is also, however, one of the great craftsmen of our time. His use of slant and oblique rhymes is wonderfully subtle (lives/ leaves; stone/moon; all/temporal); the villanelle form in "The Waking" and his ballad and song forms of "The Saginaw Song," "A Wheeze for Wystan," and "My Papa's Waltz" are extraordinary. In Roethke's poems, finally, the ideal is delineated only by the identity the poet makes between his psyche and the world. As in a dream, we break through to the beauty of "The Moment"—the moment in which events, things, persons, and feelings are transfigured to become All:

We passed the ice of pain,
And came to a dark ravine,
And there we sang with the sea;
The wide, the bleak abyss
Shifted with our slow kiss.

Space struggled with time;
The gong of midnight struck
The naked absolute.
Sound, silence sang as one.

All flowed; without, within;
Body met body, we
Created what's to be.

What else to say?—
We end in joy.

John Berryman's *Dream Songs* (1964) is one of the great achievements of American poetry.

Turning it over, considering, like a madman
Henry put forth a book.
No harm resulted from this.

Neither the menstruating   stars (nor man) was moved
   at once.
Bare dogs drew closer for a second look

and performed their friendly operations there.
Refreshed, the bark rejoiced.
Seasons went and came.

Leaves fell, but only a few.
Something remarkable about this
unshedding bulky bole-proud blue-green moist

thing made by savage & thoughtful
surviving Henry
began to strike the passers from despair
so that sore on their shoulders old men hoisted
six-foot sons and polished women called
small girls to dream awhile toward the flashing &
                              bursting tree!

Curiously, *Dream Songs* perfectly exemplify the suggestions
Roethke addressed to himself in his "Open Letter" on how a poet
can derive his important powers. The poet, Roethke writes,

> must be able to telescope image and symbol, if necessary, without
> relying on the obvious connectives: to speak in a kind of psychic
> shorthand when his protagonist is under great stress. He must be
> able to shift his rhythms rapidly, the "tension." He works intui-
> tively, and the final form of his poem must be imaginatively right
> . . . obscurity should break open suddenly for the serious reader
> who can hear the language: the "meaning" itself should come as
> dramatic revelation, an excitement.

Berryman, in a note of introduction to his early poems of
1940, wrote of the "strain," the "torsion" of his poetry. In retrospect, we can see how the poet's now-famous twisting, elliptical
style emerges in the fourth and fifth sections of Berryman's first
volume, *The Dispossessed* (1948); for example, "Rising wind rucks
from the sill/The slack brocade beside/the old throne he dreams
on," from "The Long Home." *Homage to Mistress Bradstreet*,
published in 1956 and unfortunately little read, is a magnificent

poem of fifty-seven eight-line stanzas of shifting end rhymes in which the phrasal cadence of the speaking voice conflicts violently with the iambic line. Berryman's latinate diction, wrenched accents, and occasional sprung rhythms combine to produce the haunting study of the torn and deracinated early American poetess. In monologues and interspersed conversations with the poet himself, the poet's heartbreakingly exposed love for and understanding of Anne Bradstreet is revealed:

> Outside the New World winters in grand dark
> white air lashing high thro' the virgin stands
> foxes down foxholes sigh,
> surely the English heart quails, stunned.
> I doubt if Simon than this blast, that sea,
> spares from his rigour for your poetry
> more. We are on each other's hands
> who care. Both of our worlds unhanded us. Lie stark, . . .
>
> *(Stanza 2)*

> Veiled my eyes, attending. How can it be I?
> Moist, with parted lips, I listen, wicked.
> I shake in the morning & retch.
> Brood I do on myself naked.
> A fading world I dust, with fingers new.
> —I have earned the right to be alone with you.
> —What right can that be?
> Convulsing, if you love enough, like a sweet lie.
>
> *(Stanza 27)*

It is in the *Dream Songs,* however, that Berryman finds the perfect vehicle for his style and vision. The eight line stanza becomes six-lined. The "roiling & babbling & braining" (a Berryman phrase) is spoken and sung by Henry, the dreamer of the *Dream Songs.* He talks about and converses with himself, but also with Mr. Bones, perhaps of minstrel show derivation, who is somewhat an alter ego: "Easy, easy, Mr. Bones. I is on your side," says Henry. Sometimes Henry becomes an animal like Henry Pussy-cat, or even the tail of a dog. As Roethke wrote:

The revelation of the identity of the speaker may itself be a part of the drama; or, in some instances, in a dream sequence, his identity may merge with someone else's, or be deliberately blurred. The struggle for spiritual identity is, of course, one of the perpetual recurrences. . . . *Disassociation often precedes a new state of clarity.*

("Open Letter"; emphasis added.)

For there is a marvelous clarity to these songs. They abound, of course, in the condensation and displacement of dream-work. But loneliness and despair have rarely been expressed with such quietness and restraint as in the song titled "Snow Line":

It was wet & white & swift and where I am
we don't know. It was dark and then
It isn't.
I wish the barker would come. There seems to be to eat
nothing. I am unusually tired.
I'm alone too.

If only the strange one with so few legs would come,
I'd say my prayers out of my mouth, as usual.
Where are his notes I loved?
There may be horribles; it's hard to tell.
The barker nips me but somehow I feel
he too is on my side.

I'm too alone. I see no end. If we could all
run, even that would be better. I am hungry.
The sun is not hot.
It's not a good position I am in.
If I had to do the whole thing over again
I wouldn't.

Beyond performing in complete darkness "operations of great delicacy/on myself" for the sake only of his Self, Berryman approaches our life today with the moral stature and compassion of Sam Johnson and Gibbon. He goes naked to show our "moral nudity." In many respects he has an eighteenth-century mind although his speaking voice is the singing brawl of the declamatory sot (Pope's "sot as hero"). It is through these drunken lurchings of syntax, however, that the extirpation of our respect for ourselves and others is witnessed and proclaimed. I have heard Berryman read his *Dream Songs* in public—intoxicated, slurring, emphasizing words so wilfully as to destroy the "line"—yet the majesty of his vision finally broke through like his "flashing & bursting tree." Nothing less than the decline and fall of the contemporary West is revealed in Berryman's "non-tipsyish" drunken songs.

Sometimes Berryman rages against the "teen set":

"Scads of good eats," dere own t'ree cars, the 'teens
(until of them shall be asked one thing, they romp or doze)
have got it made;
no prob. was ever set them, their poor ol' jerks
of parents loved them, with deep-freeze, & snacks
would keep a Hindu family-group alive.

Well, so they're liars & gluttons & cowards: so what?
. . . It's the Land of Plenty, maybe about to sigh.
Why shouldn't they terrify
with hegemony Dad (stupido Dad) and "teach"? . . .

One waits for the Houyhnhnms to set the "teens" to "hard work."

Berryman realizes that our "squeamish comfy ruin-prone proud national mind" is the small cause from which extend the greater evils. But the cocktail parties go on, parties like the one in which "Henry's pelt was put on sundry walls" (one is reminded of Roethke's "The flying fabric stitched on bone"):

Golden, whilst your frozen daiquiris
whir at midnight, gleams on you his fur
& silky & black.
Mission accomplished, pal.
My molten yellow & moonless bag,
drained, hangs at rest.

Collect in the cold depths barracuda. Ay,
in Sealdah Station some possessionless
children survive to die.
The Chinese communes hum. Two daiquiris
withdrew into a corner of the gorgeous room
and one told the other a lie.

And finally we have Berryman's songs of grief for those like Roethke and Robert Frost who are "in friendlier ground"; for their virtues and feelings were so "unusual," patent and open-to-wounding in the face of everyday evils. About Frost, Berryman writes:

> His malice was a pimple down his good
> big face, with its sly eyes. I must be sorry
> Mr. Frost has left:
> I like it so less I don't understood—
> he couldn't hear or see well—all we sift—
> but this is a *bad* story.

Berryman faces ruin and frustration with high comedy and low comedy and sorrow; with "ancient sighs, infamous characters, new rhythms." How can we help but be moved by the courage of:

> The high ones die, die. They die. You look up and who's there?
> —Easy, easy, Mr. Bones. I is on your side.
> I smell your grief.
> —I sent my grief away. I cannot care
> forever. With them all again & again I died
> and cried, and I have to live.

And even when we read lines like these, we know that John Berryman's fortitude and artistic power will endure the clawing degenerations of these years:

> these fierce & airy occupations, and love,
> raved away so many of Henry's years
> it is a wonder that, with in each hand
> one of his own mad books & all,
> ancient fires for eyes, his head full
> & his heart full, he's making ready to move on.

Of the several women who in the past few years have emerged as among the most interesting of American poets, the best of them, Sylvia Plath, who died at thirty-one in 1963, appears already to be one of the most startling women poets of any time.

Her predecessor, the late Dilys Lang, in her *Poems from a*

Cage (1961) once wrote of a poetry in which "the idea of a cage, or of captivity, is paramount," as well as a poetry of "release." Her verse, however, only occasionally exemplifies her ideal. The two women who realize these kinds of poetry most successfully, however, are Anne Sexton and Sylvia Plath. The former's collections —*To Bedlam and Part Way Back* (1960) and *All My Pretty Ones* (1962)—display a concern with madness, despair, and the attempted breakthrough out of bedlam. Her poems, like those of Frederick Seidel, too often explore one depressive state without relief or variation and thus dissipate their intended power through a kind of emotional stasis.

Sylvia Plath succeeds in accomplishing what Anne Sexton has attempted and Dilys Lang hoped to accomplish. Like Gaspara Stampa, the great Venetian cinquecentist courtesan poet, Sylvia Plath died terribly young at thirty-one, extending Gaspara Stampa's themes of "fever and love" into the areas of terror and suicide in finished, corrosive poems of almost unimaginable intensity. She published one collection of poems, *The Colossus,* in 1961; but her most startling verse appeared in magazines like *The New Yorker* and *Encounter* shortly after her death.

Sylvia Plath's poems betray her own awareness of an impending early death. "I am terrified by this dark thing/That sleeps in me," she writes in "The Elm Speaks." "All day I feel its soft, feathery turnings, its malignity." In "The Manor Garden," the first poem of *The Colossus,* she shows the influence of the early-to-die Georg Trakl:

> The fountains are dry and the roses over.
> Incense of death. Your day approaches.
> The pears fatten like little buddhas.
> A blue mist is dragging the lake.

And her poems do display the deracinated sensibility of many of the German Romantics. One cannot help wondering whether she did not also absorb the child-rhythms and cadences of German traditional rhymes and folk songs which occur as distinctive elements in her work:

The little toy wife—
Erased, sigh, sigh.
Four babies and a cocker!

Nurses, the size of worms, and a minute doctor
Tuck him in.
Old happenings

Peel from his skin.
Down the drain with all of it!
Hugging his pillow

Like the red-headed sister he never dared to touch,
He dreams of a new one—
Barren, the lot are barren!

(from "Amnesiac")

But this aspect of her poems illuminates the grim and dreadful
humor with which (more than John Clare and Roethke) she uses
the vehicle of childhood to write of her most personal and consum-
ing memories, especially of her German-born father who died when
she was ten. In "The Colossus," she attempts to reconstruct him
as if she were playing with a jigsaw puzzle:

I shall never get you put together entirely,
Pieced, glued, and properly jointed.
Mule-bray, pig-grunt and bawdy cackles
Proceed from your great lips.
It's worse than a barnyard.

Her most moving poem, entitled "Daddy," significantly begins in
nursery-rhyme manner:

You do not do, you do not do
Anymore, black shoe
In which I have lived like a foot
For thirty years, poor and white,
Barely daring to breathe or Achoo!

Daddy, I have had to kill you.
You died before I had time—

Marble-heavy, a bag full of God,
Ghastly statue with one grey toe
Big as a Frisco seal

And a head in the freakish Atlantic
Where it pours bean green over blue
In the waters off beautiful Nauset.
I used to pray to recover you.
Ach, du!

But it concludes with a self-destructive savagery and outraged
tenderness that leave one staggered:

You stand at the blackboard, daddy,
In the picture I have of you,
A cleft in your chin instead of your foot
But no less a devil for that, no not
Any less the black man who

Bit my pretty red heart in two.
I was ten when they buried you.
At twenty I tried to die
And get back, back, back to you.
I thought even the bones would do.

But they pulled me out of the sack,
And they stuck me together with glue.
And then I knew what to do.
I made a model of you,
A man in black with a Meinkampf look

And a love of the rack and the screw.
And I said I do, I do.
So daddy, I'm finally through.
The black telephone's off at the root,
The voices just can't worm through.

If I've killed one man, I've killed two—
The vampire who said he was you
And drank my blood for a year—
Seven years, if you want to know.
Daddy, you can lie back now.

> There's a stake in your fat black heart
> And the villagers never liked you.
> They are dancing and stamping on you.
> They always *knew* it was you.
> Daddy, daddy, you bastard, I'm through.

There is nothing like this in contemporary poetry. Even Stanley Kunitz's and Robert Lowell's magnificent poems about their fathers, as poignant and agonizing as they are, do not come close to the crazy humor and grief and destructiveness of this poem. Sylvia Plath faced ruin herself too many times not to wear it like a glove. From "Lady Lazarus" we read:

> I have done it again!
> One year in every ten
> I manage it—
>
> A sort of walking miracle, my skin
> Bright as a Nazi lampshade
> My right foot
>
> A paperweight,
> My face a featureless, fine
> Jew linen. . . .
>
> . . . I am only thirty
> And like the cat I have nine times to die.
>
> This is Number Three.
> What a trash
> To annihilate each decade!

Sylvia Plath is certainly a remarkable poet. Lines like: "My night sweats grease his breakfast plate"; "The air is a mill of hooks"; or "The yew's black fingers wag" are exceptional. Her construction of syllabic verse in "Mussel Hunter at Rock Harbor" and "Man in Black" and the subtle development of images in "Little Fugue" and "Mystic," for example, display a phenomenal technical mastery. Her rich and acute feel for language and disarming use of off-rhyme is excellently illustrated in the following two stanzas from "Watercolor of Grantchester Meadows":

Cloudrack and owl-hollowed willows slanting over
The bland Granta double their white and green
World under the sheer water
And ride the flux at anchor, upside down.
The punter sinks his pole.
In Byron's pool
Cattails part where the tame cygnets steer.

It is a country on a nursery plate.
Spotted cows revolve their jaws and crop
Red clover or gnaw beetroot
Bellied on a nimbus of sun-glazed buttercup.
Hedging meadows of benign
Arcadian green
The blood-berried hawthorn hides its spines with white.

Yet Sylvia Plath continually sees the moon "with the O-gape of complete despair. I live here," she tells us. We must approach her poetry with the knowledge that she suffered a sickness unto death and bore it to the surface through the discipline of her art, unveiling her sickness totally—"I am not cruel, only truthful."

So many fine essays have been written about Robert Lowell's *Lord Weary's Castle* (1946) and *The Mills of the Kavanaughs* (1951), especially Randall Jarrell's "From the Kingdom of Necessity," that it might be best merely to point to what is at once Lowell's most obvious strength and weakness—a somewhat over-violent use of language in his earlier poems as contrasted with the more subtle and powerful diction of Lowell's recent work. From the first stanza of "Colloquy in Black Rock," we read:

Here the jack-hammer *jabs* into the ocean;
My heart, you *race* and *stagger* and *demand*
More blood-gangs for your nigger-brass percussions,
Till I, the *stunned* machine of your devotion
Clanging upon this cymbal of a hand,
Am *rattled* screw and footloose. . . .

(Emphasis added)

The slashing aggressiveness of Lowell's verbs and verbals give the key to the tone and intent of most of the poet's earlier verse. "Colloquy in Black Rock," like most of Lowell's religious poems, keeps to the blazing tone to produce a magnificent poem. But in a sense, Lowell tends to limit his experience inversely as he ignites his verbs and images. Lowell's more recent verse—which some persons imagine to be more "simple-minded"—is, on the contrary, an advance over the previous verse, a true "breakthrough back into life." What we find appears at first to be the simpler, quieter, and "looser" structures of *Life Studies* (1959) and *Imitations* (1961):

> One dark night,
> my Tudor Ford climbed the hill's skull;
> I watched for love-cars. Lights turned down,
> they lay together, hull to hull,
> where the graveyard shelves on the town. . . .
> My mind's not right.
>
> A car radio bleats,
> "Love, O careless Love. . . ." I hear
> my ill-spirit sob in each blood cell,
> I myself am hell;
> nobody's here—
>
> only skunks, that search
> in the moonlight for a bite to eat.
> They march on their soles up Main Street:
> white stripes, moonstruck eyes' red fire
> under the chalk-dry and spar spire
> of the Trinitarian Church.
>
> I stand on top
> of four back steps and breathe the rich air—
> a mother skunk with her column of kittens swills the garbage pail.
> She jabs her wedge-head in a cup
> of sour cream, drops her ostrich tail,
> and will not scare.
>
> (from "Skunk Hour")

But in fact we are discovering, to use out of context Lowell's words from his *Paris Review* interview, a poem like "Skunk Hour" in which "you wouldn't notice the form, yet looking back you'd find that great obstacles had been climbed." Lowell's poems about Ford Madox Ford and Delmore Schwartz; "Memories of West Street and Lepke"; "Man and Wife"; "A Mad Negro Soldier Confined in Munich"—to name just several—manifest the "commanding, deadly effectiveness in the arrangement, and something that breathes and pauses and grunts and is rough and unpredictable to assure me that the journey is honest," to quote Lowell's own essay on Stanley Kunitz.

Lowell has published in magazines like *Partisan Review* and *Encounter* poems (now collected in *For the Union Dead*) about middle age and middle-age marriage in particular. "The Flaw" reveals all the "naked truths"; like Keats, Lowell refuses to "unperplex" bliss from pain:

> Old wives and husbands! Look, their gravestones wait
> in couples with the name and half the date—
> one future and one freedom. In a flash,
> I see us whiten into skeletons,
> our eager, sharpened cries, a pair of stones,
> cutting like shark fins through the boundless wash.
>
> Two walking cobwebs, almost bodiless,
> crossed paths here once, kept house, and lay in beds.
> Your fingertips once touched my fingertips,
> and set us tingling through a thousand threads.
> Poor pulsing *Fête Champêtre!* The summer slips
> between our fingers into nothingness. . . .

But in a group of poems about his Maine cottage, Lowell opens up, as if to the sea air, to write "The Old Flame" or the following poem entitled "Water":

> It was a Maine lobster town—
> each morning boatloads of hands
> pushed off for granite
> quarries on the islands,

and left dozens of bleak
white frame houses stuck
like oyster shells
on a hill of rock,

and below us, the sea lapped
the raw little match-stick
mazes of a weir,
where the fish for bait were trapped.

Remember? We sat on a slab of rock.
From this distance in time,
it seems the color
of iris, rotting and turning purpler,

but it was only
the usual gray rock
turning the usual green
when drenched by the sea.

The sea drenched the rock
at our feet all day,
and kept tearing away
flake after flake.

One night you dreamed
you were a mermaid clinging to a wharf-pile,
and trying to pull
off the barnacles with your hands.

We wished our two souls
might return like gulls
to the rock. In the end,
the water was too cold for us.

It is the poet's clear, open exploration of the presentness of feeling and the true discovery of the beauty and heartbreak of the reality of the "other"—Lowell's Anne Kavanaugh and Bathsheba are mostly Lowell himself—that are providing us now with the poet's fullest and most moving poetry. His unobtrusive slant rhymes (hands/islands; rock/stuck; color/purpler) and gentle but remarkably restless cadences correspond in technique to this new emotional "opening up."

Lowell's exquisite imitations—"reckless with the literal meaning" but "getting the tone"—of Heine:

> How confidingly the corrupt twin rocked me in his arms;
> his poppy garland, nearing, hushed death's alarms
> at sword-point for a moment.
> Soon a pinpoint of infinite regression! And now that incident
> is closed. There's no way out,
> unless the other turn about
> and, pale, distinguished, perfect, drop his torch;
>
> ("Heine Dying in Paris")

or of Russians like Mandelstam and Pasternak:

> Like water pouring from a pitcher, my mouth on your nipples!
> Not always. The summer well runs dry.
> Not for long the dust of our stamping feet, encore on encore
> from the saxes in the casino's midnight gazebo;
>
> (Pasternak's "Sparrow Hills")

all exemplify and extend Lowell's new "tone" and approach. Here is no withdrawal of the power that conceived the poems in *Lord Weary's Castle;* rather it is the unequivocal growth of Robert Lowell's great art. For rarely before have openness, tenderness, and understanding been so naturally wedded in poems that do not reflect self-consciously on themselves but communicate their experiences directly to the reader.

III

> "Oh to be seventeen years old
> Once again," sang the red-haired man, "and not know that poetry
> Is ruled with the sceptre of the dumb, the deaf, and the creepy!"
> And the shouting persons battered his immortal body with stones
> And threw his primitive comedy into the sea
> From which it sang forth poems irrevocably blue.
>
> *from* "Fresh Air" by Kenneth Koch

The so-called "New York poets"—its members consisting of John Ashbery, Edwin Denby, Barbara Guest, Kenneth Koch, and Frank O'Hara—is the most original "school" of poetry today.

While the members of this "school" have been influenced by the nineteenth- and twentieth-century European "avant-garde," they have absorbed, but modulated and directed for their own ends, the dazzling and unorthodox syntax, diction, and tones of Mallarmé, Tristan Corbière, Apollinaire, Pierre Reverdy, Vladimir Mayakovsky, and Pasternak.

Frank O'Hara, for example, in his best poems takes off from Mayakovsky's *The Cloud in Trousers,* which begins:

> Your thought,
> musing on a sodden brain
> like a bloated lackey on a greasy couch,
> I'll taunt with a bloody morsel of heart;
> and satiate my insolent, caustic contempt.
>
> No gray hairs streak my soul,
> no grandfatherly fondness there!
> I shake the world with the might of my voice,
> and walk—handsome
> twentytwoyear old . . . ;

and from Mayakovsky's "To His Beloved Self";

> With my eyes' rays I'd gnaw the night—
> if I were, oh,
> as dull
> as the sun!
> Why should I want
> to feed with my radiance
> the earth's lean lap!
>
> I shall go by,
> dragging my burden of love.
> In what delirious
> and ailing
> night,
> was I sired by Goliaths—
> I, so large,
> so unwanted?

This is a poetry of an explosive, high-pitched adolescent sensibility displaying and celebrating itself alone: "Where shall I find a beloved," Mayakovsky writes, "a beloved like me?/She would be too big for the tiny sky!" Like Mayakovsky, O'Hara never allows the "sluggish fish of the imagination to flounder softly in the slush of the heart." O'Hara begins his poem "Invincibility" with an epigraph from Mayakovsky: "In the church of my heart the choir is on fire." But O'Hara soars even higher and in a more urbane manner than his Russian model. Like the others in his "school," O'Hara "plays" with language with a great deal of *panache:*

> Avarice, the noose that lets oil, oh my dear oh
> "La Ronde," erase what is assured and ours, it
> resurrects nothing, finally, in its eagerness
> to sit under the widely spaced stairs, to be a fabulous
> toilette, doesn't imitate footsteps of disappearance
>
> The neighbor, having teased peace to retire, soon
> averages six flowering fountains, ooh! spare the men
> and their nervous companions that melt and ripen
> into a sordid harbor of squid-slipping tarpaulin strips,
> quits the sordid arbor of community butchers' girth. . . .

O'Hara—and the New York "school" for that matter—has been closely associated with a group of abstract expressionist painters. In fact, O'Hara's poems often communicate the glitter and energy of the paintings of Pollock, De Kooning, and Larry Rivers, the last of whom designed the cover of O'Hara's long poem *Second Avenue* (1960), "dedicated to the memory of Mayakovsky." O'Hara here handles long lines of fantastic exploding images and skittish humor, dissociative leaps of feeling, with a marvelous control. He is, like Mayakovsky, "just bare lips," open and dizzy in exposing himself to his world:

> My hands are Massimo Plaster, called "White Pin in the Arm of
> the Sea"
> and I'm blazoned and scorch like a fleet of windbells down the
> Pulaski Skyway

tabletops of Vienna carrying their bundles of cellophane to the
laundry,
ear to the tongue, glistening semester of ardency, young-old daring-
nesses
at the foot of the most substantial art product of our times,
the world, the jongleurs, fields of dizzyness and dysentery
before reaching Mexico, the palace of stammering sinking success
before billows of fangs, red faces, orange eyebrows, green, yes!
ears,
O paradise! my airplanes known as "Banana Line Incorporealidad,"
saviors of connections and spit, dial HYancinth 9–9945, "Isn't that
a conundrum?" asked him Sydney Burger, humming "Mein' Yid-
disher Mama";
I emulate the black which is a cry but is not voluptuary like a
warning,
which has lines, cuts, drips, aspirates, trembles with horror,
O black looks at the base of the spine! kisses on the medulla
oblongata
of an inky clarity! always the earlobes in the swiftest bird's-death
of night, the snarl of expiation which is the skirt of Hercules,
and the remorse in the desert shouts "Flea! Bonanza! Cheek! Teat!
Elbow of roaches! You wear my white rooster like a guerdon in
vales
of Pompeiian desires, before utter languorousness puts down its
chisel,"
and the desert is here. "You've reached the enormous summit of
passion
which is immobility forging an entrail from the pure obstruction
of the air."

A poet like O'Hara continues in his writing to get at the
"right language," while at the same time illuminating it, and to
incorporate everyday "things," like telephone numbers, into poetic
diction. One thinks of W. C. Williams' list of typical American ice
creams from "Della Primaver Transportata Al Morale." "We poets
have to talk in a language which is not English," Williams wrote in
Paterson. "It is the American idiom. Rhythmically it's organized as
a sample of the American idiom. It has as much originality as jazz.

If you say '2 partridges, 2 mallard ducks, a Dungeness crab'—if you treat that rhythmically, ignoring the practical sense, it forms a jagged pattern. It is, to my mind, poetry." And O'Hara draws not only on Williams' dicta, but on Mayakovsky's poetic exclamations like: "Yum-yum-yum!" or "Drink Van Houten's Cocoa!" and on the English poet John Betjeman's use of common commercial products' names in his work. Earlier than this, we can also witness a freeing-up of line and tone in the fine, little-read poems collected in *Initial A* (1961) by David Schubert, a true "New York poet," who lived in the city from 1913–1946. But perhaps we might wilfully see this kind of colloquial freedom emerging as far back as Byron's *Don Juan,* especially in those lines T. S. Eliot made famous in his essay on Byron:

> Who queer a flat? Who (spite of Bow-street's ban)
> On the high toby-spice so flash the muzzle?
> Who on a lark, with black-eyed Sal (his blowing)
> So prime, so well, so nutty, and so knowing?

Kenneth Koch's *Ko, or A Season on Earth* (1959) starts off from Don Juan, by way of *Orlando Furioso,* assuming *ottava rima* structure and a fantastic "mythological machinery/And very handsome supernatural scenery," to quote Byron. Koch's mock epic concerns a Japanese baseball star and an assortment of "characters" such as Dog Boss, the Action Poet Joseph Dah, King Amaranth, baseball players, and young lovers. The setting, like the plots, shifts every few stanzas—from Cincinnati to Tahiti to Pompeii to Kalamazoo—all is possible in Koch's world. The following quotation from Canto I should suggest Koch's "method":

> The cabin door shot open, and a man
> (Or was it human?) with a hairy large
> Long sloping face, which was all colored tan
> Except the blackish nose, came in the Arg-
> Entina-purchased cabin with a can
> Of worms he used to fish with from the barge
> And woofed and barked and quite upset the room
> By running 'round. Andrews, alarmed, cried, "Whom . . . ?"

Doris spoke smiling: "Dad's integrity
Makes him, unlike most poets, actualize
In everyday life the poem's unreality.
That dog you saw on deck with steel-gray eyes
Was but a creation of Dad's terrible musical potency.
Then seeing the dog there made him realize
That the dog was himself, since by himself created,
So in this poem it's incorporated!"

"But," Andrews asked, "what poem? where?" and "Ah!"
Breathed Doris, "don't you know that what you're seeing
Is an ACTION POEM?" "You mean he's Joseph Dah,"
Cried Andrews, "the creator of Otherness Being?"
"The very same," sighed Doris. "That's my pa!"
And Joseph, as if by his barks agreeing
Shook his tan head and frisked back out on deck.
He changed, then smiled: "It's a nice day, by heck!"

Koch's shorter poems, collected in *Thank You and Other Poems* (1962) and largely appearing in small New York magazines, reveal his debt to Ronald Firbank, Williams, but most of all to Apollinaire. Koch appropriates influences, radically refocusing them, however, in order to assume an adolescent persona in many of his poems, such as the one beginning: "Is the basketball coach a homosexual lemon manufacturer? It is suspected by O'Ryan in his submarine"; or "To You," which begins: "I love you as a sheriff searches for a walnut/That will solve a murder case unsolved for years. . . . I love you as a/Kid searches for a goat; I am crazier than shirttails/In the wind, when you're near, a wind that blows from/The big blue sea, so shiny so deep and so unlike us."

Seventeen years old seems to be the blissful age, a Golden Age, for Koch's poetic heroes—the age to which they longingly look back. Koch's characters, like Spenser's bridal couple in *Epithalamion,* "play their sports at will" and polymorphously delight; but unlike Spenser's couple, they do not accept the "laws of wedlock" as the *telos.* Thus Koch attacks the "restraint and mature talent" of the poetry "establishment" which represents those poets in the "kingdom of dullness" who write "on the subject of love between swans."

As with O'Hara, the word "play" is one of the keys to an understanding and appreciation of Koch's poetry. Koch manipulates language wonderfully, as in lines like: "lilac of angry fudge"; "And the fanning park/In lover's track of clacked-up snow"; or in the marvelous opening of "Summery Weather":

> One earring's smile
> Near the drawer
> And at night we gambling
> At that night the yacht on Venice
> Glorious too, oh my heavens
> See how her blouse was starched up.
> "The stars reminded me of youse." . . .

But perhaps the most fanciful word-play occurs in the one hundred, twenty-lined stanzas of *When the Sun Tries to Go On,* published in *The Hasty Papers,* a poem which defies explication and even persistent reading:

> And, with a shout, collecting coat-hangers
> Dour rhebus, conch, hip.
> Ham, the autumn day, oh how genuine!
> Literary frog, catch-all boxer, O
> Real! The magistrate, say "group," bower, undies
> Disk, poop, "Timon of Athens." When
> The bugle shimmies, how glove towns! . . .

And so on for 2,000 lines! You either enjoy this kind of "play" or you don't. Although the poem is certainly "not serious," it is also finally boring, for the desire to "play" has been played out in the extreme. In "The Artist," moreover, much of the comedy derives from the confusion Koch purposely contrives between the use and mention of the word *Play:* "I often think *Play* was my best work"; "Was this how I originally imagined *Play,* but lacked courage?"

The extraordinary "A Poem of the Forty-Eight States"— especially influenced by Apollinaire's "Zone," and to me Koch's best poem—is a crazily-guided tour around the imagined United States of the poet's true-adolescent narrator, perhaps Koch's alter ego, who has too much knowledge (in Eliot's sense in "Gerontion") to be forgiven because of his "youthful" sensibility:

> The electric chair steamed lightly, then touched
> Me, I drove, upward,
> Into the hills of Montana. My pony!
> Here you are coming alone with your master!
> Yet I am your master! You're wearing my sweater.
> O pony, my pony!
>
> As in a dream I was waiting to be seventh
> To smile at my brothers in the happy state of Idaho
> Each and every one of them condemned to the electric chair!
> What have we done? Is it a crime
> To shoe horses? Besides a lemon-yellow stream
> There seemed to be compact bassoons,
> And I was happy and a crackerjack. . . .

Koch's narrator not only travels through but also becomes the states ("My stovepipe hat! Perhaps you think I am Uncle Sam?/ No, I am the State of Pennsylvania . . ."). Koch has of course made this kind of imaginative spatial leap before in "Desire for Spring" (". . . I wish to leap to Pittsburgh/From Tuskegee, Indiana, if necessary, spreading like a flower/In the spring light, and growing like a silver stair. . . .") and this is much like the painting technique of the "felt image of the body" used by Picasso and Chagall, for instance, that extends the torso visually when the torso "feels" longer. Whitman, Mayakovsky, and O'Hara do this kind of thing frequently in their poetry. But as "Poem of the Forty-Eight States" nears its conclusion, Koch's narrator communicates an anguish of outraged adolescence, so frightening and powerful, that we are reminded not only of Whitman, but also of Villon:

5

> O Mississippi joys!
> I reckon I am about as big and dead as a whale!

I am slowly sinking down into the green ooze
Of the Everglades, that I feared so much when I was a child!
I have become about as flat as the dust on a baseball diamond
And as empty and clear as the sky when it is just-blue
And you are three, and you stand on the rim of the zone of one
    of the United States
And think about the forty-seven others; then in the evening
Air you hear the sound of baseball players, and the splash of
    canoes!
You yourself would like to play baseball and travel, but you are
    too young;
However you look up into the clear flat blue of the evening sky
And vow that you will one day be a traveler like myself,
And wander to all the ends of the earth until you are completely
    exhausted,
And then return to Texas or Indiana, whatever state you happen
    to be from.
And have your death celebrated by a lavish funeral
Conducted by starlight, with numerous boys and girls reading my
    poems aloud!

8

I did not understand what you meant by the Hudson Tunnel,
But now I understand, New Jersey, I like it fine,
I like the stifling black smoke and the jagged heave-ho of the trains,
I like the sunlight too at the end of the tunnel, like my rebirth in
    the poems of Kenneth Koch,
I like the way the rosy sunlight streams down upon the silver
    tracks,
I like the way the travelers awake from their dreams and step upon
    the hard paving stone of the station,
But I reckon what I should like best would be to see Indiana again,
Or Texas or Arkansas, or Alabama, the "Cotton State,"
Or Big Rose Pebble Island off the coast of Maine
Where I used to have so much fun during the summer, cooking and
    kidding and having myself a good time,
I like Pennsylvania too, we could have a lot of fun there,
You and I will go there when Kenneth is dead.

John Ashbery, the foremost poet of this school and today's most radically original American poet, writes of characters who operate in a drama without a story. His method is somewhat like that of certain serial composers—a-thematic and discontinuous—but more obviously like that of "abstract" painters who, when they title a painting "White Rose," are concerned more with connoting White Roses than in designating them in a more literal or representational sense. Ashbery is not expressly interested in the sound and texture of words, as is Gertrude Stein in *To Do* and *Tender Buttons*. His language is, word-by-word and image-by-image, always simple and elementary: "The pest asked us to re-examine the screws he held"; "Just then the barman squirted juice over the lumps"; "It decided to vote for ink (the village)." The surprise comes when we realize that these three seemingly unrelated fragments comprise the first three lines of Ashbery's "Landscape."

Anyone who attempts to apply Yvor Winters' dictum—that a poet should attempt to make in his poem a rational statement of a specific experience, thus defining it, and manifest in the poem those feelings that constitute an exact correspondence to the poet's particular understanding of that experience—to Ashbery's poems might as well not even begin to read them. Winters' theories help us to explicate Ben Jonson's "Elegy on the Lady Jane Pawlet" or Fulke Greville's "Down in the depths of mine iniquity," but they cannot deal with Mallarmé and certainly not with Ashbery—the first of whom Winters does and the latter of whom he undoubtedly would condemn, unfairly I think, just because their poetry does not "fit" his esthetic prescriptions.

Ashbery's quiet, elegant, and often refractory lines suggest those of the early poems of England's F. T. Prince and, most especially, those of Pasternak's, one of Ashbery's important influences. When not employing these long lines, however, Ashbery has invented a "notation" that sounds at times like the englyn form of old Welsh poetry: "Boots and aprons and crows and a blowing/ and cats from Rome. . . ./"; or like some of Kafka's sentence fragments: "Carried forward on the horse—"; "To sit in the corner of a trolley, your coat wrapped around you." *Europe,* a poem

in 111 parts, represents, like Koch's "The Islands," which it somewhat resembles, Ashbery's difficult but adroit construction of a
disconnected journey:

<pre>
              1
         To employ her
         construction ball
         Morning fed on the
         light blue wood
         of the mouth
                     cannot understand
         feels deeply)

              2
         A wave of nausea—
         numerals

              3
         a few berries

              4
         the unseen claw
         Babe asked today
         The background of poles roped over
         into star jolted them

             55
         mood seems the sort
         to brag
         end

             56
         songs like
         You came back to me
         you were wrong about the gravestone
       that nettles hide quietly
       The son is not ours
</pre>

Now while it is true that Ashbery discards logic, he does not
discard meaning, even if it proves difficult to get at. "Much that is
beautiful," Ashbery writes in "Illustration," "Must be discarded/

So that we may resemble a taller/Impression of ourselves." About painters like Grace Hartigan and Larry Rivers, O'Hara once wrote:

> In this pocket-abyss where one doesn't know where one is at, where a large red painting may be a Grace Hartigan or a howitzer, where one has nightmares about not knowing what one is looking at, the only thing you have to hold onto is your own natural savagery, and your ability to recognize your own *natural* savagery has been given to you by this art which in turn is the cause of your anxiety about not being able to recognize anything but yourself. And that is the last thing one wishes to recognize. . . .
>
> (From School of New York: Some
Younger Artists; edited by B. H.
Friedman)

Ashbery's poetry does not arouse this much anxiety in us, but it has the quality of a dream which begs to be interpreted, since we dreamt it, and yet whose most fascinating and wondrous quality is that it resists being interpreted—for why else have we dreamt it? As the first lines of *"Le livre est sur la table"* begin:

> All beauty, resonance, integrity,
> Exist by deprivation or logic
> Of strange position. This being so,
>
> We can only imagine a world in which a woman
> Walks and wears her hair and knows
> All that she does not know. Yet we know
>
> What her breasts are. And we give fullness
> To the dream. . . .

And the dreams are "beautiful"; they are more real than reality:

> I have lost the beautiful dreams
> That enlisted on waking,
> Cold and waiting. . . .
>
> ("The New Realism")

But anyone who reads Ashbery's two published collections, *Some Trees* (1956) and *The Tennis Court Oath* (1962), must be struck by the hidden but, as one gets accustomed to making connections and following poetic "leads," the perpetual divulgence of the theme of lost innocence; this theme operates in subservience to and as example of the poet's central idea that "as change is horror,/Virtue is really stubbornness/And only in the light of lost words/Can we imagine our rewards." Thus in many ways Ashbery is concerned with the same feelings and issues found in O'Hara's and Koch's poetry, but Ashbery distances himself through his "hard" tone and problematic syntax from these feelings, becoming in a fashion an "effigy of indifference"—a quality he ascribes to the novice in "Illustration"—for the purpose of dealing with them with greater power.

In "Le Livre" Ashbery writes that "Men appear, but they live in boxes." Girls, in the beautiful "And You Know," "protected by gold wire from the gaze/Of the onrushing students, live in an atmosphere of vacuum/In the old schoolhouse covered with nasturtiums." And Ashbery asks in the poem whose first line designates its title: "How much longer will I be able to inhabit the divine sepulcher/Of life, my great love?" The breaking-out of childhood, represented as a box, the sepulcher that "hid death and hides me"—an action which above all insists on the "horror" of change from innocence to experience, and which occurs in "The Picture of Little J.A. in a Prospect of Flowers," "Grand Abacus," "The Instruction Manual," and "Our Youth," for example—exposes the horror of the "dark elders" to the child. In the extraordinary poem "Our Youth," death in the guise of dead animals and decaying objects reveals itself when the bubble of childhood bursts—actually, when we are born:

> Of bricks . . . Who built it? Like some crazy balloon
> When love leans on us
> Its nights . . . The velvety pavement sticks to our feet.
> The dead puppies turn us back on love.
>
> Where we are. Sometimes
> The brick arches led to a room like a bubble, that broke when you
>   entered it
> And sometimes to a fallen leaf.
> We got crazy with emotion, showing how much we knew.

The Arabs took us. We knew
The dead horses. We were discovering coffee,
How it is to be drunk hot, with bare feet
In Canada. And the immortal music of Chopin

Which we had been discovering for several months
Since we were fourteen years old. And coffee grounds,
And the wonder of hands, and the wonder of the day
When the child discovers her first dead hand. . . .

Ashbery employs children's exclamations and a distancing tone to emphasize his sense that death and corruption emerge as our sub-consciousness unsuccessfully attempts to ward off the inexorable fact of change, of growing:

Heh? Eh? Our youth is dead.
From the minute we discover it with eyes closed
Advancing into mountain light. . . .

He is dead. Green and yellow handkerchiefs cover him.
Perhaps he will never rot, I see
That my clothes are dry. I will go.
The naked girl crosses the street.

Blue hampers . . . Explosions,
Ice . . . The ridiculous
Vases of porphyry. All that our youth
Can't use, that it was created for.

It's true we have not avoided our destiny
By weeding out the old people.
Our faces have filled with smoke. We escape
Down the cloud ladder, but the problem has not been solved.

Ashbery, writing of "The Pied Piper" in a poem beginning "Under the day's crust a half-eaten child," tells of children "coupling as the earth crumbled." The Piper's love was "strongest" Ashbery writes, hardening his attitude, because the Piper "never loved them [the children] at all . . . his notes/Most civil, laughing not to return." In the face of the horror of growing up, Ashbery finds it necessary to pose himself as distant from the horror, which merely re-emphasizes the horror. This is why the most beautiful and "romantic" images of Ashbery's poems are continually juxtaposed with ugly and terrifying ones or, as Ashbery writes, with the "spoiled, sordid"; as examples, "carnation world" with a "hair or a sneeze"; a "garden in mist" with "mush raging, the stump again."

In this poetic landscape, Ashbery also suggests the necessity of reaching for the "other," and he does so very often by mentioning in his poems the writing or reading of a letter to or by someone else. "The Tennis Court Oath" seems, for all its discontinuity, to be about the writing and the reading of a love letter. One of Ashbery's most moving love poems, "Thoughts of a Young Girl," a poem for an imaginary daughter, begins with a letter:

> "It is such a beautiful day I had to write you a letter
> From the tower, and to show I'm not mad:
> I only slipped on the cake of soap of the air
> And drowned in the bathtub of the world. . . ."

"The Ticket" begins: "The experience of writing you these love letters . . ."—a statement tantalizingly indefinite about time, place, or object. Then, too, in "Rain" we read: "The missing letter —the crumb of confidence," and are reminded of the renovating virtue of "lost words."

What is particularly jolting to us as we read Ashbery's poems is the possibility that his "you," to whom the letters are addressed, may well be Ashbery himself; there is, in fact, no reason to suggest otherwise. And this kind of awareness makes Ashbery's poems more puzzling and disquieting than we might have at first imagined. Nevertheless, that striving for "touching" and meeting never disappears from Ashbery's poetry; and this striving can best be seen in one of the poet's first works, "Some Trees"—a poem of subtlety and beauty that is at once a wish for and an arrival at communion:

> These are amazing: each
> Joining a neighbor, as though speech
> Were a still performance.
> Arranging by chance

To meet as far this morning
From the world as agreeing
With it, you and I
Are suddenly what the trees try

To tell us we are:
That their merely being there
Means something; that soon
We may touch, love, explain.

And glad not to have invented
Such comeliness, we are surrounded:
A silence already filled with noises,
A canvas on which emerges

A chorus of smiles, a winter morning.
Placed in a puzzling light, and moving,
Our days put on such reticence
These accents seem their own defense.

The "New York School" also includes some other fine poets: Edwin Denby, whose *Mediterranean Cities* (1957) shows us how an ebullient and imaginative poet can transform the formal sonnet forms:

A governing and rouged nun, she lifts the cubed
Jewels, garlanded heavy on hair, shoulders
Breasts, on hands and feet, the dark-blue the cell-roomed
Splendor's fountain lifts sunken to Him who holds her;
But the emperor is running to his pet hens
Cackling like a hermit, and his foolish smile
Alone in the vacancy of noon-glazed fens
Haunts a blossoming water-capital's guile;
Holy placidity of lilylike throats
Ravenna of fleets, silent above the cows
A turnip plain and stagnant houses floats
Exultance of sailor hymns, virginal vows;
In a church's tiered and April-green alcoves
Joy rises laughing at ease to love God's loves;

("Ravenna")

Barbara Guest—*The Location of Things, Archaics, The Open Skies* (1962)—who writes of an "atmosphere of wings," of a world somewhere above the "real" one:

> Parachutes, my love, could carry us higher
> Than this mid-air in which we tremble,
> Having exercised our arms in swimming,
> Now the suspension, you say,
> Is exquisite . . . ;
>   (from "Parachutes, My Love, Could Carry us Higher")

Ted Berrigan, editor of "C" magazine (a kind of "house journal" for the younger poets of this "school," including Joseph Ceravolo, Dick Gallup), whose own poetry displays an exuberant use of language with what is often an underlying penetrating directness:

> Time flies by like a great whale
> And I find my hand grows stale at the throttle
> Of my many faceted and fake appearance
> Who bucks and spouts by detour under the sheets
> Hollow portals of solid appearance
> Movies are poems, a holy bible, the great mother to us
> People go by in the fragrant day
> Accelerate softly my blood
> But blood is still blood and tall as a mountain blood
> Behind me green rubber grows, feet walk
> In wet water, and dusty heads grow wide
> Padre, Father, or fat old man, as you will,
> I am afraid to succeed, afraid to fail
> Tell me now, again, who I am;
>   ("Sonnet XXXIV")

and Ron Padget, who has learned most successfully from Ashbery, but whose own poems communicate a unique commingling of humor and of quiet and moving feelings, as his elliptical poem "I'd Give You My Seat If I Were Here" reveals:

> The shadows these flowers are making on each other,
> The wild and sleepy eyes they make
> Are being thrown against the notion *de voyager*
> My fingers that are not silver or blue and they point

This keeps happening for eleven months.
But tonight she's in her grave at the bottom of the sea,
Leaving us at that.

If I could tell you why
The delicious crunch of feathers
Through fifteen heads of yours
Can encourage and surround
Then there would be no need for this needle in my head
Or the electricity that is not really mine.

Though it is only real,
My dream to raise no curtain on the other stage
That isn't there, but there
Under the breeze of a handkerchief
That is brushing against the temple you will find
On either side of your head—

And you know and you know.

IV

By the secret that holds the forest up,
no one will escape. (We have reached this place.)
from "Reporting Back" by William Stafford

Our third and last group of poets presents to us a world that
is becoming increasingly difficult to see as reality. In this world the
most obvious source of value derives from the poet's identification
with and acceptance of his environment. The universe is considered neither good nor bad. The poet neither superinduces meta-
phorical attributions of human emotions to his existing surround-
ings nor wanders through Baudelaire's hermetic "forest of symbols." The direct contacting of the actual universal situation, whose
values never change, reveals the beauty and the ugliness, the joy
and the grief that human beings feel when they function as natural
living organisms in a world that exists. Plato's philosophical dualism which rejected the material world in favor of that supra-
sensory world apprehended by reason, or the teachings of the
Arabic philosopher Al-Ghazali which stated that if what is present

is sought for, it becomes oblique and lost, are not issues—esthetic, philosophical, or otherwise—for this group of poets. In a time when Hegel's suggestion that man not only exists but also exists as an object of his existence has come to imply an alienation of the self—man observing the movements of his small toe—the poets of this third group assume a quasi-religious role, for they "sing" of that whole natural world of multiplicity and differentiations which is, on the deepest level, the only thing that exists for us; without it there would be nothing, for we would not be alive.

It is not surprising that the poet perceives the importance of Nature and imbues it with a religious consciousness. Scholars of comparative literature who are concerned with the early stages in a society's cultural history have constantly been hard put to distinguish between the functions of priest and poet, whether in pre-Roman Welsh poetry; the Greek tragedies; or the Indian *Rig-Veda* (Verse-Wisdom). Like these early religious-literary achievements, the poems of the writers of this group whom we shall mention later, though they are writing in a much more literarily refined time, are highly religious in the same way as the above poetic examples because in all of them, the individual souls of men and, in fact, of all things are thought of as identical with what the Hindus call the Highest Soul. The Supreme Being or Principle is seen as the whole universe, animate and inanimate; He or It is the originator, the sustainer, and the destroyer of the individual creature. (In his essay, "The Theme of the Three Caskets," Freud conceives of an inherently similar pattern, although psychologically conceptualized in terms of the mother, the beloved, and finally Mother Earth—the "silent goddess of Death.") Poets like James Wright and William Stafford are our poet-priests because their recognitions and realizations of the particular aspects of Nature transfigure and, ultimately, transcend the objects they describe, so that the more acute their involvement, the more "religious" their utterances.

Paradoxically, this "new" development in American poetry returns us to the prevailing esthetic world—the great international sensibility—of the Chinese *Book of Songs,* Japanese *waka* and *tanka,* the *Greek Anthology,* the *Rig-Veda,* Virgil's *Georgics,* the

Balkan ballads, and American Indian songs. A poem like the
American James Wright's "In the Cold House," for example:

> I slept a few minutes ago,
> Even though the stove has been out for hours.
> I am growing old.
> A bird cries in bare elder trees . . . ;

is of the same "world" as the twelfth century Japanese Prime Minister Kintsune's

> The flowers whirl away
> In the wind like snow.
> The thing that falls away
> Is myself . . . ;
>
> > (translated by Kenneth Rexroth)

as Sappho's

> The moon slides west,
> it is midnight,
> the time is gone—
> I lie alone!
>
> > (imitated by Robert Lowell)

or as the Papago "Dream Song of a Woman":

> Where the mountain crosses,
> On top of the mountain,
>   I do not myself know where.
> I wandered where my mind and my heart
>   seemed to be lost.
> I wandered away.

Three American poets are predominantly responsible for
opening this "world" up for us. All of William Carlos Williams'
poems reveal this poet's beneficent relationship with the "natural"
world, and thus his indictment of our personal and social demoral-
ization emerges as trenchantly as it does—in the Corydon and
Phyllis "Idyll" in Book Four of *Paterson,* for example—because
he knows exactly where we have strayed from. Williams represents
the world in which one joyfully sneaks "sweet and cold" plums

from the icebox in mock-imitation of the eating of the fruit of the tree of knowledge, as opposed to that world where, as in Eliot's *Prufrock,* one does not "dare" to eat a peach.

Yvor Winters' poems, seemingly far from this "world" with their emphasis on "mind" and "will," actually manifest at their best a total concentration of senses and mental faculties on one realization of a particular aspect, a pure distillation, of the "natural" world. His one-line poems such as "The Aspen's Song":

The summer holds me here . . . ;

or "Noon":

Did you move, in the sun?

communicate a subtle but veritable numinosity.

The most adventurous of these three poets (and our most inspiring man-of-letters) is Kenneth Rexroth. His extraordinary essays, translations from at least six languages, and a body of poetry begun over forty years ago comprise the finest testament to a constant uncovering, re-evaluation, and protection of the esthetic and moral values of Tu Fu, Homer, Samuel Johnson, and anyone else, as Rexroth would put it, "worth his salt."

Some of the best American poets writing today are following the example of these three poets and are returning us to that world which many of us assume to be "lost." Carolyn Kizer's poems "In the Japanese Mode" in *The Ungrateful Garden* (1961) and imitations of Tu Fu; Paul Goodman's "Evening (Gavotte and Variations of Rameau)"; Barbara Howes' "In Autumn"; Hayden Carruth's *The Norfolk Poems* (1962); Robert Duncan's *The Opening of a Field* (1960); Gary Snyder's *Myths and Texts* (1960); and Denise Levertov's *The Jacob's Ladder* (1961); and especially the beautiful *O Taste and See,* published in the spring of 1964, all return us to this "natural" world.

Of all these poets, Denise Levertov seems to me the most moving. Her work from *Here and Now* (1957) and *With Eyes at the Back of Our Heads* (1959) through the two latest volumes named above continues to develop a graceful but intense verse of communion with the "other"—a verse which encounters her subjects in a "green airy space, not locked in." It is in this space that Miss Levertov's poems contact the "natural world" without masks or ambiguities, for as she writes in "The Runes" from her latest book: "In city, in suburb, in forest, no way to stretch out the arms —so if you would grow go straight up or deep down."

Even a poet like Richard Wilbur, who is generally admired for his calculated and "small perfections" of form and content, writes his loveliest poems—"Cicadas," "Winter Spring," "Driftwood," and "The Beautiful Changes"—in this "tradition," even though he too often indulges himself in hollow lines like: "And the soul bathes in warm conceptual lakes" or "A giant absence mopes upon the trees." His simple but unostentatious poem "Exeunt" suggests his kinship with this group:

> Piecemeal the summer dies;
> At the field's edge a daisy lives alone;
> A last shawl of burning lies
> On a gray field-stone.

> All cries are thin and terse;
> The field has droned the summer's final mass;
> A cricket like a dwindled hearse
> Crawls from the dry grass.

The two finest young American poets of this "style" are James Wright and William Stafford. Wright is associated with The Sixties Press (edited by the poet Robert Bly) which—with its original publications of the verse of Wright, Bly, and William Duffy, for example, and its volumes of translations of Cesar Vallejo, Pablo Neruda, Machado, and others—has defined and purveyed these poetic values.

Wright was not originally a poet whose world view or poetic diction would have suggested his affinities for these new-old values of literary creation. His first collection, *The Green Wall* (1957) contained fairly traditional poems written in a torpid, flat style. But in his latest volume entitled *The Branch Will Not Break* (1963) —one thinks of Lorca's "Along the groves of the Tamarit leaden dogs have come to wait for the branches to fall, to wait for them to break by themselves"—Wright breaks through to a verse that sounds at times like Antonio Machado or Francis Jammes, but a verse that expresses a sensibility more kindred to that of the great Chinese poets Tu Fu, Mei Yao Chen, or Su Tung-P'o:

> The white house is silent.
> My friends can't hear me yet.
> The flicker who lives in the bare tree at the field's edge
> Pecks once and is still for a long time.
> I stand still in the late afternoon.
> My face is turned away from the sun.
> A horse grazes in my long shadow.
>
> > "Arriving in the Country Again"

This seems to come right out of the Sung period; but Wright has unaffectedly and against all odds made it part of his experience as an American mid-Westerner. His themes of friendship, growing old, lonesomeness, and inebriation are those of the Chinese poets; and although not the "Ancient Chinese Governor"—or any governor—he writes about, he is also as subtly "politically conscious" as the Chinese, in poems such as "Eisenhower's Visit to Franco, 1959" and "The Undermining of the Defense Economy." Wright's worst poems tend to be overly prosaic descriptions. But his best ones are those in which he perceives a correspondence between loss and a phenomenon of nature, as in the beautiful poem "Rain":

> It is the sinking of things.
>
> Flashlights drift over dark trees,
> Girls kneel,
> An owl's eyelids fall.
>
> The sad bones of my hands descend into a valley
> Of strange rocks . . . ;

or in which he, like Winters, concentrates his senses and mental faculties on one intense realization, so that in the quiet but exultant poem entitled "The Jewel," Wright transfigures and purifies the object into a sacramental hypostasis:

There is this cave
In the air behind my body
That nobody is going to touch:
A cloister, a silence
Closing around a blossom of fire.
When I stand upright in the wind,
My bones turn to dark emeralds.

William Stafford won the 1963 National Book Award for his *Traveling Through the Dark* (1962), a volume of poems that sees, as one of the poems is titled, the "Universe Is One Place." Stafford is not simple-mindedly "agin' city folks," but rather against the pretensions and lack of genuineness of most of our lives. Stafford is a self-styled "conservative" and against those who live their "city ways" because they "cannot hold thought ways to hold/the old way steady; nowadays/you cannot hear the songs we sang/or know what glaciers told. . . ." Stafford is "for" a contacting of the "real" world—a world of "things we did that meant something," to borrow one of his poem's titles. And Stafford, employing a wonderfully unsentimental, rugged, often elliptical language, reveals in these poems an understanding of death, love, lust, guilt, and making the "responsible act" that gives the lie to the suggestion that this poetry is "naïve." The poet lives in a world in which one has "to stand in absolute rain/and face whatever comes from God,/or stoop to smooth the earth over little things/that went into dirt, out of the world."

Stafford sees the violence of a world where he must push a dead but still-warm pregnant doe over the edge of a cliff, a world where the cheetah kills the deer in that moment of the "one launched look"—the "moment of choice" that occasions a "glance" of love and personal commitment or a life of loneliness and death. Stafford sees life as a "night desert" in which only human connections, which have been betrayed, create any and all of those meanings that enable us to exist in the body of love:

The Apache word for love twists
    then numbs the tongue:

Uttered once clear, said—
        never that word again.

"Cousin," you call, or "Sister" and one
        more word that spins
In the dust: a talk-flake
        chipped like obsidian.

The girl who hears this flake and
        follows you into the dark
Turns at a touch: the night desert
        forever behind her back.

"We shall live again," sing the Plains Indians in their Ghost Dance ritual. In "Reporting Back," Stafford is writing not only of his sense of life but also, we might suggest, of the complexities, strivings, and fulfillments of contemporary American poetry:

By the secret that holds the forest up,
no one will escape. (We have reached this place.)

The sky will come home some day.
(We pay all mistakes our bodies make when they move.)

Is there a way to walk that living has obscured?
(Our feet are trying to remember some path we are walking
        toward.)

THE NEW AMERICAN

MODERN DANCE

JILL JOHNSTON

The story of dance in this century is the record of upheavals
in form and content paralleling the revolutions in the other arts.
New developments in the traditional ballet were partly responsible
for this contemporary upheaval; but it was the modern dance, in
Europe and America, that made a major breakthrough in the be-
lated arrival of individual forms in dance.

It took dance in the Western world a long time to accept the
possibility of individual styles. In a Christian world dance was
always suspect as an agent of corruption. Thus, the first secular
manifestation of dance as a theatrical art form was the ballet, which
was sanctified in the strict, hierarchical enclosure of the royal
courts as a decorous and proper form of exhibiting oneself. The
immediate codification of steps and attitudes kept dancing within
the safety limits of moral restraint. The system, even as it became
more elaborate, was never conducive to the development of individual desires. Moreover, the entire setting of the ballet was that

of a spectacle. The earliest ballets were presented on the occasions of great feasts celebrating royal events; they were spectacular entertainments, and to the present day they have not lost this original function of giving pleasure on a grand scale, with all the finery and accessories and virtuosic accomplishments derived from aristocratic expectations. The finest ballet masters were slaves to these expectations.

It is amusing and pathetic to read about the painful contortions of Marius Petipa, the famous master of the late nineteenth century in Russia, who was an innovator in some respects, but who could never escape the pressures from public and nobility to titillate them with fantastic novelties. Yury Slonimsky, a Russian dance historian, wrote that one of Petipa's ballets "survived but briefly, in spite of an electric aurora borealis, effective mass dances on ice, and a group of lively gypsy dances in the harbor." Another ballet was successful because it had a "high waterfall, occupying the entire width of the stage and cascading over a huge sheet of glass into a mirrored pool, lighted from top and sides by electric batteries." Petipa is described without disguise as a *maitre des menus plaisirs* of the imperial court.

Even now, in the most advanced ballet company that exists, in the advanced city of New York, the chief choreographer must devise a certain number of frankly appealing spectacles to keep the box office satisfied; and although the personal mark of George Balanchine is apparent in whatever he does, a mark by which he has transcended many traditional limits of the ballet, the works of pure originality and personal coherence are scattered throughout the repertory like diamonds in the rough.

For these reasons, the first modern dancers had no real historical precedents upon which to base their personal adventures. Isadora Duncan, the great catalyst of the revolution in dance in this century, was a free agent, and her chief source of inspiration was ancient Greece. On the vases in the museums she found something that suited her own natural impulses. There was little about her dancing that related, except in the most general sense, either to the iconoclastic activity in the other arts of her peers, or to the immediate and more distant past of theatrical dance. Since she did not structure her dances beyond the simple form of flowing from one movement to the next with an instinctive grace, and a loose, dynamic correlation with the music, her legacy to dance was not in the realm of structure. Rather, she released the possibility of movement according to individual taste; and although her art was not directly a rebellion against the ballet, it is clear that she shattered the prevalent notion that theatrical dance could only be a spectacle and an academy of prescribed steps.

In some sense Duncan was an anomaly because her work was not continuous with what preceded or followed her. It is impossible to locate her as one places a Cézanne or a Matisse as part of a continuous, evolutionary process. This process in dance did not begin until the emergence of Martha Graham, Doris Humphrey and Charles Weidman in this country and Mary Wigman in Germany. With these artists came the first intensive explorations of formal design in space and movement. The Denishawn era, which preceded the Graham and Humphrey-Weidman periods in the United States, was of high importance as an eclectic clearing house for many ideas, a melting pot of dances inspired by forms ranging from the American Indian to the Orient. As early moderns, neither Ruth St. Denis nor Ted Shawn, like Isadora Duncan, was concerned to develop a concentrated theory of movement or composition. But in their panoramic interests they planted possibilities for departure in the minds of the young talents—Graham, Humphrey, Weidman—who danced in their company and toured the world with them.

Technique, form and subject matter assumed a programmatic design with the advent of Graham and Humphrey. Their immediate concern was to find a way of moving that suited their individual temperaments. The techniques that evolved from their experiments were formal exaggerations of the natural breath impulse. Graham's battery of contractions and releases was an involuted, floor-bound technique to begin with, organically motivated and shot through with psychic connotations of pain and ecstasy. Humphrey's "fall and recovery" syndrome was a more generalized, extroverted form of the same impulse. She considered the theatrical appeal of the technique immediately. Crudely speaking, there was the kinesthetic pleasure of being suspended in what she called "the arc between two deaths"—of standing still and lying down. The constant recovery from the imminent danger of inertia projected the pleasure of success over the death of gravity, and, by social or psychological extension, the success of man over the powers that be. But beyond this obvious source of identification were the details of theatrical effectiveness which Humphrey elaborated in a theory of contrasts applied to the four components of movement as she analyzed them: rhythm, design, dynamics and gesture. The structure of her dances evolved quite naturally from the technique.

Similarly, of course, the structure of Graham's dances was largely determined by the inventive exploration of her technique; but the theory that substantiated the invention came from Louis Horst, her composer, mentor and musical director for many years. Like Humphrey, Horst developed a theory of composition based on thematic coherence and variation, going back for his models to the pre-classic dance forms. ("Pre-classic" refers to the decorous, highly stylized court dances of the fifteenth and sixteenth centuries which preceded the ballet proper as institutionalized during the reign of Louis XIV.) Horst extracted the rhythmic, structural and emotional characteristics of these forms to stimulate structural design in the compositions of his students. The *Pavane,* for instance, was a dance of proud, ceremonious dignity; its rhythm was a very slow 4/4 or 2/2 meter; and its structure consisted of two or three strains of eight, twelve or sixteen bars each. Adhering to this basic formula, the student must invent a simple motif and develop it in an interesting manner, and in the two or three part forms the variations would become more complex. The concentration of the early moderns on "natural" movement (i.e., walking and running, as distinct from the stylized distortions of the ballet) here came under formal scrutiny.

The old and the new were curiously interwoven in the works of the first modern dancers. The movement itself was absolutely new, and for dance the subject matter was new in so much as it directly reflected the social concerns of the times. These dancers were not interested in ethnic sources or fairy tales, and when they did turn to classical subjects it was to internalize them in their personal vocabularies. Graham made *Herodiade* a modern heroine of self-conscious recognition, confrontation and resolution.

Neither Graham nor the social realists so fashionable in the thirties had anything in common with the great structural and esthetic upheavals that had been going on in France since the turn of the century. The music of Satie, the poetry of Apollinaire, the plays of Jarry, Cubism and Surrealism in painting, the various Dada manifestations, all expressed the radical shift in emphasis from the rational, securely focused, unitary concept of composition to the fragmentation and juxtaposition of elements with no essential beginning or ending, no transitional continuity, no focal climaxes and no dramatic resolutions.

(The early modern dance in several of its aspects could have been created in the seventeenth century. If dancing at that time had proceeded as the music did, instead of getting tangled up in court festivities, it is likely that choreographers would have made dances that paralleled the inventions of composers, whose music, ironically enough, originally derived from the pre-classic dance forms—the Suite, Sonata and Symphony followed these forms. Had that happened the history of theatrical dance would have been quite different. As it is, the early modern dancers compressed a possible history of structural concentration in two short decades.)

Yet the early modern dance in this country was in step with the progress of the other arts here. One might expect dance in Europe at this time to have exhibited some parallel activity. But there was no serious choreography in Europe that corresponded to the radical activities there in painting, music, literature and the theatre. The Diaghilev period in ballet is often referred to as a modern renaissance in choreography. It is true that Fokine introduced some novel concepts to the ballet. It was certainly a renaissance for the ballet; but there was no significant relation between the new ballet and the iconoclasm of the far-out Frenchmen mentioned above. The great collaborations with Stravinsky, Cocteau, Picasso and Satie gave the Diaghilev period an aura of modernism that was deceptive. Fokine continued to produce spectacles and fairy tales. Massine created huge symphonic ballets. And the occasional experiments, such as Nijinsky's startling *L'Après-midi d'un Faune,* did not represent a major direction beyond the tradition, even as that tradition was given a new face, which was to show itself finally in the modernism of Balanchine—a revolution more in the style of movement than in the choreography.

In this country the transition from the old to the new modern dance occurred precisely at the time when the old was really beginning to look its age. By the early forties the energy of the original drive was spent: Weidman was gradually dropping out of the picture; Humphrey had consolidated her position, stopped dancing in 1945, went on to make some fine dances for José Limon, and fell into a decline of the imagination in the fifties; Graham had become an academy and a national institution with an international reputation; Hanya Holm had defected to the musical comedy business; and most of the dancers who had worked with these pioneers, as they are called, and who struck off on their own, were still too close to the original sources to think for themselves. Thus the scene through the late forties and fifties was dominated by the memory of old times, the persistence of those times in the same approach to technique and composition, and the pale reflections that crossed the stage year after year. Even Louis Horst, who was indefatigable in his support of everybody who emerged from one school or another and who had studied his pre-classic forms, was looking around for a fresh impulse. Although there was general agreement that the modern dance was defunct, nobody knew where to look for its revival.

Merce Cunningham did not explode on the dance world the way Jackson Pollock struck the world of painting. After a short but brilliant career as a dancer in Martha Graham's company, Cunningham left, in 1944, to present his own solos. The dancers and critics could not tolerate what they assumed to be his whimsical disregard for established laws of composition.

I mention Cunningham in the same breath with Pollock to

underscore Cunningham's position as an innovator who rocked the establishment with another kind of space and order and influenced a whole new generation of artists. The insurgent Cunningham and the entrenched traditionalists were dramatically juxtaposed at the ANTA Festival, a two-week season of modern dance on Broadway in 1955. Graham and José Limon were the leading dancers of the series. Limon's *The Moor's Pavane,* created in '49, was acclaimed as a great masterpiece of the times. Cunningham's *16 Dances* was received with a torrent of indignation.

Limon and Cunningham, as two prominent contemporary male dancers, make an interesting study in contrasts. Limon emerged from the Humphrey-Weidman company with a unique style of movement that was fluid, weighted, aggressive and literal. In his style the breath impulse as he knew it from Humphrey and Weidman was retained, but the sharp attacks and spatial delineations became blurred in the opulence of swells and curves, and a sensual orchestration of the parts of the body. Limon's image of himself derives from tragi-heroic visions of grandeur as he located it in the baroque, the classical tragedies, the Bible and his own Mexican heritage, which combines the Conquistador and the Indian underdog. Elegance and brutality are typical of his dances. In the abstract solo, *Chaconne,* a dance that might have pleased the Sun-King himself, Limon makes a formal essay in his massive, contained magnificence. In the *Emperor Jones* he made a satire on that magnificence in a message of sado-masochistic fury. In *The Traitor* he elevated brutality to the plane of sacrifice and tragic self-recognition.

Limon has always been interested in the literary concept. The problem was to find the proper vehicle, in form and content, for his image. *The Moor's Pavane,* based on *Othello,* remains one of his most successful dances. Bound by the Rondo form of the piece, the dancers keep returning from their narrative interpolations to a variation on a formal walk-around (a slow, elegant pin-wheel) in the center of the stage. The drama is enhanced by the relief, which is like a choral declamation of the characters on their own destinies.

Moreover, Limon makes an excellent Othello. The role of the stricken aristocrat suits him perfectly.

Insomuch as Limon extended the ideas and theories of Humphrey in his own style, his work is a culmination of the early era of American dance. The humanitarian message is explicit. The dances are centrally focused. The space is used for its dramatic potential to enlarge or diminish the figures as befits their status in the dance at any moment. The movement is emotionally motivated, organically developed, and visually designed to please the eye with contrasts of unison and opposition, vertical and horizontal, and so on. And the progress of each dance is determined by statement, development and resolution.

Cunningham's first point of departure from all these concepts was to make an arbitrary time structure for his dances. The time was not determined by a piece of music selected in advance to accompany the dance, nor by the dance itself as he was making it. Rather, he would sit down beforehand and say the dance would consist of five parts and each part would be three minutes long. Deciding on such a structure, he and his composer, John Cage, would work independently to fill in the structure with sound and movement. This was the first example in dance of putting things together, or letting things go together, that are not logically thought to have any business being together. Actually, it was the logic of a simultaneous vision, and it seemed only necessary to recall a theatre ticket and a landscape postcard appearing side by side in a collage by Kurt Schwitters to get the logic of it straight, or to watch your hand move from stove to sink and hear the children screaming in the other room at the same time. Similarly, Cunningham's art is actually a complex mixture of personal adjustments and random inclusions.

His adventures with chance began in 1951 with *16 Dances*. When he had made the dance he saw no reason why the parts should occur in any particular order, so he tossed coins to determine the sequence. This piece also included a small section in which the sequence of the movement itself was determined by chance. The following year, in 1952, he made several dances entirely by chance. *Variation* became a collage of ballet movement as the movements were broken down into a gamut of possibilities and put together again by tossing coins. The procedure began to involve time, space and movement charts. Each chart contained a number of predetermined possibilities, and the coin then decided what the movement would be, at what time and in what space it would occur. The method became more elaborate when it was applied to each dancer in a group piece. The resulting dispersion of the dancers projected a new kind of open space that is characteristic of Cunningham's work.

Since the sound and the movement were independent of each other there seemed no reason why the dancers themselves could not move independently. When the dancers are moving thus around the stage the effect is something like what you might see in a train terminal where the people are rushing, walking, waiting or sitting as they are, isolated in their own destinations. The result is also analogous to a Pollock painting where the colors are dripped independently on the canvas and converge and disperse in their own rhythms.

In the simultaneous vision there is no central focus, except where the observer, if not basking in the total effect, concentrates at any moment. The values become equalized; there are no climaxes or resolutions, which means that there is no necessary beginning or ending. It has often been remarked that Pollock's paintings suggest an infinite extension beyond the picture plane. Cunningham's dances suggest the same extension; and since he often juggles the order of the parts by chance, it is clear that he considers one beginning as good as another.

The containment of a picture within its frame, or the dance within the proscenium stage, is a practical expediency. But since that is, at the same time, all we see, that is all there is. We sense the boundless and see the limits. The facts are essential. The point is to accept what the immediate presence offers us and not judge that presence by the consideration of possibilities other than what we see in the presence. The judgment which applies to traditional forms, where the progression of one step to the next is understood as inevitable, must here be suspended, since there are only facts, no inevitabilities. The facts are interchangeable. There are no laws governing the sequences or juxtapositions. The dances are lawless.

Cunningham's fourth step in liberating movement from conventional logic was to apply the simultaneity of action to a single body. He did this with *Untitled Solo* in 1953. By tossing coins to establish a movement of the head, then the arms, the torso, etc., he made a superimposition of motion which was a more concentrated fragmentation of elements. The resulting coordinations were so unusual as to render the performances of them extremely difficult.

The idea was not to make things impossible, but to find new ways of moving. Devising a certain gamut for each part of the body (i.e., the head twists, or rolls, or snaps in staccato from right to left, etc.), then putting the several parts together in simultaneous action, provided the possibility of movement beyond the habitual preferences of personal taste.

There is some analogy in Cunningham's method to the Cubist analytical breakdown and reorganization of images. But a better relation is to the chance methods of the Dadaists. Hans Arp composed collages by picking up scraps of paper, shuffling them, and gluing them down just as they fell. The chance methods of the Dada painters and poets were primitive devices compared to the refined, elaborate chance methodology evolved by John Cage, Cunningham, and a number of avant-garde composers here and abroad. The devices then were usually as simple as pulling words out of a hat to make a poem (Tristan Tzara); and if one reads Jackson Maclow's essay (printed in La Monte Young's *Anthology*) on the involved procedures he employs to make poetry now, one can see the difference. The complexity of present methods is the result of analyzing the various components of a medium and applying the devices, which may be various in themselves, to the different components. The attitude behind the method in either case is the same, but what has happened in the past fifteen years, which accounts for the complexity, is the programmatic extension of those early ideas.

The attitude is really the central issue. John Cage picked up where the Dadaists left off. His inventive experiments with sound, and his studies in Zen, led him to the philosophy of indifference that Duchamp has so beautifully exemplified for many years. Dada wished to recover the natural, unreasonable order in the world, to restore man to his humble place in nature. The chance gesture became a spiritual insight into the condition of chaos, which is the natural order of the world. Cage has said that, "Form is what interests everyone and fortunately it is wherever you are and there is no place where it is not." Chance was a gesture of affirmation and acceptance; for to remove oneself, to whatever degree, from the means and ends of a composition, meant to identify oneself with the ground of existence. The heresy of Dada and Cage is the abdication of the will. In a culture brought up on the pride of accomplishment in subduing the brute forces of nature, the admission of chaos seemed like madness from the beginning. But the philosophy has persisted and Cage has had an enormous influence on contemporary artists. The madness has become a new kind of order, and the possibilities extend in every conceivable direction.

Through chance Cage arrived at his position of "letting sounds be themselves rather than vehicles for emotions and ideas." Sounds, for Cage, are not structurally connected as in the melodic and harmonic designs of the past. Each sound is heard for itself and does not depend for its value on its place within a system of sounds. Similarly, Cunningham's movement is a series of isolated actions, and the connection is simply that of sequence or juxtaposition or whatever the observer wishes to make out of it. The emphasis is on movement as movement. "I don't look in a book," he says, "I make a step."

It is easy to understand why the older modern dancers viewed Cunningham's work as de-humanized. Gone were the old connections and transitions and representational gestures. Gone the dramatic narrative and the idealized expressions of pain and ecstasy that were the stock-in-trade of the modern dancers. But Cunningham notes that it is impossible for the human body not to be expressive. A number of his early works were expressive in the more obvious, traditional sense, in that he would make a dance that referred to a specific emotion, like fear; but the emotions never appeared in narrative sequence and they were never developed thematically or in phrases. Even before he employed chance methods his inventiveness was toward making one movement after another rather than in "melodically" linked continuities. Later on there was greater abstraction. The space became a field of pure movement and dramatic "incident." The incidents might come about fortuitously, where the paths of two or more dancers coincided in some way, or they might occur as a result of allowances for contact or unison in the chance method for any one dance. *Crises,* of 1960, contained much contact between the dancers, because Cunningham made a gamut of predetermined possibilities of contact in his original calculations. *Rune,* 1959, by a similar token, contained a lot of unison movement. Suddenly, as it were, several dancers might be facing on a downstage diagonal with their hands folded at the waist. The effect is something like the emergence of figurative elements in an abstract painting. This particular incident reminded me of what one might see in a dance like Martha Graham's *Appalachian Spring.* The difference, of course, is the context in which it appears. As an incident in Cunningham's dance it has no specific meaning, becoming entirely suggestive, and open to multiple interpretations. Even *Antic Meet,* which was not composed by chance and which is an episodic piece of highly specific incidents, is extremely ambiguous. In one episode the dancers wear sun glasses. It is impossible to know why exactly. (One might ask Arman, the French maker of assemblages, why he put a lot of eye glasses together in a box.) Yet the slight, tentative arm gestures of the dancers seem appropriate to the shades, as though they were partially blind. In the same dance Cunningham exits after a solo and re-enters promptly with a small table (covered with white table cloth) which he sets in a polished fast manner with napkins and silverware. As he exits again, a dancer, who enters with a black umbrella lit underneath with small blinking lights, moves horizontally across the stage in a solo of intricate, staccato foot and leg action. At the end of a funny gymnastic encounter with another dancer Cunningham exits and re-enters in a big raccoon coat to drag off his flattened opponent. All these incidents are provocative images. I don't believe the observer tends to take time out to analyze or interpret what he sees. More often he probably notes a novel combination of facts and relaxes to enjoy the image.

I am reminded of two Happenings by Claes Oldenburg, called *Fotodeath* and *Ironworks,* in which each episode contained several isolated and simultaneous actions. In one a young man examined himself in a small mirror and a larger mirror lying on the floor, while another man, in tights, wrestled ferociously with a dummy bag, and a lady dressed as a man removed her clothes and put them back on in front of a dressing table. The incidents just mentioned in Cunningham's dances are related to the entire movement of Collage, Assemblage and Happenings extending from Braque and Picasso to the present. The first motion to incorporate life into the picture plane by way of "found" objects and materials was the beginning of a vast enterprise by many artists in this century to extend art into the environment. The fast distinction between art and life has melted into a fluid transaction between the two, and in some cases the observer is hard pressed to call a thing art or life. Duchamp's famous Readymades remain a classical challenge.

But the revolution in materials is central to the whole development. The entrance of life into music first meant noise, and Cage has described this entrance as "the acceptance of all audible phenomena as material proper to music." The painters and sculptors recognize the same of visual phenomena. It is, in fact, often impossible to say whether a work is more painting or sculpture, and when Robert Rauschenberg puts a radio behind one of his canvases the visual work is clearly entering the domain of music. When Jim Dine attaches a big hatchet on a chain to a canvas divided down the center by a rough beam of wood, the paint-construction becomes music and movement as well as paint and objects. The observer is implicitly invited to pick up the hatchet and try his hand at the wood. Just as the boundaries between art and life have become confused, so the sacred limits defining one medium as distinct from another have dissolved. The only limits remaining are those imposed on the artist by his choice of materials.

In certain Happenings all the media are happily combined to make a theatrical situation of light, sound, movement, paint and objects. But where the emphasis remains centered on a particular medium—Cunningham makes dances, and Cage is primarily interested in sound—the collage inclusions are like putting your hand in a churn of butter and finding forks. Mostly, you see and feel the butter. Cunningham feels free to do what he pleases; but he is a dancer, he has always been a brilliant dancer, so what interests him is movement. He trains his dancers in a rigorous technique designed to encourage the greatest possible range of movement and control. In some respects the movement is akin to ballet, with which it has more in common than with the early modern dances. The lines are crisp and clean. He likes the elegant, attenuated line typical of the ballet, and there are extensions, attitudes, positions of the arms, and allegro footwork which are similar. Yet they are rarely exact facsimiles. The overall look is simply cool and classical, and there are many movements alien to the ballet. From his Graham period, for example, he retains a contraction of the torso, his own reduced version of it, which is quite abstract in the context of his dances. And there are many personal gestures, like the faces he makes (the traditional "tragic" and "comic") in *Septet,* or the delicate jerks of head and hands as he walks off stage concluding a solo in *Aeon.*

Unlike the ballet or some other modern dances the movement never looks romantically idealized. Where there is romance, it is matter-of-fact. A section in *Aeon* is concluded by the dancers moving off stage in unison with high jumps and falls. As they exit one dancer is left inert on stage in the fallen position. Cunningham walks over and regards her in a silent moment. He picks her up, carries her a short way, puts her down again. . . . Cunningham is not entering any lion's den to rescue a princess. The appearance of such incidents in an abstract context makes them exciting enough in the melodramatic light of the conventional drama of the past.

For the same reason Balanchine's *Serenade* is exciting, even now, thirty years after its premiere. There is an event in that ballet strangely like the fallen girl in Cunningham's dance. A ballerina is left on stage as though literally swept off her feet by the voluminous rushing exit of the other dancers. The following interlude—beginning with a male dancer walking blindly toward her, his eyes shielded by another ballerina—is a vestigial remnant of an old fairy tale ballet. The suggestion of a plot is unmistakable; but it appears from no place, so to speak, and it doesn't go anywhere. The movement and the music continue as though nothing had happened. It seems more like life than a story, for stories in life don't have the pat statements and conclusions that stories on the stage do.

Balanchine, like Cunningham, considers movement first, but the differences in their work are striking. Balanchine, as is well known, always sets his ballets to music. Since he is a fine musician, the coordination of movement with music is exceptionally perfect. Moreover, he is always an inventive master, never dominated by his habits. Even his most classical ballets are full of unusual phrases, and the ballets in his modern disjointed style—*Four Temperaments, Agon, Episodes*—can be dazzling in their inventions. Yet his space remains as traditional as his musical affiliations. The patterns are the geometric formations known from the earliest court ballets. The symmetrically balanced disposal of dancers is always maintained. The soloists keep the focal centers intact. The frontal orientation is absolute. The counterpoint is musically derived, usually in short fugal patterns, and the ballets are often climaxed in the grand, symphonic tradition, as befits the particular music he uses.

The dynamics of Cunningham's dance make the difference in the kind of space he creates. The fragmentation of movement by chance projects a dynamic of alternating qualities quite unlike the regular rhythmic expansion and contraction of a melodic phrase. Brief sections in a dance like Balanchine's *Agon* are close to this dynamic. Edwin Denby described such action as follows: "Each phrase, as if with a burst, finds its new shape in a few steps, stops, and at once a different phrase explodes unexpectedly at a tangent. They fit like the stones of a mosaic, the many colored stones of a mosaic seen close by." When several dancers at once are engaged in this action and are doing it in a contrapuntal canon form, the mosaic becomes kaleidoscopic. Yet the dancers remain in formation (i.e., a line), the movement is frontally directed, and the pattern is a formal construction.

Cunningham's counterpoint is the result of the independent action of the dancers all around the space which I described a while back. And although he does often adjust the movement according to the frontal focus of the audience, especially in those dances not composed by chance, much of the action has what I might call a revolving orientation. The proscenium stage is as important as the painter's canvas in delineating space (I am not suggesting that his dances could as easily be appreciated in the round); yet the directional values tend to be equalized. An arabesque line in profile is as pleasing as it is in ballet, but that line is never struck as a "home base." The foreshortening of the body in an arabesque facing upstage is just as important as the attenuation of an arabesque facing stage right or left. The chance procedure itself creates this equalization of values. One might ask why Cunningham's dances could not be received in the round. They could be, they have been; yet the limits of the stage create a tension, a frame of reference, that would be lost in the round.

One might also ask, at this point, what the unifying factor is in Cunningham's work. His own style as a dancer—the lightness, the levelled gaze, the taut concentration, the relaxed confidence, the clean delineations, the comic absurdities, the nervous tension, the slow sustained qualities, the rough-edged nonchalance, the hard thrusting qualities—partially defines the unity of his work. And all the facets of his composition that I have mentioned are also essential. A large part of his complete stylistic consistency is the result of the special action exerted on his chosen material by chance. That material is a cool breakdown of the qualitative possibilities of movement of all parts of the body, in place or in getting from one place to another. The choices are clear in what you see. The chance operations tend to make a rich complexity out of these choices. From this point, coherence is a problem of performance. Cunningham himself always makes everything look right. Where the movement is disconnected, it is performed with perfect kinesthetic continuity. His dancers rarely look as individual as he does. But they execute the same rightness of continuity in their own ways. Carolyn Brown, for one, is a superb technician. She has the poise and line of a ballerina. Her dancing is crystal clear, and she exemplifies to an extreme degree that aspect of Cunningham's work which is an impersonal concentration on the material at hand.

It is this aspect, as much as anything else, which confirmed the opinion of the modern dance establishment that Cunningham's dancers were de-humanized. This opinion is a silly side issue and reveals only the historical difficulty of moving on from one kind of expression to another. The problem was to accept the human state in its simple condition of existing. To walk across the stage the way one walks across a street, or to stand still the way one stands when there is no place to go, seemed like a bad way to be human. The cultural burden is too much with us. Walking across the street is not enough. There has to be a goal on the other side. Where are we going and what are we doing? The older modern dancers were plagued with these questions. The plight of the poor in England. The state of the union in America. Guilt, conscience, loneliness, ennui, dreams, hopes, denials—the list is endless, and the modern dancers made up a lot of stories to make the whole grab-bag of emotions and social affairs a palatable artistic transaction.

There were some great dances in that idiom. My concern is not to disparage that period, but to illustrate the difference. Where the tone indicates a personal preference, it exists and reflects my engagement in what is going on at the present moment. Also, it seems eminently human to me to stand still and let the world go about its business. The world remains a stage and the stage of a theatre can be a beautiful place to be if that is the only problem: how to be beautiful on your own stage. The special originality of Cunningham was to appear on his own stage with no cultural encumbrances. He comes on the stage as himself, and one could draw a deep breath of relief that there is nothing else to think about. For all its complexity and sophistication, Cunningham's work engages you in the simple pleasure of existence.

Alwin Nikolais, associated with the Henry Street Playhouse, has also been the object of a controversy about what is human and what is not. His work has been damned as de-humanized and hailed as a new kind of integrated theatre. He is, in fact, considered by many to be as far-out as you can get. *Newsweek* printed a photograph of Nikolais' company with a caption explaining that Nikolais is to dance as Beckett and Ionesco are to the theatre. This is pure foolishness. Although he has made something altogether original in his combination of movement, lights, costumes, props and sounds, his concepts of drama and development are quite traditional. In any case, there is nothing absurd about it.

The de-humanized aspect of his work is rather interesting. The term does apply in a way that it does not apply to Cunningham; and although I cannot see why people should think of disparaging the dances because the dancers don't look particularly human (performers are often disguised in bags, barrels or other paraphernalia), it is true that Nikolais' concentration on props and costumes has immobilized him in a formula that has no place to go beyond the increasingly inane manipulation of these materials. This is *not* so interesting. Still, Nikolais is a fine teacher, and the concept of "extensions" (to the body, of materials) originally developed as a teaching device to help his students and dancers to "project themselves more heroically into space." The later esthetic, theatrical use of these devices evolved into *Masks, Props and Mobiles* (1953) and a series of works since then, right up to *Sanctum* of 1964.

There are two strains in all these works. On the one hand, there is the manipulation of materials. On the other, there is the pure dancing of his soloists. The movement is typically light and lyrical. It is often very inventive; but it is always organically expanded from one or several motifs, and it always echoes—in dynamic, qualitative changes—the electronic sound score. In its own way the movement unencumbered by props does what the movement encased in props does. As for the latter the idea is to exploit the possibilities of design suggested by the color-shape of each prop or costume. In a quintet for men in *Imago* the arms were extended in three long segments (the outermost like an exaggerated bone, or plunger) to obliterate the arms and make them anonymous appendages. In a frontal position these appendages were extended in all positions, or twirled slowly, or made to form a successive wheel pattern as the men stood one behind the other. In profile they made a design of placing one end on a hip and the other end on a knee. In a circular formation they moved with the appendages placed end to end, and so on. Each section of a dance has a specific project for development. Although the costumes, props, lighting effects are often strikingly beautiful, one can see immediately what is going to happen as soon as the eye absorbs the novelty of shapes and colors.

A number of dancers at the Henry Street Playhouse have been given the opportunity of developing their talents in concerts of their own. Only one of these, however, Beverly Schmidt, has come from that situation with any marked individuality and contemporary outlook. This low ratio is not unusual. Since the forties and up until the past few years the serious individualists have numbered a mere handful.

Meanwhile, it is important to note that Cunningham is not the only choreographer to emerge from the early modern dance with a mind of his own. Sybil Shearer and Katherine Litz had worked with the Humphrey-Weidman company in the thirties. By 1941 Shearer was presenting her own work. These solos were uniquely lyric and personal. Katherine Litz first gave her own solos in 1948. Both dancers developed movement in their own ways according to musical principles of thematic variation. But the immediate difference between their work and the work that resulted from Horst and Humphrey methods was in the movement itself, which became abstract in the intimacy of personal gestures that did not refer beyond the self to socially understood gestures of ritual, work and emotion. The difference is not always easy to grasp at a glance. But the subtleties, the elusiveness and ambivalence become apparent as the atmosphere spreads. In some sense the style of Shearer and Litz was a return to the romanticism of Isadora Duncan. It was definitely a reaction to the tortured introversion of Graham, and to the broad, open extroversion of Humphrey, and to the technique of both, which were sharp, angular and dissonant. Yet, unlike Duncan, their romanticism is refined and distilled by its formal containment, and by the concentrated internalization of gestures. The art of Shearer and Litz is a solo art. Although they have both choreographed for groups, they were never interested in the massive, symphonic forms that were so popular in the thirties.

The new lyricism in modern dance is consummately realized in the dancing of Merle Marsicano, who gave her first solo program in New York in 1953. With Marsicano the gestures are even more abstracted, and the reference beyond movement itself is totally absent. Her dancing is like Mark Rothko's painting, or Morton Feldman's music. The pure lyrical impulse spreads and suffuses like some luminous, internal light that soaks the space with gradual, subtly persistent intensity. Within the dynamic of a low-keyed, continuously flowing gesture, Marsicano explores infinite possibilities. It is a rare thing in art to find so much interest in a quality that centers on itself without pushing and pulling into the more obvious excitement of dynamic contrasts. Philip Guston's paintings of the early fifties had this same lyrical intensity. The glory was in the paint itself as it mutated in a soft, plastic reverie.

James Waring and Aileen Passloff also arrived in the fifties as important individual artists. Waring has made many dances in his fifteen years as a choreographer, and he has not been bound by any particular idiom. He was exposed to the various influences of the traditional modern dance, but he choreographed from the beginning in the way that he saw fit and that had little to do with the conventional modes of composition. He took one of Horst's classes when he came to New York and discovered immediately that he had no interest in making dances that way. Until '55 his work often had a narrative thread. He says that Horst described his early movement as "shuffling and huggling" and that later on he moved out into a more obvious energy, especially when he had banished the narrative ideas and implications. By the late fifties the influence of ballet and Cunningham and Happenings became more dominant in his work. The space of his dances often looks like Cunningham's space, but Waring doesn't make his space look that way by chance—he always invents his movement on the spot, intuitively. A pure dance like *Dromenon* (1962) is very close to Cunningham in style. At the same time, it is peppered with personal gestures unique to Waring. Some of Passloff's group dances are similar in space and gesture. Both choreographers work from ideas more than from method. Waring, among other things, has a special talent for the ridiculous. *Extravaganza* was a wild and hilarious burlesque. *Hallelujah Gardens* (1963) was a massive rollick of objects and persons in absurd situations. Waring's follies go back at least to *Dances Before the Wall* of the fifties, which was an extraordinary dance-happening performed before a wall of whisky crates filled with objects. I believe this is one of the important and influential contemporary dances.

Passloff's greater talent is for lyric dancing. In her personal lyricism she is related to the contemporary tradition of Shearer, Litz, Marsicano, Midi Garth, Beverly Schmidt and Erick Hawkins. (Hawkins is another isolated figure who went his own way after a career as a ballet dancer and a leading member of Graham's company. His lyric duet, *Here and Now With Watchers,* is another major work among the new modern dances.)

Along with Cunningham, Waring and Passloff contributed to the climate that made the Judson Dance Theater possible. The new American modern dance at last assumed the dimensions of a full-fledged movement when a group of dancers who had been studying composition with the composer, Robert Dunn, launched a series of concerts at Judson Memorial Church in New York. From 1960–62 Dunn, assisted by his wife, Judith Dunn, taught this free-wheeling course in choreography at Cunningham's studio. Dunn was not interested in presenting any choreographic formulas to the group; at the same time he saw the opportunity of stimulating activity by exposing the dancers to the methods of avant-garde music here and abroad, methods largely the result of Cage's influence. Because this was the first class in choreography to offer an approach to composition related to the whole contemporary art scene of the late forties and fifties, inadvertently, perhaps, it spelled the end of the dynasty of Horst and Humphrey whose classes had held sway over two or three generations of modern dancers.

The time was auspicious for a class that would focus contemporary ideas for the dancers who were already aware of what
was going on around them, but who needed, as Dunn said, a
"clearing house for structures" derived from the various sources of
contemporary action. I have outlined the importance of Cunningham and Cage as one source of inspiration. The Happenings and
Events by painters, sculptors, poets and composers are another
vital source. Several dancers in the course had studied with Ann
Halprin on the West coast. For some time Halprin has experi-
mented with improvisation and with theatrical situations that are
more like Happenings than dances. Simone Morris, who had
studied with Halprin, and who was in Dunn's class, gave a seesaw
event on a program of Happenings in 1960. She also made several
dance "constructions"—written as simple instructions for action
that could be construed as events (i.e., "One man is told that he
must lie on the floor during the entire piece. The other man is told
that during the piece he must tie the first man to the wall.").

In Dunn's class the limits of dance expanded to include any
kind of activity at all. Non-dancers participated from the beginning; and by the time they began presenting concerts at the church,
the non-dancers were almost as prominent as the dancers, both as
performers and as choreographers. Gertrude Stein's question about
prose and poetry might be put to the dance. What is dancing, and
if you know what dancing is, what is non-dancing? The trained
dancer is an exceptional creature who can do many things a non-
dancer can't do.

But if a performer walks across a stage and calls it a dance,
who is to say it is not a dance?

In several of his early Happenings Robert Whitman did some
spectacular leaps and falls. He would project himself in the air like
a dolphin and land with a crash the length of his body. Aileen
Passloff did a solo called *Asterisk* in which she simply walked
briskly around the stage in heels and a dress. In the late fifties Paul
Taylor presented a concert which included a dance of ordinary
pose changes, performed in a business suit, accompanied by reiterated telephone time signals. The recent history of everyday

activity as material for dance goes back to Cunningham's *Collage* of 1953, composed for the first Creative Arts Festival at Brandeis University. Fifteen people from the university who were not trained dancers performed a number of natural gestures, like washing the hands, combing the hair, powdering the face or filing the nails. They also skipped, walked, ran, turned somersaults and stood on their hands. This part of the dance was a collage of ordinary activity.

The "natural" movement of the Judson group is neither like the romantic lyricism of Isadora Duncan, nor like the formal abstraction of real gestures that followed Duncan. The gestures tend to be completely abstract or completely natural. Yet both are out of the ordinary when they appear on stage in an art structure. The dancers do not mind adjusting their clothes or brushing their hair out of their eyes if it makes them more comfortable. These are inadvertent everyday gestures. One recognizes them for what they are and accepts them in the context of the structure. I suppose it is something like the inadvertent drip of an Action painter, who leaves the paint where it drips if he likes it that way. The performer can do that too, if he does it in perfect confidence and permits the spectator to accept it as part of the composition.

Real situations and gestures are incorporated in a dance and often form part of a complex mixture of invented action and dancing as we know it from the professional studios. Three situations in Judith Dunn's *Acapulco* are a fair example. A woman irons a dress in a natural manner, but the dress she irons is on her body, and she does it while leaning on a diagonal tilt. Two women sit down together and play cards the way they might on the floor of anybody's living room. A girl in a nightgown rises in slow motion on the chair where she had been seated, immobilized, for some time, and turns her torso, arms in second position, until she falls off balance into the arms of a man who has been standing for quite a while waiting for her to fall. This particular piece is more in the nature of an event than a dance. Yet the emphasis rests on movement. In a collaboration between the Judson Dance Theater and sculptor, Charles Ross, the space was similar to the environments of objects and constructions created by the painters in their Happenings. At the end Ross made a huge sculpture of chairs piled on top of his platform construction. Here the emphasis was obviously on the visual impact of jumbled chairs; yet Ross's functional movement in piling the chairs was no more nor less of a dance than another section of the collaboration where the dancers pushed a big iron trapezoid end over end around the space.

The natural movement of the Judson group has often been the raw, rugged action of running at top speed, falling in disorganized heaps, or rolling and sliding the way a child might roll down a hill or slide into home base. The excitement is in the sheer informal physicality of it. The formality of dance movement is another kind of excitement. The synthesis of both kinds of energy can produce a vital dynamic. Deborah Hay's *All Day Dance* combined these energies to make a field of inter-penetrating dance and non-dance activity. Judith Dunn concentrated only on the raw aspect of movement in *Speedlimit,* in which there was not a dance proper at all. She and Robert Morris performed in white jump suits on gymnasium mats. They pushed, pulled, braced, leaned, balanced, fell, rolled, bumped and grappled in a quiet duet of impulse and counter-impulse.

Speedlimit, like many other dances by the Judson Dance Theater, included objects (cart, pole, flag, rope) which were manipulated in a simple, functional manner, much the way Ross handled his chairs. The use of objects is, in fact, an important aspect of the whole movement. During the past decade objects have figured in painting, sculpture and music for their natural value as they exist or function in the world, and for their associational potential as they have been coordinated in collage, and assemblage, of which the Environments and Happenings by the painters were a natural outgrowth. Both aspects of real objects have been exploited by the Judson choreographers. Alone or in association, objects have been projected as facts. On a program in May, 1964, David Gordon and Valda Setterfield presented a television dance, *Silver Pieces.* The television set was tuned to various stations at whim while the two dancers performed ten sequences of action of an indeterminate order. As a mass media product the fact of the TV set loomed large in its ironic presentation before a captive audience. The association of images—the movement of the dancers and the picture on the screen—was intentionally haphazard (life in the living room has the same quality) and produced some interesting, often hilarious, results. In one performance a commercial advertising a cure for headaches was accompanied by a sequence of repetitive head-clutching and bellyaching gestures. On the same program Lucinda Childs presented *Carnation,* a remarkable dance with objects. She used foam rubber curlers and sponges, a salad colander, a plastic bag, a sheet and two socks (attached to the sheet). The manipulation was restrained, precise, economical. She stayed close to the facts of the objects, at the same time making a zany abstraction out of the realistic possibilities.

Steve Paxton, one of the outstanding dancers of the group (he is also in Cunningham's company), has done something else with found objects by making dances in which certain actions are taken from photographs of sports or other activities.

In her evening-long work, *Terrain,* Yvonne Rainer's play with a red ball was a factual presentation of the object with the kind of movement appropriate to the use of that object. Here, she elaborated the play in a long group section in which the performers called for red balls from a supplier stationed in the balcony, and made games of bouncing, chasing, throwing, and catching. Sometimes the action was perfectly natural. At other times the movement was an imaginative take-off, a slight exaggeration of the natural, establishing a subtle interplay between dance movement and ball play. In another section of the dance a yellow street horse was used as a functional property to lean on or sit against. Occasionally the dancers moved it from one place to another. As a piece of decor, aside from its functional value, the street horse had something in common with the atmospheric properties of ballet or the traditional modern dance; but the street horse had no symbolic significance. By contrast, most of Martha Graham's decor, whether employed functionally or as pure setting, supports the dramatic connotations of the dance. Rainer's street horse was more like the grey painted boxes in many early Humphrey-Weidman dances. The boxes served the space sculpturally, in their architectural arrangements and as supports to provide changes of level for the dancers. Yet nobody ever sat, leaned or stood on the boxes as they might in a rehearsal or on a street corner waiting for a bus. This ordinary activity in Rainer's dance was in keeping with the horse as a "found" object. The fact of the object and the functional activity suitable to such an object is a kind of realism (Pop artists have been called "New Realists") unknown to the older modern dancers, whose "realism" consisted of social and psychological statements in idealistic terms. In one sense the contemporary attitude is more direct and realistic. In another sense it is more abstract, since there is no contextual logic, no narrative sequence, no reference to any ideas or attitudes beyond the fact of the object or the movement.

Even the presentation of emotions has been factual. This is one of the most curious and startling aspects of the new movement. Rainer first made it explicit in another dance from *Terrain,* a love duet, which was a sequence of frank gestures, more like lovemaking than the courtship gestures familiar in romantic duets. Rainer was, in fact, inspired by the gestures and poses of reproductions of Hindu erotic sculpture.

As they performed, Rainer and her partner, William Davis, made a dialogue of the conventional, hackneyed phrases of love. "I love you," "I don't love you," "I've never loved you," "Do you love me?", etc. They spoke in flat tones. They could have been ordering groceries for all the words had to do with the feeling normally associated with them. The movement itself was performed with the same bland, impassive expression. Clearly, what Rainer did in this duet was to offset the high charge of intimate gesture and words with a matter-of-fact delivery. I did not read the dance, the way some did, as a commentary on the impossibility of love. Actually, many people were moved by the duet. Both the expression and the absence of it pushed against each other so that the form became paramount as it hung balanced between the two; and the novelty of the situation, this new form, revitalized a very common emotional content.

A year later, in *Dialogues* (1964), Rainer did something quite similar in three sequences of words and movement. In the first sequence she and Judith Dunn performed innocuous dance movements while they alternated in utterances of social and personal importance ("I need help," "I am desperate," "I am torn between duty and ennui," etc.) in tones of phony desperation, or the factual manner of making a statistical tabulation of the world's urgencies. The third dialogue was an expert imitation of Gertrude Stein, all about changing, growing, loving, thinking, becoming, stopping and so on. As they spoke, normally or in falsetto, the dancers performed the same movement phrase over and over. This reiteration of words that have potency in the language, as they signify essential states or processes, was another way of flattening the verbal content.

There is some irony in the deadpan delivery of crucial issues. People take life seriously. A tour of the theatres would convince anyone that the psycho-social issues are placed high on the hierarchical scale of things to be considered. Yet since the turn of the century many artists have been levelling objects and events on a single plane of value. It is not that the emotional life of people has significantly changed. People remain the same. People have the same desires and frustrations and gratifications; but their intellectual attitudes have changed and so have the forms and structures. Thus there is no intentional irony in Rainer's factual delivery of emotional words and movement. The structure is the important thing, and the attitude behind the structure is that red balls and Coca-Cola are no more nor less significant than fear and rage. There seems, then, no necessity to treat any object or event with conventional reverence. Andy Warhol makes a monumental image of a Campbell soup can. Rainer reduces love to a plan of action. People are moved by the new context in which they find their familiar objects and events. It has been one aspect of Rainer's originality to re-locate emotions. By pitting an emotion against its natural connotation she jolts the observer out of his habitual expectations into a novel experience of the commonplace. The method is a dissociation of form and feeling, as though you were to tell somebody you were crazy about them in a monotone of embalmed apathy. The reiterated insistence of such a split has an evocative power which somehow brings the feeling into sharp relief by its very absence.

The use of objects by the painters, sculptors and composers has resulted in some of the most interesting and progressive work at the Judson Dance Theater. The point at which these artists have become involved in performance is the transition from a static construction to the kind of construction that invites manipulation. Jim Dine's hatchet canvas did not require participation by the observer to be complete; but if the observer did attack the wood with the hatchet, it became a performance. Most of the events in the Happenings—by Claes Oldenburg, Dine, Robert Whitman, Allan Kaprow—involved the manipulation of objects which constituted the Environment for the Happenings. The Environment was a natural extension of Collage, and the Happening was a mobilized extension of the Environment. The performers were not actors in any conventional theatrical sense. They were more like objects themselves, or agents in the manipulation of materials, or regular people in ordinary activities. Two women in Whitman's *E. G. Opera* were transformed by huge burlap sacks stuffed with paper balls. Two women in *Mouth* sat down on the floor to eat a picnic lunch. Two women in *Ball* fried eggs on an electric pan. Several people in one of Oldenburg's Happenings sat for a long time at a table full of fake food. Their activity was not unusual; but they moved in slow motion and they wore tinfoil masks. All these Happenings were rich in the association of images, either by sequential or by simultaneous juxtaposition. The artists also tended to push real situations into fantasy, by exaggeration, distortion and unlikely combinations.

Several works presented by the Judson Dance Theater have something in common with the Happenings. Carolee Schneeman's *Chromolodeon* was a wild and lyrical assemblage of rags, hemp, costume, paint, movement, and objects. Philip Corner (composer) mixed dance, props, instrumentation, painting and slide projections in *Flares,* a long piece alternating black-outs and flashes of those combined images. Elaine Summers' *Fantastic Gardens* was an evening-long work of films, dancing, words, sculpture and sound. On an early program, in 1962, Robert Morris and Bob Huot, dressed in a fantastic panoply of found objects and materials, brandishing wooden weapons, made serious *War* for about 60 seconds.

Morris is a brilliant young sculptor who has made some of the most significant contributions to the new dance scene. His work also involves objects; but unlike the creators of the Happenings, he does not assemble a personal, environmental atmosphere, nor does he extend his images into fantasy. His performances are like his grey boxes, plaques, portals, columns and platforms—neutral, geometric, impersonal, matter-of-fact. In 1960, in presenting an event at The Living Theatre, he placed a light grey column, eight feet tall, two feet square, in the center of the stage. The column stood for 3½ minutes. Then, by means of a string attached to the top of the column Morris pulled it down and it rested in the fallen position for 3½ minutes. Morris said he wanted a change from the vertical to the horizontal with a rest in each position. His own role as a performer was simply that of facilitating the fall of the column. *Arizona,* presented at the Judson Church in 1963, was in four simple parts and not unlike the column event. In the first part Morris stood in the center of the performing area and moved his torso very slowly, twisting front to left, accompanied by a taped description of cows being herded into a corral. The second part was an overhead swing in the darkness of two blue lights on a rope. In part three he threw a javelin. In part four he placed a T-form of two blue sticks in the center, then alternated adjusting the top stick and walking to each corner of the area. This was a dance of great economy and precision. The severe reduction of activity is analogous, not only to his own sculpture, but to certain forms of Hard-Edge painting in which the personality of the artist sits like a Sphinx behind the work. The free play of an intuitive coordination of materials is replaced by the hard core of a mathematical object. These exercises in neutrality arrive at a still point similar to Cage's position of attempting to eliminate the personality by chance and indeterminacy. The art object is not a direct exposure of the personality and the object tends to speak for itself. Morris' poise and concentration as a performer are that of a person fully engaged in any ordinary activity. As such, it is certainly expressive. The body is always expressive. But the emphasis rests dramatically on the simple existence of a body in space—the silent presence or the functional action or the difference between a business conversation and a private harangue. Where business becomes art it is still a matter of choice and placement; Morris makes a considered choice of materials and places them with esthetic discretion.

The eye of the painter was well-defined in a dance by Alex Hay called *Colorado Plateau*. The objects in his dance were six people, whom he dragged and carried, according to the taped instructions of his own voice, from one position to another around the performing area. The space became a changing sculpture of diagonals, verticals and horizontals. The performers were neutral objects in this visual exercise.

The painter Robert Rauschenberg has also been involved in the Judson Dance Theater. In Washington, D.C. he made a dance on roller skates (the dancers gave a concert there in a huge roller rink) with a parachute strapped to his back. On a series of concerts at Stage 73 in New York he presented a dance in the dark with a flashlight strapped to his leg, accompanied by a Lecture On Birds in Swedish.

It should be clear by now, from the above descriptions, that the structure of works by the new modern dancers is wide-ranging. Thus far there are no theories of composition and no attempts to pour material into pre-established molds. The idea is that each dance is a new problem with its own formal requirements. The structure might be as simple as a single action repeated over and over from entrance to exit. That was the form of Fred Herko's *Once or Twice a Week I Put on Sneakers and Go Uptown*. He did the Suzie-Q in semi-circular transit with no alteration of pace or accent. Repetition is a favorite device of many of the choreographers. Unlike traditional modes of composition, the idea is not to repeat movements to enhance the thematic coherence of a dance. Rather, a repeated action, especially as it is an exact repetition and occurs in an unbroken sequence, is a means of engaging the observer's involvement in the specific "thereness" of that one action.

The composer, La Monte Young, is well known for his commitment to the kind of event that devolves on a single action or sound, his aim being to entice the participant into an ever-increasing state of awareness of that one particular sound or action so that he becomes One with it—what Young means when he says he likes "to get inside a sound." One might also notice how an action is never the same. What appears to be identical becomes a study in depth as the eye steers through minute changes, revealing the manifold aspects of a single activity.

More complicated structures are often the result of improvisatory elements in a dance. Sally Gross made a clock diagram for six performers, specifying a two-hour span of the day for each person. Extracting movement from the kinds of activities they were accustomed to doing in those two hours, the performers improvised from there and the result was a random juxtaposition of six bodies with occasional unison as two or more performers did a pre-established movement on the circumference of the clock. In Elaine Summers' *Instant Chance* the performers tossed boxes of various sizes, shapes, colors and numbers to determine what they should do from one moment to the next. Like the clock dance, the structure was a complex field of action that would never be the same from one performance to another. Both dances were typical of a variety of chance devices, usually including improvisation, employed in the sessions of Dunn's composition course, as well as in the early concerts by the Judson Dance Theater.

The wedding of chance techniques with improvisation produced a new scheme of action which Yvonne Rainer called "spontaneous determination." In most cases this meant that the movement was composed and given, but the sequence of phrases was left to the choice of the performer, who made his choices on the spot during the performance, according to some pre-determined ground rules or signals. Cunningham, it might be recalled, sets both movement and sequence by chance, although a recent dance, *Story* ('63), included some improvisatory choices. With "spontaneous determination" the movement is set beforehand and chance becomes improvisatory as it is transposed to the performance itself in the choice of sequence.

The objective in the use of any variation of this method is to produce a partially unforeseen situation. The more elaborate the devices the more complex the results tend to be. The effect is to minimize the expectations of performers and audience alike. Familiarity with the phrases is deterred by the constant unpredictability of sequence and spatial relationships.

Although indeterminacy of one kind or another has played an important part in the compositions by the Judson choreographers, it has by no means overshadowed other interests. There have been at least as many, if not more, works made in which the results conform completely to prior calculations.

I have discussed certain common tendencies and preoccupations of the Judson Dance Theater. Yet the scene keeps changing and there has been a tremendous variety of structure and styles. No doubt the best way to define the movement is to indicate the variety and freedom and wide-open policy of the group. It is their mobility as well as their exposure of contemporary attitudes that has projected the modern dance into a new era of unlicensed activity. The only prediction I would hazard for the future is that the major directions in the dance of the next decade or two will be largely the result of the adventurous work of members of this group.

THE NEW AMERICAN

FICTION

RICHARD KOSTELANETZ

> *Let us finish with a positive assur-*
> *ance that the stories that we offer*
> *today will be absolutely new and*
> *in no way embroideries of known*
> *sources. This quality is of some*
> *merit in an age when everything*
> *appears to have been done.*
>
> Marquis de Sade,
> "Essay on the Novel" (1800)

In retrospect, we see that Sade's contemporaries were naïve to think that writers had milked dry all of fiction's possible resources, even if, as Sade put it, "The exhausted imagination of authors [of his time] seems no longer able to create anything new." In literature, as well as in science, incapacity is no proof of impossibility, and the future showed literature what it continually demonstrates to all arts: that everything has *not* been done. In fact, the major revolutions in fiction took place in the last quarter of the nineteenth century, as thinkers and writers began to explore with increasing insight the subtle realities of consciousness and the complex nature of society—in intellectual thought, Nietzsche and Freud, Weber and Marx; and in fiction, Dostoevsky and Zola. Thus, just as Sade himself, who in the above quotation was introducing his own fiction, added new dimensions to that underground tradition of prose literature which is more concerned with recording a personal fantasy than with accurately depicting external reality; so his own work in this direction was, in turn, surpassed by more extreme fantasies—Poe's stories, Apollinaire's *The Debauched Hospodar,* Kafka's fiction and Jean Genet's *Our Lady of the Flowers.* In the same fashion, just as the proclamations of some contemporary critics and thinkers that nothing new could happen in the post-Joycean, -Gidean, and -Faulknerian novel are, with each passing year, more decisively repudiated, equally irrelevant are the oft-heard claims that the "New French Novel," our lump-name for a variety of trends, represents the end of fiction. The point is that an achieved originality always inspires, not stifles, further invention. As Sade's fiction led to, and was superseded by, artworks possessed of a distinctly different originality, so the literature of modernism's major phase—the 1920's—has by 1964 become a segment of the total literary tradition upon which contemporary writers selectively draw. As the possibilities of life have changed and esthetic ideas in the other arts have been assimilated by novelists, fiction has been similarly transformed; and in decisive respects, the books that comprise the new American fiction move beyond the literature of this modern period, as well as beyond the post-World War II phase of American fiction, to chart in form and content new directions in both streams, the sociological and the psychological, of modern fiction.

I

What might first suggest that there *is* no new American fiction is the widespread opinion that *nearly all* the promising novelists of 1946–58 have not, as of mid-1964, equalled their earlier pieces. The grotesque novelists, whose big splash in the late 1940's has smoothed out to a faint ripple in our literary history, have all but ceased imaginative writing; and their few later books, such as Carson McCullers' *Clock Without Hands* (1961), are disappointing. The recent fiction of their most promising, albeit eccentric heir, the late Flannery O'Connor, does not match her previous achievements. James Agee, Isaac Rosenfeld, and John Horne Burns all died in the mid-fifties, just as they were finally gaining control of their promising talents. J. D. Salinger remains silent after the debacle of *Seymour: An Introduction* (1959), though his admirers have high hopes for his long-germinating next book. Robert Penn Warren, despite his immense talent and sophistication, sinks with each novel deeper and deeper into the groove of high-handed, semi-Christian romance; and both Mary McCarthy and James Jones exhibit similar failures of narrow range and repetition, the former offering in "The Fact in Fiction" a ridiculous defense of nineteenth-century principles as contemporary ideals. With each new novel, Wright Morris predictably creates another colorless microcosm of modern sterility, and Louis Auchincloss another portrait of moral ambivalence in upper-class, old-line America.

Few would defend, to list several sets of recent disappointments as opposed to previous achievements, William Styron's *Set This House on Fire* (1961) as better than his brilliant *Lie Down in Darkness* (1951), J. F. Powers' *Morte D'Urban* (1962) against *The Prince of Darkness* (1947), Delmore Schwartz's *Successful Love* (1961) against the more successful stories of *The World Is a Wedding* (1948), Herbert Gold's *Salt* (1963) against the similar "Love and Like" (1958), Frederick Buechner's unread *The Return of Ansel Gibbs* (1958) against his much-heralded but hardly read *A Long Day's Dying* (1949), Leo E. Litwak's *To the Hanging Gardens* (1964) against "The Solitary Life of Man" (1959), or Nelson Algren's recent work against his *Man with the Golden Arm* (1949); and even fewer would favor J. P. Donleavy's *The Singular Man* (1963) against *The Ginger Man* (1955). Alas, even Herman Wouk and Leon Uris have declined. Andrew Lytle, whose unduly neglected *The Velvet Horn* (1957) was the best work of his long novelistic career, has not published a book since assuming the editorship of *The Sewanee Review,* nor has Robie Macauley, author of the well-realized *The Disguises of Love* (1952), published long fiction since becoming editor of *Kenyon Review.* Whatever hope Jack Kerouac and those trailing behind him ever offered American fiction has, by 1964, thoroughly evaporated. Norman Mailer's fiction career, which became more interesting as he moved away from the naturalism of his early novel to the more mythic fictional universe of *The Deer Park* (1955), abruptly stalled around

1957 when he began concentrating his immense energies on essays; and the story "The Time of Her Time" (1959) and *The American Dream* (1964) are less realized achievements than public warm-ups for future work.

On the other hand, some writers of that generation born in the early 1920's have matured. Vance Bourjaily, for one, records with increasingly accurate realism the typical experiences of our time; no American novel I know has such a convincing portrait of life at an American men's college as his *Confessions of a Spent Youth* (1959). Evan S. Connell, Jr., for another, after writing a series of rather realistic and conventional stories, collected as *The Anatomy Lesson* (1957), and novels, *Mrs. Bridge* (1959) and *The Patriot* (1960)—each book more ambitious than its predecessor—created in *Notes from a Bottle Found on the Beach at Carmel* (1963) a collage of images of the decline of modern civilization, all told through notes left behind by a quest hero. A third, James Baldwin, wrote his most honest and, despite disintegrating structure, his best novel in *Another Country* (1962), an eloquently written protest fiction on behalf of Negroes *and* homosexuals that is a vital complement to his polemical writing. In any event, but for Connell, none of these writers, in my opinion, has recently, even in his less successful work, done anything decisively new in fiction.

In our time "new" has become so honorific a word, particularly in the non-literary arts, that even in literary criticism it is applied with such cheapening indiscriminateness that it verges on joining "great," "wonderful," and "exciting" in the dustbin of platitudes. This is unfortunate, for the epithet must be used with extreme precision if it is to be used at all. I do not, for instance, find anything truly new in most of Bernard Malamud's fiction, though I think him one of the most accomplished storytellers of our time. His moral concerns and fictional style, derived it seems largely from Gogol and Yiddish fiction, strike those of us who have come of age in the sixties as, like Isaac Bashevis Singer's work, more an archaic remnant than a contemporary voice. The prime exception, of course, is his *The Natural* (1952), his most original work, in which absurd details do not create an absurd vision. The young and over-praised John Updike, despite his gift for language, continually overblows the trivial and skips over the significant until his fiction becomes lumpy, bloated and artsy-craftsy. The fiction of an older novelist, George P. Elliott, is wildly uneven, particularly falling off, I find, once his religious impulses overwhelm his fictional sense.

As a general rule, I would say that writers who emphasize their ability to render the external details of life today, rather than create a vision of existence, penetrate the human psyche, or achieve a formal originality do not belong among the new American novelists. This judgment includes, to mention several young novelists, Philip Roth, whose ability to reproduce in detail contemporary mannerisms and idiom is extraordinary; Warren Miller, whose ersatz-sociological study of divorcée culture, *The Way We Live Now* (1958), fulfills its limited, almost reportorial intentions, as does Richard Yates' portrait of young suburbia, *The Revolutionary Road* (1961); John Knowles, whose two well-crafted novels, *A Separate Peace* (1959) and *Morning in Antibes* (1962), seem a trifle too pat; Clancy Sigal, whose *Going Away* (1962) in its realism, linguistic energy and obsessive self-concern greatly echoed Thomas Wolfe's writings and Sigal's own *Weekend in Dinlock* (1961), George Orwell's *The Road to Wigan Pier* (1937); John Rechy, whose field in *City of Night* (1963) is male prostitution and whose style is awful; and Wallace Markfield, whose satirical, mildly comic novel *To an Early Grave* (1964) propagates the theme that New York Jewish intellectuals find mass culture more enjoyable than high art.

Those pretenders to newness whose admirers base their claim on esthetic criteria can usually make a stronger case, though sometimes not a convincing one. John Hawkes, for instance, has since 1948 regularly published a kind of dream fiction in which usually, if not predictably, a group of grotesque characters is coupled with strongly visual, bizarre images, all rendered with a precise rhetoric filled with odd, jarring metaphors. These stylistic gimmicks, serviced by a disjointed narrative, produce a vague sense of nightmare; but just because Hawkes is the only novelist doggedly exploiting this style does not, as some of his admirers think, make him a new and/or important writer. To my taste, his fictional style was more successfully realized, with greater thematic resonance, in Djuna Barnes' *Nightwood,* (published way back in 1936); and Hawkes in his later novels, *The Lime Twig* (1961) and *Second Skin* (1964), seems to debase his formula by introducing elements, such as a more cohesive narrative, that make his recent work more accessible to the larger public. Susan Sontag, who exchanges admiring words with Hawkes, wrote in *The Benefactor* (1963) a depressingly dull, oddly written, thoroughly ironic novel about a decrepit man's unfulfilled love-life, the irony being doubled by an inverted Albertine strategy—that "male" narrator seems to be a woman in disguise. A critic-turned-novelist-turned-critic, Miss Sontag performs more successfully in her primary profession.

Several other writers, hailed here and there as "new," likewise seem on second examination to use their predecessors' techniques with less success. Terry Southern, whose satirical technique in *Flash and Filigree* (1958) and *The Magic Christian* (1960) eschews the creation of sympathetic characters to contrast with those he mocks, strikes me as essentially imitating what Nathanael West achieved in *The Day of the Locust* twenty years before, as do the stories in John Anthony West's *Call Out the Malicia* (1963). While Jerome Charyn in *Once Upon a Droshky* (1964) and Grace Paley in the best stories in *The Little Disturbances of Man* (1959) have not fully enough emancipated themselves from Isaac Babel's example; Elliott Baker's funny but trivial *A Fine Madness* (1964), Stanley Elkin's mildly comic *Boswell* (1964), and Thomas Berger's intellectually interesting but fictionally soporific *Crazy in Berlin* (1958) and *Reinhart in Love* (1962) seem spun wholecloth out of Ellison, Bellow and the fifties' picaresque. The same failure—derivativeness—is characteristic of two other remarkable writers, Tillie Olsen and John F. Gilgun, both of whom published in *New World Writing #16* (1960), respectively, the intensely moving "Tell Me A Riddle" and "A Penny for the Ferryman," stream-of-consciousness short stories that excessively reflect the influence of William Faulkner (of *The Sound and the Fury* and *The Bear*) without achieving, particularly in Gilgun's case, the master's breadth and depth. Faulkner of *As I Lay Dying,* along with Gide and the other great modern practitioners of the multiple point-of-view, seems the omnipresent guide behind promising books by other young writers who have learned their lessons well: William Melvin Kelley's uneven *A Different Drummer* (1962); Peter Sourian's *Miri* (1957), a neat demonstration of how to create three convincing narrators; Benjamin DeMott's obtuse *The Body's Cage* (1959), Norman Fruchter's intelligent *Coat Upon a Stick* (1963), to which are added dashes of Malamud and Robbe-Grillet; and Charles Haldeman's impressive *The Sun's Attendant* (1964), an ambitious novel with a flighty point-of-view that fails to keep all its weighty political baggage from dragging.

Other interesting, but hard-to-classify, new novelists include the critic Leslie A. Fiedler, whose novella *Nude Croquet* (1957) is the most realized application I know of Westian satirical technique to another social milieu and who created in *The Second Stone* (1963) a rather suggestive, ironic and befuddling novel; John Yount, whose superbly comic, deeply moral tale, "The Scattering," in *Contact* (July, 1963), displayed both command and style; Arno Karlen and Ivan Gold, two younger writers whose mastery of the resonant symbolist tale, as in Karlen's "The Clown" (1957) and the latter's "The Nickel Miseries of George Washington Carver Brown" (1960), marks remarkable, if so far limited, achievement; and Jack Gelber, more noted for his play *The Connection,* whose *On Ice* (1964) appears, I think, to be an ambitious attempt to pattern a novel after the structures of serial music. Perhaps because most contemporary minds do not retain and reorganize fictional motifs as easily as they can those of music, the novel seems, at least to this reader, disintegrating and dull. But possibly, in the hands of another writer, the same attempt could be better realized; and in any case, *On Ice* establishes Gelber as capable of producing fiction as experimental in intent as his plays.

Of course, not all attempts for true originality are even faintly successful. William Gaddis' *The Recognitions* (1956), which many fervently admire, strikes me as incoherent for any two of its 956 pages, as do the much shorter, potentially more interesting, sup-posedly subliminal writings of Arlene Zekowsky, *Concertions* (1962) and *Abraxas* (1964), and Stanley Berne, *The Dialogues* (1962). Richard Stern's *Golk* (1960), despite blurbs, did not jell as a satire of television, capitalism or even the semi-cultured sons of rich men. Alan Harrington's *The Revelations of Doctor Modesto* (1955), a satire of conformity, sank into all its over-intellectualized trappings; while Douglas Woolf's dullness, exhibited all though his two novels, rivals that of nearly all the contributors (Hubert Selby and Michael Rumaker excepted) to LeRoi Jones's collection of late-beat "New [Prose] Writing in America," *The Moderns* (1963). Against this background of declining older writers and the heralded prophets of the pseudo-new, the derivative and the pretentious—against the waves of novels that flow out of New York each Sep-tember—what little that is new and worthwhile in recent fiction collects in an isolated eddy to attract a following slowly but, in all cases, surely.

Of the older writers, the two who seem most likely to hurdle the barrier of 1959—if not the two most significant of that genera-tion now about fifty—Ralph Ellison and Saul Bellow have each been working on a novel for several years. The sections of Ellison's work I have seen in print, especially the breath-taking "And Hick-man Arrives," in *Noble Savage #1,* and those I have heard him read aloud, suggest it will be a superior novel, resembling perhaps the absurd fiction of recent years. Bellow's oft-announced and much-postponed *Herzog,* which finally appeared in the autumn of 1964, is a disappointment. In attempting to portray a deranged man as hero, Bellow compromised both efforts, creating a character whose derangement is too mild to disturb and whose heroism con-sists largely of tilting with windmills.

The one older writer who has successfully bucked the trend, Vladimir Nabokov, was probably saved by the singularity of his career. Literally reborn as an American novelist in the early fifties, with a command of an adopted language that includes words found only in an unabridged *O.E.D.,* Nabokov produced in *Lolita* (1955) and *Pale Fire* (1962) two works superior to what earlier Russian writing I have read in translation (rumor has it that his best Russian works remain untranslated), the second of which, more than the first, belongs with the new American fiction.

In retrospect, 1959 clearly emerges as the turning point; for just as the older novelists find it a barrier, nearly all of the best fiction written since then is by previously un- or little-known writers. Moreover, despite the wide range of personal styles and subjects, nearly all the most interesting and original of recent works fit into two distinct patterns, one concerned with depicting the absurdity of life in an appropriate form and the other with the madnesses of the individual. This is not to suggest that the patterns were pre-established by critical fiat—they were not—but that the novelists today seem to find certain areas of concern more congenial than others. Each pattern includes works which are, in crucial dimensions, unprecedented and successfully realized. In general, their newness stems less from formal revolutions—these are not entirely absent, though—than from their metaphysical theme, absurdity, and the ways this theme is realized; and, in the other strain, their rendering of a certain range of universal experience, mental derangement.

The first group, which includes the novels of John Barth, Joseph Heller, Thomas Pynchon and Mordecai Richler, resembles the absurd theatre of contemporary Europe in that the author creates a series of absurd (i.e., nonsensical, ridiculous) events—repetition of similar action forms the novel's structure—to depict the ultimate absurdity (i.e., meaninglessness) of history and existence. Thus, these works embody absurdity both in the small events and the entire vision, the subject matter and the form. In world literature, their ancestors include James Joyce's Nighttown sequence and, especially, French 'Pataphysics which, in Martin Esslin's summary, "like its sister philosophy, existentialism, . . . sees the universe as absurd; unlike existentialism, though, it does not take that knowledge as tragic but, on the contrary, as a matter for laughter." Its spiritual father, Alfred Jarry (1873–1907), once, in a preposterous imitation of mathematics, "proved" that "God is the tangential point between zero and infinity." In American literature, progenitors include Nathanael West's *The Dream Life of Balso Snell* (1931) and, in key spots, the works of William Faulkner, S. J. Perelman, and Henry Miller. In contemporary world literature, its analogue is Samuel Beckett's masterpiece, *Comment C'est* (1961), in which the absurd situation of a lone man crawling through mud becomes a paradigm of existence (How It Is).

The second trend includes Vladimir Nabokov (in his American genesis), Bruce Jay Friedman, Walker Percy, Irvin Faust, Michael Rumaker, and William Burroughs, all of whom create realized *internal* portraits of mental distress, running from mild neurosis to hallucinatory insanity, with a sophistication, depth, accuracy, intimacy and/or terror that is, in crucial degrees, unprecedented. Its ancestors include that long line of European works that descend from Dostoevsky's *Notes from Underground* (1864), and probably the best of the few American portraits, the Jason Compson section of *The Sound and the Fury* (1929). These Americans, it should be pointed out, diverge from the Jamesian tradition exemplified today by Nathalie Sarraute, which is concerned with the subtleties of normal consciousness.

The absurdity of society, the madness of the self—these are the over-arching themes of an American fiction considerably different from both postwar American writing and trends in contemporary European fiction.

II

John Barth is unquestionably the most brilliant and promising novelist to appear in America in the past ten years. No other writer as young as Barth (b. 1930) is so thoroughly equipped with the verbal resources and energy, imaginative range, literary sophistication, intellect, courageous originality, independence and, most important, the literary genius to transform these virtues and talents into fiction that continually reflects his capacities. Moreover, Barth has distinctly and considerably matured in the course of his three-novel career—*The Floating Opera* (1956), *The End of the Road* (1958), and *The Sot-Weed Factor* (1960); and since the third of these novels is one of the greatest works of fiction of our time, the potential limits of Barth's achievements are beyond pre-definition, if not comprehension.

Set in late seventeenth- and early eighteenth-century England and Maryland, filled with characters who speak accurately rendered eighteenth-century dialect with appropriate contemporary references, *The Sot-Weed Factor* (an archaic term for a Tobacco merchant) for 806 large pages tells of the adventures of one Ebenezer Cooke who at the age of thirty makes a two-fold vow—to preserve his treasured virginity and to devote himself to poetry. Having convinced a rather dumbfounded and generous Lord Baltimore to be his nominal patron, Cooke confers upon himself the rather dubious title of "Poet and Laureate" of Maryland and sets out to write an epic in praise of the New World, his Marylandiad. A summary of all the twists and turns of the maze-like plot, all the little digressions, disguises and coincidences, and the natures of all the characters is, for the moment, unfeasible; suffice it to record that Stanley Edgar Hyman attests that "The plot contrivance is the most fantastic of any book I know."

On its most basic level, *The Sot-Weed Factor* is a mockery of written history; for Barth systematically distorts—mostly debunks —the accepted versions of the past. In this narrative, Sir Isaac Newton and Henry More, the Cambridge neo-Platonist, emerge as lubricious pederasts who provide refuge for orphaned boys. The intellectual coffee-house conversation which Addison described, actually, says Barth's novel, soon turned to sex. The third Lord Baltimore, known to history as an undistinguished Catholic ruler, runs a network of spies and saboteurs in his war against the Protestants, and he informs Ebenezer that in the New World poets are as rare as virgins; and the most successful and self-confident woman Ebenezer encounters in Maryland is Mary Mungummory (note her initials) who claims to have been "swived" 28,000 times. Boatloads of whores regularly arrive in America, and at one point American pirates intercept a ship carrying Moorish virgins to Mecca and take their pleasure until "The deck looked like a butcher's block." Barth's most extensive debunking comes with the piece-by-piece discovery of the *Secret Historie* of John Smith and *The Privie Journall of Sir Henry Burlingame,* both written in magnificently faked seventeenth-century prose. These "authentic" documents, to deny the accepted version, reveal that John Smith was a lecher who first obtained Powhatan's friendship by giving him pornographic pictures, later won his confidence by satisfying the chief's otherwise insatiable wife, and, finally, thanks to a secret "Egg-plant" potion manages to deflower the much-tried, but previously impenetrable virgin Pocahontas. The Indians, likewise untrue to historical form, confiscate Smith's immense collection of erotica. Whereas Ebenezer Cook (without the "e") is known to history as the pseudonymous author of *The Sot-Weed Factor* (1708), a bitterly satirical attack on life in Maryland, Barth's Cooke writes a mildly unfavorable, Hudibrastic ditty that Londoners interpret as a sign of Maryland's high cultural achievement —it even persuades some of them to settle in the New World. ('Pataphysical proverb: "Only the unusual exists and . . . everything is unpredictable, especially the predictable.") Among other historical figures, William Penn, John Coode, Sir Edmund Andros all make their appearance, albeit in somewhat unfamiliar dress.

Though one character rejects sentimental interpretations of history, saying, "More history's made in the bed-chamber than the throne room," Barth is sophisticated enough to suggest that not much history is made in bed either. To Barth, history is thoroughly disordered; and the search for first causes or definitive interpretations uncovers only confusion. A chapter heading near the book's end expresses the reader's befuddlement as well as Ebenezer's:

> The Poet Wonders Whether the Source of Human History Is a Progress, a Drama, a Retrogression, a Cycle, an Undulation, a Vortex, a Right- or Left-Hand Spiral, a Mere Continuum, or What Have You. Certain Evidence is Brought Forward, but of an Ambiguous and Inconclusive Nature.

In addition to burlesqueing written history, *The Sot-Weed Factor* thoroughly ridicules literary conventions and, thus, undercuts art's ways of understanding life. The satirical blade is aimed obliquely at all fat popular historical novels (this being too fat, too difficult, and totally faked as history) and particularly at the eighteenth-century novel whose chapter headings and pet plot devices are exaggerated *ad absurdum:* the search for the father, reversal of roles, the accidental recognition scene, transformation through disguises (Burlingame, Cooke's Sancho, assumes a plethora of identities), moments of near incest, and, especially, preposterous coincidences all appear with excessive abundance. Thus, Barth successfully transforms a serious two-fold quest—Cooke's for his muse and Burlingame's for the identity of his parents—into a long series of incidents so incredible that high comedy becomes the book's overall tone. The traditional picaresque structure is further subverted by making the book's main character a congenital unsuccess, a *schlimael,* whose innocence, in another inversion, turns out to be the single quality that saves him in the rough, cynical, greedy society of America. Indeed, one of the book's main themes is that in a world which throws up hazards and sharpsters at every turn— the novel is almost a catalogue of man's sins—innocence is stronger protection than the mild worldliness of, say, the diseased prostitute, Joan Toast.

Finally, Barth's debunking is universally extended—it starts with the novel's main character, includes the most minute facets of society, ends in the book's final passages with Barth himself, spares no one, and offers no reforms. In mocking the conventions of the eighteenth-century novel, by overusing them to absurd lengths, in suggesting that the history we know is as unlikely as his rewriting of it ("This Clio was already a scarred and crafty trollop when the author found her."), in mocking both Ebenezer's quest and the society that is inhospitable to poetry—in doing these things with such a thoroughness and breadth of reference, Barth ultimately says, not only that the single events of life are preposterous (i.e., absurd), but also that life as a whole, which resists any ordering interpretations, is likewise totally absurd.

As well as being thematically neat—indeed, it seems to be a programmed illustration of a pre-determined theme—*The Sot-Weed Factor* displays on nearly every page Barth's verbal brilliance. It is, at once, one of the most eloquently written books of our time and one of the funniest. Few writers can turn as many striking phrases as Barth or coin as many quotable aphorisms, such as the double-entendre of: "Who gives a man horns must beware of goring." And nobody else would have written this or many other scenes:

> *We were fetch'd into the small circle and station'd before the altar of* Venus *(to look whereon brought the blush to my cheeks), whereupon the Salvages lay'd hands upon my Captain, and with one jerk brought his breeches low. From where I stood, wch chanc'd to be behind him, the sight was unprepossessing enough, but the Salvages before all suddenlie put by there clamour. The Emperour shaded his eyes from the morning Sunne, the better to behold him, and Pocahontas, maugre her bonds (wch netted her as fast as those, that* Vulcan *fashion'd for his faithless spouse), this Pocahontas, I say, came neare to breaking her necke with looking, and the unchast smyle, that erst had play'd about her mowth, now vanish'd altogether.*
>
> *My Captain then turning half around to see, Whether I was at hand? I at last beheld the cause of all this wonder, and as well the effect of all his magick of the night past—the wch to relate, must fetch me beyond all bownds of taste & decencie, but to withhold, must betray the Truth and leave what follow'd veil'd in mystery. To have done then, my Captains yard stood full erect, and what erst had been more cause for pity than for astonishment, was now in verie sooth a frightfull engine: such was the virtue of his devilish brewe, that when now his codd stood readie for the carnall tilt, he rear'd his bulk not an inch below eleven, and well-nigh three in diameter—a weapon of the Gods! Add to w^{ch}, it was all a fyrie hue, gave off a scent of clove & vanilla, and appear'd as stout as that stone whereon its victim lay. A mightie sownd went up from the populace; the Lieutenants, that had doubtlesse been the Princesses former suitors, dropt to there knees as in prayer; the Emporour started up in his high seate, dismay'd by the fate about to befall his daughter; and as for that same Pocahontas, she did swoone dead away.*

More than just mere joking, this is truly superior comedy, stemming from Barth's ability to mesh frustrated expectation, witty language, vivid description, timing, parody; so that, one kind of joke enhances another (just as Harpo complements Groucho) and all the comic effects fall together into a neat whole. As sophisticated comedy, it is funnier if one reads the archaic language with some ease, is familiar with the conventions of pornography, colonial history, the literary references and the geography of Eastern Shore Maryland; but even without this erudition, the novel is often hysterically funny. Though capable of a wide variety of comic tricks and of turning nearly everything he touches to laughter, Barth never makes what is, to my taste, a cheap joke, and rarely does he concoct an unsuccessful or a corny one.

As well as being one of the funniest, most erotic and pervasively scatological novels since Henry Miller's best gems, *The Sot-Weed Factor* is also one of the intellectually richest. Not only is Barth acutely aware of how ideas can function in and be illustrated by fiction, he is also, without doubt, the most erudite novelist of excellence we have ever had in America; perhaps only Vladimir Nabokov and Thomas Mann could rival him among modern writers. In his work, especially in *The Sot-Weed Factor,* there is conspicuous evidence that he is extensively knowledgeable in music (in fact, he studied composition at Juilliard), English literature, pornography, ethics and the history of philosophy (he was once a Ph. D. candidate in "aesthetics-of-literature" at Johns Hopkins), American colonial history, English cultural history (his characters of both centuries familiarly refer to the music, books and popular ideas of their respective times), the development of the English language and etymology (he literally seems to have checked the accuracy of every archaic word and the origin of every modern one in the *O.E.D.*), existentialist philosophy, and a variety of critical theories of the American mythos, ranging from Philip Young's reinterpretation of Pocahontas and R. W. B. Lewis' *American Adam* to Leslie A. Fiedler's insight into our writers' preoccupation with the inter-racial homosexual romance and Ralph Ellison's image of the trickster as archetypal American (tricksters and Adamic innocents prosper in the novel; others don't). Thus, *The Sot-Weed Factor* inspired Fiedler to report that it embodies "all the obsessive themes common to our classic novel: the comradeship of males, white and colored, always teetering perilously close to, but never quite falling over into, blatant homesexuality; sentimentalized brother-sister incest or quasi-incest; the anti-heroic dreams of evasion and innocence; the fear of the failed erection"; and, thus, as Fiedler added, it is "closer to the 'Great American Novel' than any other book of the last decade." Stanley Edgar Hyman, surely among our most erudite critics, wrote, "The novel has so many literary sources that it would be easier to list the books that it does *not* copy or burlesque." The book, I predict, will become a gold mine for symbol-, source- and influence-hunting academic critics, all of whom will be implicitly mocked with each discovery they make. Yet, as remarkable as Barth's knowledge is, more extraordinary is his ability to use it in fiction—to use it at the same time he parodies and debunks it. All his academic interests are at the service of a true fictional energy; and in this respect, although the book is far from what is called a dry, academic novel, it is still the kind of book only an academic could write.

In comparison to the lushness of *The Sot-Weed Factor,* the earlier novels are distinctly minor works in which Barth seems to be lightly, if not blithely, testing his talents and his ability to win publishers. *The Floating Opera* is a rather conventional absurd novel, outfitted with an unconventional twist that makes it a parody of Camus' *The Myth of Sisyphus.* Its narrator is a typical twentieth-century middle-class man—Todd Andrews, a fairly eminent lawyer in the small Maryland town of Cambridge, born in 1900 (and, thus, a child of the century), a bachelor, an adulterer, a man of little religion and no family. Writing in 1954, he remembers the day, seventeen years before, when he planned to commit suicide. Discovering his own inability to explain life, that the reasons people have for attributing value to things are ultimately arbitrary, and that nothing around him is truly important, he considers taking his own life; but being fairly logical, Todd then discovers there is no justification to death either. "Hamlet's question is, absolutely, meaningless." A very neat novel—the intellectual joke is clearly and efficiently made—*The Floating Opera* is stylistically undistinguished and, once the joke is fathomed, not very interesting.

Although it contains some scenes more brilliant than those in the earlier book, *The End of the Road* is the weakest of the three novels because of its inability to coalesce around anything, even the theme Barth has publicly attributed to it. Its narrative center is the psychic health of Jacob Horner, an indolent graduate student and sometime teacher of "prescriptive grammar" at Wicomico State Teachers College. Suffering from emotional paralysis, which seems to stem from existentialist *angst,* he is remobilized through therapy with a Negro witch-doctor. Finding himself in need of an abortionist for a friend's wife, whom Horner probably impregnated, Horner selects the witch-doctor, who bungles the abortion, killing the woman and leaving Horner suffering from paralysis again. The novel ends with him hailing a taxi to drive him to the "terminal," ambiguously either to his death or to the train headed for the witch-doctor's Remobilization Farm. Unnecessarily uneven in tone, uninteresting in language, never quite focusing on the announced theme —Horner's evasion from responsibility—and lacking any other unifying thread, the novel has one brilliant chapter. The therapy scene is brilliant absurd comedy—two desperate people talking at cross-purposes; and it stood as an excellent short story in *Esquire.*

Coming after the earlier novel, *The Sot-Weed Factor* leaves the critic with the same impression that Joyce's *Ulysses* must have implanted after its first appearance—that nothing, but nothing, is beyond the competence of its author. He has the literary intelligence, the fictional adroitness, the self-awareness, the mature control, the ideas—indeed, all the basic virtues (except, perhaps, psychological insight) to produce fiction more extraordinary and more original than any other writing today. Unlike too many American novelists, he seems to plan his fiction well in advance, announcing with the publication of *The Floating Opera* that it was the first in a series of novels concerned with various aspects of nihilism: "Each will concern some sort of bachelor, more or less irresponsible, who either rejects absolute values or encounters their rejection." So far, he has shifted emphasis from the first pattern to the second, defining in progressively larger chunks a world without order or value.

The author of three novels before he turned thirty, Barth has since 1960 slowed down his pace. Only two of his short stories have appeared, rather undistinguished pieces in *Esquire* (February, 1963) and *Southwest Review* (Summer, 1963); and he has also published an obtuse essay on his native Eastern Shore Maryland, the locale of his three books, in *Kenyon Review* (Winter, 1960) and an immensely illuminating (on his own works too) afterword to the Signet edition of Smollett's *Roderick Random*.

Still, his forthcoming novel promises to be more extraordinary, if not larger, than *The Sot-Weed Factor*. In a letter to me, dated August 7, 1964, Barth described *Giles Goat-Boy* as follows:

[It] will be a two-volume work, each volume consisting of three reels, each reel consisting of seven chapters. It isn't an easy book to synopsize sensibly. George Giles, the narrator of the story, is a young fellow whose complex fate it is to have been raised as a goat on the stockfarms of New Tammany College, one of the richest, strongest, and largest colleges in the whole University. As a kid, George learns from his keeper (a pacifist polymath named Dr. Max Spielman) that the modern University is divided into two armed campuses, presently pitted against each other in a kind of Quiet Riot, but perennially on the verge of EATing one another alive. (EAT stands for Electroencephalic Amplification and Transmission, the ultimate weaponry of WESCAC—the West-Campus Automatic Computer—and equally of its counterpart EASCAC: Dr. Spielman helped invent it during Campus Riot Two.) Many are convinced that only a new Grand Tutor can lead studentdom away from the wholesale flunkage of modern terms and set it on the way to Commencement Gate; and a great many signs indicate —to George at least—that he himself may be destined for that hero-work: that indeed he may be no mere Goat-Boy but the true GILES—the *G*rand-tutorial *I*deal, *L*aboratory *E*ugenical *S*pecimen—prepared some years earlier by WESCAC in a supposedly **abortive experiment**. In the first volume George leaves the goatbarns, makes his way to the Great Mall of NTC, and after sundry encounters and vicissitudes contrives to pass the Trial-by-Turnstile, slip through Scrapegoat Grate, and matriculate as a Special Student, not without having met a rival claimant to Grand-Tutorhood. In volume two he must address himself to his Assignment, which he conceives to be (perhaps mistakenly) passing the finals himself, declaring his Grand-Tutorhood, descending into WES-CAC's *Belly*—the basement chamber where its EATing-tapes are stored—and changing its AIM, or Automatic Implementation Mechanism, to more passèd purposes: something only a Grand Tutor might presumably accomplish without being EATen alive. He may fail.

The twenty pages of discarded fragments Barth enclosed hinted that the novel would be even more imaginative (is that possible?), more difficult and just as comic as *The Sot-Weed Factor* and that the book would describe a world just as nihilistic and absurd.

Barth's plan, I conjecture, is to follow his demonstration of the absurdity of history with a novel about the absurdity of technological science, both novels taking faint swipes at religion and academia. To pursue the logic of his plan, he could then progress to philosophy or to various modes of art, or even to language itself, again to expose his theme, always illustrated with encyclopedic learning, immense imaginative energy, and unquenchable wit, that human culture is ultimately as absurd as life itself. The world yields to our efforts no ordering scheme; there is no central truth, only nonsense, with each twist of complexity multiplying itself to infinite degrees.

Like *The Sot-Weed Factor,* Joseph Heller's *Catch-22* is a rather unrealistic narrative of supposedly historical happenings which becomes the author's stylized vision of life as absurd; but where Barth sees absurdity in history's disordered confusion and man's inability to understand it, Heller in his portrait of American soldiers in World War II describes a world which is absurd because there is no relation between intention and result. This is the law of Catch-22, the book's central symbol, introduced in the following dialogue between Yossarian, Heller's main character, and Doctor Daneeka:

> "Is Orr crazy?"
> "He sure is."
> "Can you ground him?"
> "I sure can. But first he has to ask me to. That's part of the rule."
> "Then why doesn't he ask you to?"
> "Because he's crazy. . . . He has to be crazy to keep flying

combat missions after all the close calls he's had. But first he has to ask me."

"And then you can ground him?"

"No, then I can't ground him."

"You mean there's a catch?"

"Sure there's a catch. Catch-22. Anybody who wants to get out of combat duty isn't really crazy."

Thus, in a world ruled by Catch-22's law, it follows that Major Major Major Major should impress people by "how unimpressive he was," that "Colonel Cathcart was so awful a marketing executive that his services were much sought after by firms eager to establish losses for tax purposes," that the same Cathcart who ruthlessly sends his pilots on an excessive number of missions will become a hero in the eyes of the *Saturday Evening Post,* that Yossarian should be told he is jeopardizing his traditional freedoms by exercising them, and that syllogistic logic is destroyed by contradictions: If war is crazy, the book continually says, and if soldiers go to war, then soldiers are crazy; but all soldiers who, like Yossarian, want to run away from war are abnormal—therefore, crazy. Of course, Heller's principle of opposites does, in fact, govern much of modern behavior. The army hospitals are rated, I am told, by how few deaths take place within each of them; thus, authorities quickly transport all near-death patients elsewhere, thereby increasing the likelihood of death. Or, in a more heroic example, President Kennedy in the Cuba *affaire* of October, 1962, had to use the threat of violence to reduce tensions. In an interview, Heller speaks of a more mundane example: "There is a law of life: People in need of help have the least chance of getting it."

Heller's polemical point, as I get it, is that a society that has so distorted the natural correspondences between intention and result, between need and fulfillment, is thoroughly absurd; and in this respect, *Catch-22* is not at base a war novel. "Certainly," Heller has written, it "is not about the causes or results of World War II or the manner in which it was fought. *Catch-22* is about the contemporary, regimented business society." The book also has a secondary, unabsurd theme: nothing, but nothing, is worth a human death. But this theme is undercut by the absurd paradox, suggested by Heller's Major Danby, that the Second World War had to be fought, that there was in Nazism a real enemy who had to be destroyed, that people had to *die* to *preserve* human life.

The novel itself exhibits a rich talent for comic invention, exemplified by Heller's ability to run the whole gamut of comic devices from pun to slapstick to irony. Many of the characters, most of them defined by single passions, are memorably resonant; and though slightly preposterous, most are imaginatively convincing. Heller's failings stem more from a want of craft. No other recent novel I know has such a needlessly wild discrepancy in the style of representation, running from naturalism through surrealism, from the grotesque to parody and comic satire to symoblic fantasy; moreover, the book's structure shifts from a series of vignettes that jell into common themes (the influence here, Heller says, was Celine's *Journey to the End of Night*) to, in the last seventy or so pages, something of a conventional narrative; and coupled to this is a shift in authorial stance from Olympian detachment to social-protest engagement. For these and other reasons, Heller's literary future remains unpredictable. In the spring of 1964, some three years after the completion of *Catch-22*, Heller told a *Book Week* reporter that he had not yet started writing his second novel. Yet it is hard to believe that Heller could not do as well again.

Closer to *The Sot-Weed Factor* in style, if not, indeed, influenced by it, Thomas Pynchon's *V.* is a lushly brilliant novel, exhibiting on every page its author's huge and versatile talent and erudition. At first, the novel seems to evade coherence with every ridiculous turn of its incredible plot; but precisely in this incoherence and preposterousness is the key to the book's theme. Very much like Barth, Pynchon relentlessly illustrates—through two separate and faintly inter-connecting plots, one American and the other international in scope, through a variety of absurd quests and counter-quests, a gallery of inane characters, and a plethora of pseudo-factual details that give the book a pretense of historical narrative—his personal vision of human life as thoroughly and irrefutably nonsensical.

Two-thirds of the way through the book, one of Pynchon's internal narrators, who has his own story to tell—Fausto Maijstral —writes clumsily and suggestively: "No apologia is any more than a romance—half a fiction—in which all the successive identities taken on and rejected by the writer as a function of linear time are treated as separate characters." A few lines later he adds, "It isn't so much to pay for eyes clear enough to see past the fiction of continuity, the fiction of cause and effect, the fiction of humanized history, endowed with 'reason.' " Maijstral, then, is one of Pynchon's identities, creating an incoherent story within an incoherent story; and his tale, like Pynchon's, is a calculated denial of the principle of continuity in fiction and, thus, its usefulness as a way of understanding human history.

Like Barth, Pynchon endows his theme with a wealth of original inventions, burlesques of religious practices and literary styles, and absurd events. Of the two key images, a yo-yo and the letter V., the first, which previously and tellingly appears in Barth's second novel, is used to describe the book's characters, particularly Profane, as they bounce from one place to another, spinning free on the string of life, coming to rest only through the exhaustion of energies. The letter V. is Pynchon's most imaginative projection, the central symbol of the book, first introduced as the object of Stencil's search (indicatively, he was born in 1900, another child of the century); and like much else in the novel, V. is capable of meaning many things: a wide variety of similar, perhaps successor, characters, ranging from Victoria, an English girl seduced in Cairo in the late nineteenth century, to the grotesque Veronica Manganese with a jewel in her navel; as well as, in Stanley Edgar Hyman's summary, "Some great female principle [the searchers are all male], . . . she is the goddess Venus and the planet Venus, the Virgin, the town of Valetta in Malta, the imaginary land of Vheissu with its iridescent spider monkeys and Volcanoes. She is Vesuvius, Venezuela, the Violet of the vulgar mnemonic; ultimately, she is the V of the spread thighs and the mons veneris." Pynchon's special achievement is devising a symbol for metaphysical reality defined not by ambiguity as, say, Moby Dick is, but by nonsensical multiplicity.

Behind *V*. is a superior intelligence, perhaps not quite equal to Barth's, but still capable of making familiar references to a wide variety of historical, scientific and social phenomena and of using phrases from Latin, Yiddish, Spanish, German and French with facility and appropriateness, steeped in modern world history, widely and eccentrically familiar with contemporary literature and thought and, most unusually, knowledgeable in science. Not only did Pynchon study engineering at Cornell, before enlisting in the Navy and transferring to literature upon his return, but more than any other American novelist today he uses scientific ideas to understand reality. Surely, his knowledge of Quantum theory must have influenced his desire to reject causality in literature, and his short story in *Kenyon Review* (spring, 1960) entitled "Entropy" expresses a two-fold image of that scientific concept—one side from thermodynamics and the other from information theory. In the first sense, the story depicts the possibility that if the earth's temperature stays constant at 37° F. then human life will become, on its surface, randomly disordered and, at its base, stasis. Second, entropy is, in information theory, a measure of the disorder present within language, and in the story the term refers to the failure of Saul and his wife to communicate with each other. The story, then, describes a scene in which entropy, in both senses, has reached its maximum levels. (If absence of motion is the apocalypse of "Entropy," a vision of universal violence concludes a story Pynchon published as an undergraduate in *Epoch* [Spring, 1959], "Morality and Mercy in Vienna," which seems an early draft of the style of *V*.)

The failures of *V*. are perhaps unavoidable, given the nature of Pynchon's attempt; portraying incoherence, he succumbs to incoherence himself. The book is wildly overdone and, to my taste, better on the page than as a whole. At times Pynchon seems to have little control over his imagination's excesses, piling unclear images and references upon obscure bases, until some paragraphs are needlessly impenetrable. Not only does he create some of the most unimaginably complicated visual descriptions I have ever read; he also spins off an unusually high number of what strike me as unsuccessful jokes.

On the one hand, I suspect that Pynchon's characters would be more engaging if he paid more attention to human essences than to surfaces; Pynchon probably understands people less well than any other writer discussed here. On the other hand, *V.* is in many ways a story about its author's not-understanding things—as Benny Profane, Pynchon's main character, comments upon his own experiences, "I'd say I haven't learned a goddam thing [about life]." Still, Pynchon has faced the problem of depicting human absurdity and his own incomprehension of life quite successfully, perhaps not wrenching it as neatly into form as Ionesco does in *The Chairs;* but Pynchon's strategies, like Barth's, are towards statement by overstatement, rather than understatement; by reference to a wealth of images, rather than a single pregnant scene. In many ways, this is an extremely impressive book, making Pynchon, who was born in 1937, easily the most accomplished and original very young American writer today, whose *V.* seems, as "Morality and Mercy in Vienna" did in 1959, an imposing sign of wonderful books to come.

Like the other novels here, James Purdy's *Malcolm* (1959) describes the voyage of an innocent young man into the absurdity of society; but in contrast to Pynchon and Barth, Purdy employs a wispy, low-keyed style, keen psychological and emotional sensitivity, a knack for creating the telling moment and the resonant line—in general, a greater artistic control—to produce a more pruned absurd novel. Malcolm, a fifteen-year-old boy stranded alone on a park bench, is befriended by a Professor Cox, an astrologer, who in turn instructs Malcolm to visit all his friends. They include Estel Blanc, a Negro undertaker; Kermit Raphaelson, a midget artist, and his wife Laureen; Girard Girard, a tycoon; and Melba, a teen-age popular singer, whom Malcolm finally marries. Each wants something of him; and though Malcolm responds to their needs—having no essence and being passive towards others, he is capable of a wide variety of responses—he still never thor-

oughly adjusts to any of his masters. This is why the novel is, as
Jonathan Cott suggests, an allegory of growing up into an absurd
world, one which offers a young man neither satisfaction nor frustration of his needs and ambitions, has nothing worth his clinging
to, and also evades his understanding; and in allowing Malcolm to
die in his teens of an excess of alcohol and sex, Purdy seemingly
says that these retreats from life are inevitably the only outlets for
a young man. *Malcolm* is by far Purdy's best work; his other novel,
The Nephew (1960), is just another savage portrait of the emptiness of mid-western life, albeit with a few nice moments; and of
his stories, which are, in general, extremely uneven, the best, such
as "Goodnight, Sweetheart" and "Don't Call Me by My Right
Name," depict in muted tones persons in extreme distress and are
realized by Purdy's uncanny ability to strike a perfect moment in
which human tensions are implicitly and resonantly announced.
Though some of his work is marvelous—a few of his scenes are
truly great—his work, I find, lacks the immense verbal resources,
the grandness of vision, the sheer imaginative energy that I admire
in Barth, Heller and Pynchon.

Of all the young Canadian writers, the one whose work seems
especially promising is Mordecai Richler. On the one hand his
The Apprenticeship of Duddy Kravitz (1959) strikes me as highly
derivative, its hero a compound of Augie March and Sammy Glick;
its prose undistinguished and its minor characters undefined. In
contrast, his more recent and most interesting fifth novel, *Stick Out
Your Neck* (1963), shows that Richler has abandoned his preoccupation with heroism for a fiction that focuses upon the situation—
the absurdities of Canada's love-hate dependence upon American
culture. An Eskimo, Atuk, takes Toronto's literary society by
storm, wins the high-minded national heroine, a swim champion,
for his mistress, becomes the founder of a prosperous Eskimo-
trinket business and, subsequently, an inhumane capitalist, is ac-
cused of the murder (by cannibalism) of an American colonel, and
finally becomes the martyred hero of Canadian nationalism.
Against Atuk's career, Richler creates a gallery of Canadian hypo-
crites—a rabbi who champions national culture also invites "Jerry

Lewis to give readings from the Book of Esther at the up-and-coming Israeli bond drive"; an entrepreneur encourages at-cost prostitution for male teenagers in hopes they will "acquire a taste that in later, higher-income years, they would find hard to give up," and so forth. The polemical point, made quite strongly, is that Canadian society has fallen into the particularly ridiculous situation of denouncing with one hand what it imitates with the other, a situation that creates an emptiness of value which makes the society absurd.

In his first forays into fiction, Kenneth Koch, whose mock-epic poem *Ko* (1959) is a comic masterpiece, has written some realized, though minor absurd fiction. His novella, "The Postcard Collection," first published in the first issue of *Art and Literature* (March, 1964), is a tight, ingenious parable of Koch's major idea about the nature of artistic understanding: true art, truly experienced, produces ambiguous responses that signify the observer's ultimate non-comprehension; thus, any clear meaning one discovers in an artwork is forcibly imposed on it and is, therefore, a violation of art's inherent ambiguity. Creating a perfect vehicle for embodying the theme of the absurdity of trying to understand art definitively, Koch has his first-person narrator examine a collection of postcards, written some time ago, filled with hand-scrawled French (art is a foreign language), only to find himself unable to decipher their messages; thus, the narrator uses the fragments he can comprehend as touchstones for writing his version of the message; and throughout the story, Koch continually draws the necessary analogy between the postcards and art itself. Although the esthetic thesis, for a variety of reasons, strikes me as untrue—indeed, Koch's neatness of composition verges on an implicit denial of his polemical point—the story is, on its own terms, a successful absurd parable. What I have seen of Koch's projected novel, *The Red Robins*—those sections published in the first issue of *Location* (Spring, 1963) —suggested the book would be an attempt to dispense completely with plot, character and definite setting and create a fictional world of pure spatiality, complete possibility and underlying absurdity. Such a novel could quite easily disintegrate into its own method or, more likely, attain the richness, comedy and scope of the best absurd novels; even in fragments it is another sign of the ambition for artistic originality that informs all of Koch's work.

Though, of course, attuned to the same impulses in contemporary culture to which the absurd novel responds, several recent works in this strain seem considerably less successful, if not embarrassingly imitative. The polemical point of Ken Kesey's *One Flew Over the Cuckoo Nest* (1962)—it is absurd that the guards of a mental institution should be more insane than the inmates—is enhanced by some marvelous comedy but considerably blunted by a relative absence of true and deep madness anywhere in the book. His second novel, *Sometimes a Great Nation* (1964), hardly rises above being an energetic, obfuscating exercise in rapidly shifting the point-of-view. Jack Ludwig's *Confusions* (1963), whose narrator tries to define his own identity through a mass of superficial, conflicting signs, never lived up to the promise of the brilliant short story, "Confusions: Thoreau in California" (1960). The best stories in Donald Barthelme's collection, *Come Back, Dr. Caligari* (1964), such as "To London and Rome," employ absurd surfaces to depict the absurdities of affluence; but Barthelme so far has created just a series of eye-catching tricks, useful only once, rather than an interesting or personal style. Also, George Moorse's story, "Hub Caps," in *Transatlantic Review* (March, 1962), shows faint signs of a developing absurd style. Both Lawrence Ferlinghetti's *Her* (1960) and Harry Mathews' *The Conversions* (1962) are often originally comic, but lacking in consistency, resonant symbols, stylistic variation and other undergirding necessities. *Cat's Cradle* (1963) by Kurt Vonnegut, Jr., fails to transcend its surface confusions and fix absurdity in a viable form. Finally, William Peter Blatty's *John Goldfarb, Please Come Home* (1963) is probably the first of many watered-down, denatured novels which absurd fiction will spawn. As the new absurd novels attract more of a following—nearly all have appeared in paperback—more imitations, we should expect, will flood the market until its conventions, like the patterns of late nineteenth-century writing, will become fossilized.

Still, at the moment the American absurd novel thrives, both in distinguishing itself from the small-scale European absurd novel and in attracting publishers, readers and critics alike. More than anyone else in America, these novelists announce, collectively, that the novel is neither stale nor dead, nor has the audience for high-quality fiction disappeared into the void in front of the TV screen. In his introduction to the Signet edition of *Roderick Random,* John Barth wrote a "post-naturalistic, post-existential, post-psychological, post-antinovel novel in which the astonishing ('out-wandering'), the heroical—in sum, the adventurous—will come again and wel-comely into its own." Though a question rises whether these major characters are heroes—they seem too slight for the role and are used more to reveal the character of the world—the kind of novel Barth describes is blossoming in force.

III

As the absurd novelists sometimes defend personal eccentric-ity, if not madness, as the most viable strategy for encountering absurd life, so the other stream of new novelists explores these madnesses *from the inside;* that is, they depict the workings of the mad mind itself, rather than carefully noting external symptoms. This internal-external dichotomy illuminates the crucial difference between the progenitors of inside portrayals of madness, such as Nikolai Gogol's "The Diary of a Madman" (1835) and the first part of Dostoevsky's *Notes from Underground,* and the rather ob-jective observation of a madman's odd behavior, such as Her-man Melville's "Bartleby" (1856), Hendrik Ibsen's *Rosmersholm* (1886), and Sherwood Anderson's *Winesburg, Ohio* (1919). A third tradition was initiated by Kafka, whose greatest works symbolically objectify the patterns of a neurotic mind. Neither an external rec-ord nor an inside portrait, Kafka's fiction is like dream-work itself, a conscious ordering of psychic symbolism.

Although a few novels of the early fifties had realized por-traits of mental derangement, such as Salinger's *Catcher in the Rye* (1951), Shirley Jackson's *Hangsaman* (1951), and William Styron's *Lie Down in Darkness* (1951), only in recent years have so many striking novels dealt with madness. The most original, especially in form, is Vladimir Nabokov's *Pale Fire* (1962). Its protagonist is the most recent incarnation of the figure that haunts so much of Nabokov's fiction—from the early Russian novels through *Lolita* (1955) to the present—the writer as fool; and not only is Charles Kinbote psychologically the most interesting of these creations, he makes *Pale Fire* Nabokov's best work as well as one of the most hysterically funny novels in contemporary literature. Incidentally, this novel belongs to American literature, rather than Russian, because its frame of reference, its language, its realm of action and its expressed values are primarily American.

Developing an idea faintly presented in *The Gift* (1937), that the act of literary criticism could be the novel's subject and determine its form, Nabokov gives *Pale Fire* an unprecedented structure of three unbalanced parts: a 999-line poem entitled "Pale Fire" by the American poet John Shade (who considers himself second only to Robert Frost), a foreword to it and a critical commentary. These are the work of Shade's admirer, Kinbote, who for a semester was guest professor of Zemblan, his native tongue, at Wordsmith College, where Shade himself taught. The poem itself is a prolix, occasionally tender piece about Shade's development, written in a fairly orthodox form, which at various times echoes (and implicitly parodies) Alexander Pope, T. S. Eliot, Robert Frost, and Wordsworth's lines about the growth of the poet's mind.

Whereas the best comedy in Nabokov's early books stemmed from his cutting descriptions of external phenomena, here the satirical blade is swallowed, so to speak, by an ironic narrator who unintentionally wields it against himself. The third section, Kinbote's line-by-line commentary, is the comic center, for his remarks are a masterful example of what in graduate school is glumly called "over-reading," in the outside world "egomania," and in literature, brilliant comic irony. Most of the humor stems from the ironic relation between what Kinbote sees and what the reader perceives is actually happening. A passage from the foreword—Kinbote describing his early days at Wordsmith—is a sample of Nabokov's technique:

> On one of my first mornings there, . . . I noticed that Mr. and
> Mrs. Shade . . . were having trouble with their old Packard in the
> slippery driveway where it emitted whines of agony but could not
> extricate one tortured rear wheel out of a concave inferno of ice.
> . . . Thinking to offer my neighbors a ride to campus in my power-
> ful machine, I hurried out toward them, . . . and I was about to
> cross the lane when I lost my footing and sat down on the sur-
> prisingly hard snow. My fall acted as a chemical reagent on the
> Shades' sedan, which forthwith budged and almost ran over me
> as it swung into the lane. . . .

Kinbote's characteristic fault is missing the point, and being doubly
gifted he can persuade himself that his failures are really virtues;
and Nabokov, being even more gifted, can create a commentary in
which Kinbote's blabberings consistently reveal more than they
explicitly tell.

Kinbote the egomaniac insists upon understanding Shade's
poem "Pale Fire" as a symbolic recreation of all the Zemblan history that Kinbote unloaded on Shade's disinterested ears. Therefore, in his interpretation, Shade's trivia actually tell of Kinbote's
life, perhaps fantasied, as King Charles Xavier II, the deposed
monarch of Zembla, and Kinbote pushes his self-importance
through what, at first, seems unpromising stuff. Doomed to be a
fool and not to recognize it, Kinbote can report that the first time
he read Shade's "Pale Fire" he could see no reference to Zembla.
Likewise, he fails to recognize that when someone addresses him
as "The Great Beaver" the epithet is derogatory, that his capacity
to rationalize all mistakes and criticisms is immense, that he regularly commits all sorts of mis-spellings and greater intellectual
errors (which can be interpreted as an undercurrent of ironic commentary), that he is morally arrogant and disingenuous, that he has
a natural inclination for overblown and inappropriate similes and
needlessly multi-syllabic adjectives and adverbs, and that in his
superficially correct index to Shade's poem several names, usually
those of young attractive males, do not exist in the text. Quite
accurately, Nabokov shows that his malady produces a variety of
secondary ills, including an unselfconscious, thorough insensitivity
to the written word—Kinbote's artistic judgments are ludicrous and

his quotations from Shakespeare, retranslated from the Zemblan, make one wince—and a general inability to recognize reality.

What is remarkable about *Pale Fire,* then, is Nabokov's ability to realize a three-fold effect—to sustain the sheer comedy of Kinbote's stupidity, to render from the inside consistently and subtly the meanderings of a deeply mad, but superficially functioning, intellectual mind, and to keep us aware of the inescapable terror of Kinbote's isolation and constant failure. Though *Pale Fire* is Nabokov's best work, it fails to measure up to Barth's big novel in one crucial respect—an inability to transcend the sense that it is at base faintly trivial. Whereas Barth or, say, Eugene Ionesco in *The Lesson* can lift a similar feeling about the joke of knowledge and life into a basically serious vision of the absurdity of existence, nearly every line of action in *Pale Fire* culminates in just a guffaw; so that, the humor reflects merely on itself, letting Nabokov's work fall short of what we recognize as truly major fiction.

The other novels of madness tend to be less perfect in achievement and less original in form, for their authors, seemingly less in total control of their materials, weave realized portraits of neurotics into rather disjointed contexts. Walker Percy's *The Moviegoer* (1961) depicts in a young, well-connected New Orleans stockbroker, Binx Bolling, an anomic man who finds more "reality" in a movie house than in the life around him. From the movies, he learns how to understand life—he uses film examples to understand experience around him, and the incidents in life continually remind him of more interesting events in the movies. "I keep a Gregory Peckish sort of distance," he says to describe his own behavior. In the climax of the book, a moment of desperation, he addresses his confession to a movie star: "I'll have to tell you the truth, Rory, painful though it is. . . ." But precisely because the movies do not explain life, Bolling accepts platitudes as sincere compliments, fails to recognize the ineffectuality of his own social behavior, records "happiest moments" which a detached reader can see are insignificant, and continually rationalizes a life in which nothing happens. Indeed, his apathy is a more realized and profound version of the "paralysis" Barth continually attributes to his characters.

In the novel as a whole, Percy has a religious point to make. The movies have become Bolling's church, the source of other-worldly truth (and thus to them he must confess); and in giving the book the following epigraph from Kierkegaard, Percy perhaps gives too much of the theme away: "The specific character of despair is precisely this: it is unaware of being despair." But the Christian framework seems, in my opinion, rather forced and abstract in contrast to the true feeling and terror of Bolling's neurosis. Other aspects of the novel are rather fuzzy—Bolling's intelligence seems to fluctuate wildly, as does his attitude towards sex and business; but *The Moviegoer* is never more resonant and true than when Bolling is mad about the movies.

With Bruce Jay Friedman's *Stern* (1962), the problem of imperfection is somewhat different. After a brilliant opening section, the remaining two-thirds of the novel falls apart terribly; but in that opening vignette, Friedman creates a deftly concise portrait of a man who sees an enemy behind every strange bush—in Stern's life, there is an anti-Semite behind every gentile face. His feverish mind transforms every event that has an ambiguous significance to give it an ominous meaning. Stern, a new resident of the suburbs, hears that a male gentile neighbor has seen under his wife's dress and perhaps called her a kike. In his mind, this becomes a rape. . . . Elsewhere, "As [Stern] drove by, the man was looming up in front of him, standing, hands in pockets, on the lawn and wearing a veteran's organization jacket. It meant he had come through the worst part of the Normandy campaign, knew how to hold his breath in foxholes for hours at a time and then sneak out to slit a throat in silence." But, on second thought, the fact that the gentile wears that jacket means absolutely none of these things; and Friedman shows how Stern's neurotic mind exaggerates the potency of the enemy to rationalize his own cowardice. What makes the first part of *Stern* a comic and psychological masterpiece is Friedman's ability to capture Stern's neurotic mechanisms without ever letting the characterization become a mechanically unlifelike "case study" or allowing us to believe that Stern's fears might be real. However, once the portrait of Stern's anti-Semite neurosis is complete, the book disintegrates. For some unfathomable reason, Friedman reveals that many of the fears that at first seemed products of Stern's imagination are quite real; so that the sustained brilliance of the first part is nearly massacred by the rest of the book. Friedman's collection of stories, *Far from the City of Class* (1963), is extremely uneven, full of effects too arch to be true, phrases whose flash obliterates their clarity ("pistol-like bosoms"), themes written in letters so large they blot out any need for narrative, and trick endings that give no discernible shape to the tale. Here, too, the best moments are Friedman's portraits of neurotic behavior or reactions, like "The Good Time," which tells of a young man's traumatic discovery of all the complicated underwear under his mother's dress. Out of the situation and characters of that story, Friedman fashioned his second novel, *A Mother's Kisses* (1964), a Kafkaesque exercise in psychic symbolism about a young boy's emancipation from his domineering mother. In this work too, Friedman has written some truly extraordinary scenes; but he is unable to sustain his occasional brilliance.

Though his work so far is confined entirely to stories, Irvin Faust, working with the same materials as Friedman and Percy, appears to be a considerably more promising writer, showing in *Roar, Lion, Roar* (1965) that he is capable of depicting convincingly a wide range of madnesses in stories as stylistically rich as they are well-realized. In the best of the seven I have read, "Jake Bluffstein and Adolph Hitler," originally in *Carleton Miscellany* (Spring, 1962), Faust describes, from the vantage point of an intimate third-person narrator, a mad aging Jew who fondly remembers the days before and during the Second World War when Jews found good reasons to hate the gentiles, who tries to stir anti-gentile sentiment by scribbling late at night the word "JUDE" on the window of his neighborhood butcher and who believes that all Jews who do not hate gentiles are, like his rabbi, basically Nazis. In a dream, he addresses the synagogue's members and imagines himself becoming the Jews' modern messiah: "He saw a great sea of

faces, miles and miles of faces. 'SIEG,' he roared and the uni-
formed men marching toward him out of the faces, raised their
arms for all the millions behind them and roared back, 'HEIL.' "
In the story's next and last line—"He was free at last"—Faust suggests that this dream was a catharsis for Jake and that he would
resume normality; but in none of these stories has Faust depicted
normal men.

What makes Faust such an extraordinary psychological writer
is the variety of madnesses he can describe. In the stories I read,
he portrays a Puerto Rican boy whose existence becomes so
attached to the fate of the Columbia football team that when they
lose to Princeton he commits suicide; a rather stupid, dreamy fellow who sets out, accompanied by his Sancho, to be the Albert
Schweitzer of Central Park; a lonely stockroom boy so pathologi-
cally attached to his portable radio that a girl who makes a pass at
him must first destroy the radio before she can attain her end.
Faust's wide range of psychological understanding results from
his professional work. A guidance director at a Long Island high
school by trade and author of a book of case studies in social psychology, *Entering Angel's World* (Teachers College, Columbia University, 1963), Faust advocates that the counselor must assume,
"wherever possible, the character and personality" of those with
whom he deals; thus, his fictional interests and professional talents
complement each other. But on top of his capacity for empathy,
as well as a varied social knowledge, Faust has mastered the ability
to evoke in print the frenzied mind dashing between memory and
present, fragment and thought, to report its wanderings in an appropriately intense, immediate and elliptical style and to write with a
masterful control over image and metaphor in a variety of idioms.

Though far less original and ambitious than Nabokov and
Percy and less psychologically insightful than Friedman and Faust
at their best, Michael Rumaker has created some acute portraits
of mad young men. Although he functions as a third person narrator, Rumaker gets inside his characters by sensitively reporting
their feelings in an empathetic, matter-of-fact tone. "Jim had this
tennis ball he found at the hospital," Rumaker writes in the open-

ing of *The Butterfly* (1962). "He walked around bouncing it off the sidewalks and off walls. He bounced it in the library and bugged everybody. He was wearing an imaginary baseball cap until he could get a real one." Two pages later, "Jim cocked his baseball cap back on his head and thought. . . ." Among other psychological experiences, the book contains a remarkably accurate record of a self-castration dream. Yet, as a novel *The Butterfly* seems cut in two, offering no transition between the opening three-quarters and the final fourth, in which Jim, unlike the other mad characters in recent fiction, attains a kind of normalcy. In his novel, as well as his stories, Rumaker exhibits a strong control of description, language and emotion—in short, of fictional craft—that immediately distinguishes him from the "beats" with whom he usually publishes.

Staking out its own area of pathological behavior, Burt Blechman's savage *How Much?* (1961), which is more insightful than his later *The War at Camp Omongo* (1963), focuses upon the compulsive desire to buy things "cheaply," particularly as it turns into a mania that destroys moral and emotional balance. A first story by Mrs. H. W. Blattner, "Sound of a Drunken Drummer," which first appeared in the *Hudson Review* (Fall, 1962), is a brilliant portrait of the disjointed consciousness of a suicidal alcoholic prostitute, somewhat reminiscent of Malcolm Lowry's classic treatment of the same condition in a man, *Under the Volcano* (1947), and yet extremely brilliant and promising in its own right. Indicatively perhaps, the best part of William Styron's disappointing second novel, *Set This House on Fire* (1960), is an incisive sketch of drunken impotence and disorientation originally published in *Paris Review #22* as "The McCabes."

Other writers have attempted to portray mental aberration with the same kind of depth and insight that Faust and the above writers display; and among those who do it with considerably less success I would list J. D. Salinger whose title character in *Franny* (1955) suffers from a madness too abstract, perhaps too intellectualized in Zen terms, to be convincing; Francis Pollini, who could not quite render in *Night* (1960) the experience of Chinese brainwashing; Anne Sexton, whose single story "Dancing the Jig" (1960), a first-person portrait of a drunken woman's aspiration to be an inanimate object, is too declarative for fictional effectiveness; Grace Paley, whose loony, single-obsession characters remain the cartoon vehicles of her a-moral themes; Seymour Krim, whose moving and honest "The Insanity Bit" (1959) is marred by superficiality and cultural posturing; Carl Solomon, whose "Report from the Asylum" (1950) is too sane a description of his own extensive and violent therapy (it pales next to Antonin Artaud's last letters); Joseph Slotkin, whose portraits of madness included in *The Perfectionist* (1960) were inadequately realized; and Theodore Weiss, whose narrative poem, *Gunsight* (1962), rather thinly depicts psychic disorientation. In contrast to the theme of absurdity, which attracts only a few writers, personal madness, in an age when nearly everyone considers himself afflicted, is an exceedingly popular subject with the younger aspiring writers.

IV

In the past decade, drugs have replaced alcohol and sex at the frontiers of avant-garde experience; and while one sub-strain of the new literature of the self focuses upon madness, the other turns to the new forms of experience provided by drugs. Without doubt, the most extraordinary work in this literature is William Burroughs' *Naked Lunch* (1959), a report of the hallucinatory madness he experienced during a withdrawal from narcotics addiction. The narrator is identified as William Lee; but since Burroughs used that name as a nom de plume for his earlier *Junkie* (1953), one assumes Lee is Burroughs himself. In structure, *Naked Lunch* is a collection of scenes, gathered from notes supposedly jotted down while undergoing withdrawal and not remembered afterwards; and in it Burroughs creates, like Genet, a dream universe, full of characters who have some semblance to real people but who are transformed into nightmare grotesques.

The book's characters fall into two groups, the horrendously evil and the anonymous dregs: Salvador Hasson O'Leary, the mythical international mogul, the Man behind the Man, who "held

23 passports and had been deported 49 times." Doctor Benway, Burroughs' most demonic creation, is the scientific man using his knowledge for super-evil, in charge of "interrogation, brainwashing and control" in Burroughs' totalitarian world and who in the middle of a riot samples the blood of the dead. With shrewd images, Burroughs evokes the nameless bottoms of the drug world, such as the lonely old opium addicts: "A few old relics from hop-smoking times, spectral janitors, grey as ashes, phantom partners sweeping out dusty halls with a slow old man's hand, coughing and spitting in the junk-sick dawn, retired asthmatic fences in theatrical hotels. . . ." The sterility of the external world complements the paralysis of the self; during addiction, Burroughs remembers: "I could look at the end of my shoe for eight hours."

Some of Burroughs' fantasy images are extraordinary creations, unlike, one guesses, anything that could be consciously devised. The scene of the book is an alien city:

> All streets of the City slope down between deepening canyons to a vast, kidney-shaped plaza full of darkness. Walls of street and plaza are perforated by dwelling cubicles and cafés, some a few feet deep, others extending out of sight in a network of rooms and corridors.

In the end, *Naked Lunch* becomes a vision of the world in total decay, thoroughly without redemption, any outpost of retreat or a possibility for change. Among all the modern books that envision a contemporary world of complete horror, none evokes it more thoroughly, or with such uncompromising images of decay and violence, as Burroughs' book. In this respect, *Naked Lunch* makes other "end-of-the-world" books, such as Kenneth Patchen's *The Journal of Albion Moonlight* or Nelson Algren's *A Walk on the Wild Side* (1956), seem pretty feeble. Ferdinand-Louis Céline, perhaps Burroughs' closest competitor in this respect, once boasted that yes he had imitators but no one else could keep up such intense, imaginative negation for a couple of hundred pages; well, Burroughs does. However, whereas Céline intended, perhaps pretended, to describe reality, Burroughs' world is entirely his madness's creation.

What makes *Naked Lunch* such an arresting and disturbing book, the best of all the narcotics fiction to emerge in recent years, is that Burroughs transcends a concern with narcotics as such to render the hallucinatory experience in a realized and appropriate literary style. Like other American fiction concerned with the frontiers of human behavior, *Naked Lunch* opens the reader's mind to the possibilities of perception and literary creation; and in its unfettered exploration of demonic consciousness, it resembles such great American books as *Moby Dick* and *Absalom, Absalom*.

In structure, *Naked Lunch* is a string of scenes from which emerge a coherent sensibility and a set of themes; in this respect it resembles the books of Henry Miller. But because Burroughs relies more upon an image than upon plot for unity, his book achieves an overall spatial form that justifies his boast that, "You can cut into *Naked Lunch* at any intersection point." This too is appropriate, for the heroin experience itself is the achievement of timelessness.

Although *Naked Lunch* will, I think, become a modern classic, Burroughs himself is fated, I am afraid, to remain a minor writer. His later creative works seem distinctly less impressive. *The Exterminator* (1960), *The Soft Machine* (1961; revised, 1963), *The Ticket that Exploded* (1962), and *The Nova Express* (1964) are relentless pursuits of Burroughs' faith in the theory that certain composing methods viable in painting and music can be applied to literature. Some of these books are produced with the cut-up method: Burroughs writes on several pages, cuts them up, scrambles the scraps and sets down the result in a fixed final form. Others were written with what he calls the "fold-in" method: "I take a page of text, my own or someone else's, and fold it lengthwise down the middle and place it on another page of text, my own or someone else's, lining up the lines. The composite text is then read across, half one text and half the other." Since his books regrettably do not contain prefaces explaining the method used to compose them, it is impossible to tell whether one method provides better results than another. Nonetheless, except for an occasional original image, surely an achievement that has little to do with the method, there is not much here to engage one's interest. Only when Burroughs harnesses his rich imagination and observational honesty to a confining form does he produce excellent writing, as in the letters of 1953 to Allen Ginsberg (whose own letters, in contrast, seem mannered) published as *In Search of Yage* (1963). If Burroughs rejected literature-by-chance, he could, possibly, produce some excellent writing again.

In contrast to Burroughs who records the fantasies of withdrawal, most of the other writers on withdrawal, from Alexander King in *Mine Enemy Grows Older* (1959) to more serious novelists, accent the addict's sheer pain and compulsive movements. In two stunning passages that redeem Clarence L. Cooper's confused, otherwise undistinguished novel, *The Scene* (1960), Rudi Black is described as "twisting his body in a half-figure eight," suffering from uncontrollable spasms, constant tickling sensations, shivering, sweating, vomiting, spitting and dreaming of friends who might give him dope. "He tightened his belt until the thin leather bit into his stomach like wire, establishing a new pain, one he could concentrate on to forget the others."

In a chronicle of the day-by-day details of the addict's experience, *Cain's Book* (1960), Alexander Trocchi, a Scotsman who spent many years in America, describes the sheer boredom and emotional impotence of addiction and the addict's lack of concern for past or future, or for other people, in a novel that taunts and eventually succumbs to the intentional fallacy of being a dull portrait of dullness.

The experience of using hallucinogens, non-addicting fantasy-producing drugs, while it greatly interests the educated young in America, has not to my knowledge been the subject of any American prose writing as interesting, original and unselfconscious as, say, Aldous Huxley's *The Doors of Perception* or the French poet Henri Michaux's "Experiments." Some of our poets, such as Michael McClure, have written about their use of hallucinogens, particularly peyote, usually to propagate pet theses about esthetics or existence. Paul Bowles in *A Hundred Camels in the Courtyard* (1963) has spun off rather pat didactic tales advocating kif smoking as superior to alcohol. Hallucinogen experience will, I suspect, interest many young writers in the next few years; and in all likelihood, out of this en masse derangement of consciousness some interesting writing will emerge.

v

Scattered other young writers have produced some novel and interesting fictional work which, in the end, stands outside the two main trends. If Barth and Nabokov exhibit a versatile inventiveness, Hubert Selby, Jr.'s originality is extremely narrow, confined to one aspect of his writing, his style. He has concocted a gritty, grinding, impatient, hard-edged, undertone-less idiom, with the quality of a lawnmower, to tell prosaic, violent naturalistic stories, as in the following passage from "Another Day Another Dollar" in *New Directions #17:*

> They formed a circle and kicked. He tried to roll over on his stomach and cover his face with his arms, but as he got to his side he was kicked in the groin and stomped on the ear and he screamed, cried, started pleading then just cried as a foot cracked his mouth. Ya fuckin cottonpickin punk and a hard kick in the ribs turned him slightly and he tried to raise himself on one knee and someone took a short step forward and kicked him in the solar-plexus and he fell on his side, his knees up, arms folded across his abdomen, gasping for air and the blood in his mouth gurgled as he tried to scream, . . .

Though his fiction so far offers little interest besides its language, that alone makes everything he writes very much worth reading.

In *American Contemporary* (1963), an uneven collection of portraits of modern pathos and rootlessness, Curtis Zahn creates a variety of styles to carry his basically satirical themes. "Recognition," my own favorite, is the most successful rendering I know in first-person narration of a stupid, inarticulate person's inability to cope with experience:

> When we first move here I was born in Saint Louie and Harry Ohio but met in Kansas, Mo, because I was going with this fry cook but Harry had a Chevy convertible. He got married to me in Riverside, Cal, because there is this cousin that has an Olds.

But we didn't have much else in common with Riverside except shooting, which is the main route down to Palm Springs where Tony Curtis goes.

In the other sketches, particularly those of California life, Zahn is too apt to let his bitterness obliterate his literary sense.

VI

Although the two strains of new American fiction, concerned with opposite poles of human experience, are on the surface quite different, they complement each other's view of the world. In an absurd world, man contracts the *anomie* that incites and abets mental disability; and widespread madness is one of the factors contributing to an absurd world. Indeed, in two of these novels, madness and absurdity overlap—*Catch-22* and *The Moviegoer,* each of them coming to the center from different sides. In all, then, these novelists present such a narrow vision of contemporary possibility that one suspects either their vision is severely limited or they have succeeded in penetrating to the two-fold heart of the contemporary experience. I believe that the novelist has always been more successful at grasping social essences than facts and, thus, that these writers too reflect, as well as indicate, our predicament. They present images of society which neither sociology nor newsreels can evoke or confirm and offer glimpses into madness which psychological writing does not provide.

Stylistically, too, they have much in common. Unlike the playwrights, they all seem to remain unaffected by the major trends in post-World War II European literature; neither the reactionary realism of the New University Wits, nor the objectivist novels of Alain Robbe-Grillet, the concern with semi-consciousness of Nathalie Sarraute, nor the existentialist realism of Alberto Moravia has fathered propitious parallels in recent American literature. Only one major recent European work I know, Gunter Grass's *The Tin Drum* (1959), greatly resembles the new American writing. If these novels belong anywhere, it is in the great American tradition of non-realistic romance: the novel of man and civilization (such as *Huckleberry Finn*) now receives an absurd twist and the gothic imagination has moved into the haunted house of the mind.

In nearly all these novels, the isolation of the main figure is extreme. Except for Ebenezer Cooke, the protagonist has no discernible father; except for Stern and Jake Bluffstein, he has no wife; and in general, he does not reveal his intimate self to others. Conversely, society is depicted as offering little salvation. No character explicitly considers religion or politics, though Binx Bolling and Bluffstein fantasize substitutes for each. Just as these authors make their characters and situations paradigms for the larger world, they eschew creating explicit contrasts. Sane men are never compared to madmen, rational societies to absurd ones; for what these authors describe will, they believe, inevitably exist. Although none of these writers creates life-giving heroes, worthy of imitation, nor posits a Way Out of the contemporary predicament, the sensitive protagonist in all these books but *Malcolm* refuses to die before his due, for these novels join Samuel Beckett's in speaking a single metaphysical message for our time: Although man has little reason to go on living, in a world so meaningless and hazardous, he still asserts, by the force of his essential will, the right to exist. Finally, by traditional criteria, these writers literally have "nothing-to-say," except to say, 'pataphysically, that there is nothing to say.

The writers themselves are as culturally isolated as their characters are socially; none is largely a product of that main line of American culture that runs from the universities of Boston through those in New York to Philadelphia. John Barth was born in Eastern Maryland, took his degrees at Johns Hopkins, and has taught at Penn State for a dozen years. Joseph Heller worked in advertising in New York while writing *Catch-22*. Nabokov wrote *Pale Fire* in Switzerland; Pynchon is a recluse in Mexico; Faust works in a Long Island high school; Purdy lives aloof in Brooklyn; Percy in New Orleans; etc. Yet these writers have received conventional, if not extensive, educations. All, to my knowledge, have B.A.'s, and many have advanced degrees: Barth and Heller, M.A.'s; Percy, M.D.; Fause, Fiedler and Koch, Ph.D.'s; Nabokov taught continental literature at Cornell for several years; and Pynchon was offered a Woodrow Wilson Fellowship. Most have taken courses in creative writing, if often to rebel against their teachers' pet formulas. Not only are they educated, but they use their learning so easily and extensively that their novels have, to various extents, a pedantic quality; indeed, they succeed best with educated readers.

Their education largely explains why these writers, except for Friedman and Faust, appear to start writing with a theme clearly in mind, rather than a situation, a conflict, or a single character, and then devise ways to best dramatize their point; yet it is not their themes, which are easily summarized, but the method by which these ideas are realized that makes these books interesting and artistically important. Surely, it is rather easy to plan an absurd novel, but it is enormously difficult (if not inconceivable) to give the scheme the embellishment of *The Sot-Weed Factor*. Moreover, all these books are realized primarily as novels—they contain effects only fiction can achieve; but for *Catch-22*, I cannot imagine any of them being adapted into another artistic medium without having its essence distorted or destroyed.

Finally, all of them have experienced an excess of unfavorable and/or uncomprehending reviews: the basic irony of *Pale Fire* was all but completely missed, Heller's novel was nearly universally panned, Percy's and Friedman's were hardly reviewed at all. Yet, in the 1960's, thanks largely to the perseverance of conscientious critics, the mistaken judgments of hasty reviewers—the maltreatment that plagued nearly all original American writers throughout their careers—are with each year being rectified with increasing speed. By 1964, all the novels discussed here at length are widely admired, nearly all have appeared in paperback; and all together, they make American fiction one of the most interesting arts in America and the world today.

THE NEW AMERICAN

MUSIC

ERIC SALZMAN

The problem of the "avant-garde" is, in one sense, a pseudo-problem. The classical method of defining the avant-garde stems from a kind of secondhand dialectical determinism designed to discover what sort of mouse the mountain of historical inevitability will squeak out next and how to get the right mouse-trap built first. If a composer takes a dialectical view of history and consciously acts on it, such a view can fairly be said to have influenced the history of music; perhaps (considering the success, for example, of style criticism in European art history) some such interpretations are valid for the European historical experience. But the very notion of "avant-garde," as derived from the Hegelian and Marxist-determinist synthesis, loses force and meaning in proportion to its use—the more it is invoked, the less valid it becomes. There is a kind of built-in "indeterminacy principle" operating here: you cannot stand around and observe, analyze and act on history without influencing it; you cannot define the historical necessity of the avant-garde without immediately implying some still newer avant-garde which instantly obliterates the old avant-garde one historical necessity back.

The historical-determinist way of disposing of the problem is to define the avant-garde—the American avant-garde at any rate—as John Cage. Cage is, after all, the leading young avant-gardist at 52, the granddada of New York School Avant-Garde, everything from popsters to popsicles, Zen trances to happenstance, aleators to crashing bores. (But then, how avant-garde can an avant-garde follower be?)

All good, red-blooded Americans know that history is bunk—that's what makes America great. We are entering what has been called the post-historical age, not because history is failing us but because the classical Hegelian-Marxist synthesis is no longer relevant to our experience. To paraphrase Gertrude Stein, America is the oldest country in the world because it was the first to enter the post-Marxist age. The received European notions of historical avant-garde necessity are essentially foreign to the American experience of pluralism and individualism, of optimism and alienation, of rationality and eccentricity; they are irrelevant to American technological civilization and to the American tradition of handwork, of doing things, of tinkering, of activity as a good and an end in itself; it is alien to the American experience of the frontier, of the idea of the extension of possibility, of conformity on the one hand and freedom of action on the other, of mass-cult—ugly, brutal, closed on one side—and multiplicity—always open at some other, almost unknown, outer end.

Thus, without resort to the clichés of European art history—the derivations of unique processes of historical necessity out of which the traditional notion of the avant-garde comes, we can begin to define the preconditions of the new American music in terms of pluralism and the extension of the idea of the possible. The essentially open character of the music of Ives, open in content and form in every direction; the original, intense chromaticism of Carl Ruggles; the vast accumulations of new materials and ideas by Henry Cowell; the abstract spatial concepts of Edgard Varèse with the growth of new forms out of sonority, timbre, texture and accent—all of these musical ideas and others (including forerunners of serialism and of improvisation-chance procedures) date back 40, 50 and 60 years but also carry forward into recent years the American tradition of the new defined artistically in terms of the expanding nature of aural experience. John Cage's *4' 33"*, four minutes and thirty-three seconds of musical silence, has its perfect 1920's antecedent in a book called (like a collection of Cage's own writings) *Silence* which consists of nothing but blank pages. The work of a composer like Varèse, still a vital, creative force on the contemporary scene, links right up with the music of the fifties.

The expansion of ideas and techniques in the twenties and its continuation in the late forties and fifties (interrupted by the conservatizing, classicizing and populist notions of the thirties) is characterized by the introduction of new forms and new ways of experiencing. It defined and created the conditions under which latter-day ideas have developed, conditions which can now define the very different meaning of creative possibilities today:

1.) All possible aural sensations in any sequence and in any combination are available and of equal esthetic (though not necessarily equal artistic or psycho-acoustical) validity as raw material. These include the entire range of pitched and noise sounds, artificial and "natural," recorded and live (also including non-sound or silence), up to and even beyond the thresholds of perception and pain.

2.) All levels of pre-performance control are available, from total determinism (or some close approximation thereof; e.g.: a totally predetermined electronic conception fixed in its unalterable form on tape) to improvisation and random choice within open patterns whose shape and content may be determined at any level, at any time before or during the performance of the music and to any extent by the use of performer choice and/or random and chance procedures.

3.) There are no generally accepted symbolic meanings or referents inherent in any usage. However "real" sounds or even quotes from other music may stand for themselves, words may appear as sound objects as well as meaning-conveyors, and physical pain and even boredom can be (although with more inherently questionable esthetic-psychological significance) literally evoked. Formal patterns and structures may represent or exemplify thought processes, and non-verbal mental structures may be realized as relationships of sound; such patterns may also grow out of and exemplify the range of human perceptive abilities and related states, mental and psychological.

Now this is an unprecedented state of affairs: the assumptions of the newest "new" music grow out of an awareness of the entire range of aural possibility and its meaning conveyed through heightened and widened experience. The actual content of a work and the relationships of its parts as they unfold—as they are acted upon, interact or intersect in time—are defined uniquely by each work as its own form or structure. In the end, the effect is to redefine every aspect of the creative act: the relationship between creator, performer and listener is then redefined by each new work and indeed, in the best and most important new works at least, so is the very way we perceive and understand.

In some sense, all of the new creative ideas of the twentieth century have contributed to this; particularly decisive has been the development of new, highly organized and controlled forms in the postwar serial music, of new composer-performer-listener relationships in the action music of chance and choice, and, most important, of the infinitely extended resources and controls in electronic music. The significance of electronic music in this respect cannot be overemphasized; for whatever range of possibility had been previously imagined, it was only the development of electronic and tape techniques that established at least two of the determining characteristics of recent musical thought: total possibility of aural resources and perfect control. Furthermore, electronic developments, by the mere fact of their existence—the reality, so to speak, of the potential, rather than any specific artistic achievement—have suggested new and useful distinctions between recorded and live performance and, thus, by a kind of negative influence, have had an enormous effect on performed music, producing new kinds of composer-performer-listener relationships. The new performed music has tended to grow out of the conditions and possibilities of the live performance situation: new types of control and flexibility, a new virtuosity and new improvisatory techniques, the exploration of the outer physical limits of performer possibility, the projection of instrumental and vocal sound in actual physical space and so forth.

It is interesting to note that the very first "totally organized" music was written by Milton Babbitt in 1948, the same year that the first "musique concrète" experiments with sound effects began in Paris. By the early years of the fifties, the Columbia University electronic studio was in operation and John Cage had created his *Music for 12 Radios*. All of these developments were virtually simultaneous: a series of expanding techniques and new perceptive forms, curiously parallel and mutually exclusive; carefully nourished bits of aural experience rigorously pushed on to their logical and physical extremes, much in the manner of experimental investigation.

At a certain point, the cumulative result was a new awareness which made the old narrow kinds of exclusivenesses seem no longer necessary. The creative process was reversed; it became analytic, so to speak, instead of synthetic, growing out of this new discovery and acceptance of the totality of possible experience. In the earlier new music, the materials and means of the work of art were formed by rigorous selection, often defined negatively by a strenuous, pre-compositional exclusion of possibility; in the comparable developments of the last few years, the entire range of possible experience is represented by a portion of it—a cross-grain cut, so to speak—organized, not through pre-compositional assumptions, but through musical and psychological structures established uniquely by each work itself.

This change is evident not only in the work of younger composers but in the continuing work of a group of older composers who contributed to the earlier development of new ideas. A composer like Milton Babbitt is committed, not merely to the older twelve-tone organizing principle, but to the expansion of the concept of form perception and to the idea of totally rational form and expression. The earlier classical twelve-tone music of Schoenberg and Webern grows out of the total range of chromatic material —the twelve half steps of the tempered scale—organized in each piece according to a particular ordering or grouping principle. Thus, each piece has a basic conformation of pitches and intervals which, although subject to certain transformations, retains its identity throughout the work, permeating every aspect of the music, not in a thematic way, nor as representation of some kind of scale or mode, but as a kind of defined repertoire of musical materials which inform and control the music; the technique is at once structurally analogous to the function of standard tonality in traditional Western music and to the function of the old medieval mode or the "raga" in Indian music.

With Babbitt, however, the whole principle of twelve-tone music becomes something quite different; the row—now a "set" of twelve tones with an underlying structural form—is not merely a unifying factor; it becomes in a sense identical with the music itself. That is, the twelve-tone material is really the totality of possibility within a given body of material (pitches, durations, dynamics, timbres, registers, etc.), and the subject of the piece is permutation— the unfolding of these relationships in time. Works like the Babbitt *Three Compositions for Piano,* his *Composition for Four Instruments, Composition for Twelve Instruments,* all of 1948, and his song cycle, *Du* (1951), might be described as cool, brilliant abstractions which gain tension and power from their clarity of expression; these are pieces that, in a final sense, can be said to express thought processes.

A decisive point in Babbitt's development came when, at the end of the fifties, he began working with electronic means. In 1959, the Columbia-Princeton Electronic Music Center—originally founded as the Columbia Electronic Music Studio early in the fifties—acquired a substantial foundation grant and an important piece of equipment known as the R. C. A. Electronic Sound Synthesizer. The Synthesizer was built by R. C. A. for the purpose of producing and reproducing pop music without the benefit of live musicians; it did not quite work out that way and the equipment was put at the disposal of the Columbia-Princeton studio. This remarkable machine is designed to produce electromagnetic impulses which will drive a loud-speaker or magnetize a tape to produce—in theory at least—any possible sound. Every aspect of both pitched and non-pitched sound—duration, attack, decay (dying away), intensity, timbre and so forth—is subject to the most careful and precise definition and control; and, of course, any combination of superimpositions or successions is easily achieved. Any sound possibility, once pre-set, can be immediately tested by flipping a switch; if it is not up to snuff, further setting and adjustments can be made before anything is committed to tape in final form.

Electronic techniques offer a virtually limitless range of materials, but Babbitt's professed interest in the new medium is not new sounds (he scorns the latter-day new-sound scramble) but the possibilities of complete control. The extension of resources in his *Composition for Synthesizer* (1961) and *Ensembles for Synthesizer* (1963–4) implies new forms, new ways of organizing perception and time and, thus, ultimately new ways of conveying what are essentially new patterns and meanings.

Interestingly enough, Babbitt's performed music has simultaneously taken on a new liveliness and color. Works like *All Set* for jazz ensemble, *Partitions* for piano and *Sounds and Words* for soprano and piano have acquired a richness of texture, a tension and a lively virtuosity appropriate to the conditions of live performance but largely missing from his earlier music.

Babbitt has twice combined live performance with tape: in his powerful setting of the Dylan Thomas *Vision and Prayer* for soprano with "synthesized accompaniment" and in the equally remarkable *Philomel,* a setting (for the same combination) of a poem by John Hollander expressly written for the purpose. *Vision and Prayer* is based on a complex typical twelve-tone pattern extended into every nook and cranny of the piece; the tape part, completely electronic in origin, is a masterpiece of perfectly controlled detail built up in conjunction with the vocal part into a substantial intellectual and dramatic form. The origin of the form can be found in certain sonic and structural aspects of the poem, notably its diamond and hour-glass shaped verses with increasing and decreasing line lengths. An important aspect of the tape music depends on the opposition and resolution of pitched and non-pitched sounds; thus, the electronic means permit a whole range of pitch-and-noise patterns in which one or the other aspect dominates in different degrees. This kind of subtle, controlled gradation is a natural development out of the electronic techniques; but it also parallels the movements of the vocal part from speech to *sprechstimme* to pitched song and back and it suggests how the live vocal sound and the electronic tape are interrelated—through parallelisms, oppositions and, at a higher intellectual and dramatic-structural level, resolution. Although these oppositions work in a purely formal way, they are also the source of the intense, dramatic expression of the work. Some of the same intensity on an even bigger and more dramatic scale carries over into *Philomel.* The classical story of the young lady who was ravished, had her tongue taken out and was turned into a nightingale is an image which is symbolic, not only of the poet and the condition of poetry, but also of some ultimate identity between poetic and musical expression. Thus, in the setting, the highly articulated tape part includes not only electronic sounds, but vocal sounds, run through the synthesizer: the voice of the soprano in a thousand guises, taken high up into the realm of bird song, multiplied into a forest of bird choruses echoing and reverberating across some new and imagined musical space. The conception is that of word become inarticulate and sound become articulate, of sound become structure and structure become meaning, of inarticulateness made rational and rationality made expressive through the extension of resources, of the control and unification of opposition, of the exploration of the range of consciousness at its outer limits; from all this emerges the expression of complex, non-verbal thought processes.

There is a large group of younger composers, many of them pupils of Babbitt, who have been influenced by him. Most of them —Donald Martino at Yale, Henry Weinberg at Pennsylvania, Peter

Westergaard at Columbia, Ben Johnston at Illinois—cultivate well-tended serial gardens with great skill. But Babbitt's influence seems most significant, not so much in specific matters of procedure and style, as in the more general diffusion of concepts of technique and intellectual responsibility at a time when spontaneousness and irrationality are widespread. There was, not long ago, a period of twelve-tone total determinism in European avant-garde music; but it was a mechanical idea, mechanically worked, and the reign of the numbers game was brief. It is significant that Babbitt's cool, rich and complex music has never been understood in Europe and remains peculiarly American in its boundless optimism and confidence in the rational powers of man.

We can define electronic music as organized sound, arranged and prepared for performance on magnetic tape (or some similar kind of storage device) and specifically designed to be heard through loudspeakers. Sound sources may include the "real" world, including normal instrumental and vocal sounds, and a wide range of electronic devices, from simple sine wave and white noise generators to the R. C. A. Synthesizer. Complex structures may be built up through dubbing and "contrapuntal" super-impositions; the sound material itself can be altered electronically, reverberated in any number of ways as well as arranged and rearranged through direct manipulation of the tape: looping tape to provide endless pattern repetition; changing tape speed to produce transpositions of register up to the highest peeps and squeaks and down to the lowest of low rumbles; chopping and splicing tape in limitless combinations and juxtapositions affecting the character of single sounds or whole structures. Sound transformations so gradual as to be imperceptible except over long periods of time may be placed next to the most violent contrasts followed by every perfectly controlled gradation in between, each event and motion arranged in just the precise context required. Some of these procedures, developed and used at Columbia and in European studios as well, can be bypassed with the R. C. A. Synthesizer; and the techniques being developed now at Bell Laboratories, although not as yet of any musical importance, suggest that it may be possible some day for a composer to work directly through a computer onto tape without any tape tampering at all.

This is not, it should be pointed out, music composed by machines, nor is there any implication that electronic music will "replace" live music or live musicians. The simplest isolated "live" sound is so rich and complex that efforts to duplicate it electronically, even when successful, are not worth the time and effort involved. The classical repertory, conceived with the realities of live performance in mind, remains, and there has been a remarkable growth of a new repertory intended for the conditions of live performance. The composer of electronic music creates, as the painter always has, directly with materials which he can organize, fix and set down to the nth degree of control, realizing, if he wishes, complexities and subtleties, structural forms and inter-relationships which may pass up to and even beyond the ability of the human ear and intelligence to detect. With the proper equipment, effects of incredible velocity and complexity are easy to achieve: trills between different timbres, gliding effects and subtle transformations of every kind and in every dimension, continuous stereophony extended in every direction and so forth.

French-born Edgard Varèse—who has been in the U.S. since the First World War and whose mature work is associated with his adopted country—can be said to have developed musical and intellectual ideas in the twenties and thirties which led to electronic and concrète music. Musique concrète, the sound montage idea based on recorded noises, started in Paris in 1948 but may be traced back to such Varèse works as his all-percussion Ionisation of 1930; and it is Varèse who, fittingly, has provided the movement with its only two masterpieces to date: his Déserts for tape and instrumental ensemble and his Poème électronique commissioned for the 400 loudspeakers that sent sound spinning around the insides of the Le Corbusier Phillips Pavilion at the 1958 Brussels World's Fair. These impressive and powerful tape collages are magnificently worked out of pre-existing recorded material built up into new spatial structures of great originality, breadth and scope. In its original place, inside the Pavilion and used in conjunction with Le

Corbusier's extraordinary series of projected images, the effect of the tape was overwhelming. Even in a mere two-channel stereo, there is a continuous, almost frightening power in the juxtapositions of aural images, slowly turning and colliding in spatial encounters.

Varèse has done part of his electronic work at the Columbia-Princeton studio, where tape montage methods have been extensively used together with "pure" electronic methods. Otto Luening and Vladimir Ussachevsky, who founded the studio in 1951, have tended from the very first to use live and live-recorded musical sounds in conjunction with tape techniques. Their work in this field pre-dates everything except some of the *musique concrète* and, possibly, some of the very first experimental work in Cologne; they were also among the first (following Varèse) to explore the relationship of tape music to live performance. Nevertheless, both composers have shown a decided preference for adopting new techniques and resources to old patterns.

Of the other composers who have worked at the studio, Mario Davidovsky, an Argentinian now living here, and Bulent Arel, a Turk now returned to his native country, have proved the most exceptional in their skill at building new forms from new and not-so-new electronic sound materials. Mention should be made here of Mel Powell, the former jazzman, now director of the newly founded Yale Electronic Studio and a serial composer of considerable originality who has produced electronic music of interest.

In a way, the tape-live medium is the logical one for the new ideals of the last few years. Typically, the wide-ranging but fixed and unyielding qualities of tape are set against the more "limited" but richer, more flexible virtuoso live performance. The best work of a younger composer like Charles Whittenberg is to be found in two or three pieces for solo instruments with tape which, within an extremely limited compositional technique, have nevertheless been able to achieve something valid in the way of new expressive form which does not appear at all in his purely instrumental pieces. The range of tape-live compositions runs from the carefully fixed conceptions of a Milton Babbitt to the open forms of a younger composer like Earle Brown.

There can be no doubt of the impact of tape and electronics on performed music; but the results, far from hinging on a kind of spurious negativism, have helped to bring into being a whole new repertoire of live music of great vitality. The argument (in its European dialectical form) runs about like this: since electronics can take over the job of producing perfect, total, rational order, the truly "human," non-electronic task of instrumental or vocal live performance is to do what a machine cannot do: act freely, exercise choice; in these "natural" and intrinsic conditions of freedom and flexibility each performance should presumably be as unique as the performer himself; thus the only valid live new music is a music of chance and change. The argument is false insofar as it implies, in the manner of such either-or dialectics, that the unique, "essential nature" of live music is a function of the fact that no human performance can ever be the same twice and, thus, that any new performed music must be open to chance or choice in detail or large form. The presupposition underlying this series of syllogisms is that the true condition of live performance lies in the essential irrationality of human behavior, a premise that is difficult to accept; irrationality and randomness are no more the essence of the human condition than man's capacity for imposing order on the external world even where none appears to exist. No human behavior can be really random; the mathematician must turn to the machine for true randomness as well as perfect order.

It is important, nonetheless, to recognize the new impulse to explore and define anew the conditions and possibilities of the active live performance situation. Beginning in the early fifties, Cage, Christian Wolff, Morton Feldman and Earle Brown began introducing improvisatory and chance techniques in their music on all levels from detail to big form. Conventional notation was abandoned in favor of a variety of graphic notational techniques; this music is very closely bound up with its notational devices which suggest visually to the performers the areas of choice and selection within which they are to operate. Thus, Feldman will indicate with a diagram or a schematic set of indications a typically soft dynamic range and a series of isolated entrances with no more specific indications than general areas of attack, register, timbre, etc. These limitations guarantee an atmosphere of intense, empty quiet and sparseness; all specific performer decisions in the classic chance-choice "aleatory" are equally possible and indiscriminately valid.

There are important differences between this music and the music of improvisatory freedom which is based on the interaction of the musicians in a live performance situation. The work of a "New York Action School" composer like Earle Brown is to be distinguished from the action and gesture non-music of John Cage or the quiet, schematic grandiloquent hollowness of Feldman's performer-choice "graph" pieces. Brown has been working in the last few years with a kind of controlled, random wildness in which the performers must make decisions by reacting, within a given framework, to each other as well as to set-up musical situations. Typically Brown gives the performers materials which are absolutely clear and fixed but which, as an agglomeration of independently shaped ideas, are capable of generating any number of possible forms. This process of structuring, of realizing possible forms out of the material in actual time, is built into the performance situation through a very specific system of decision making and performer interaction—in *Available Forms I*, for example, between conductor and instrumentalists; in *Available Forms II*, between the two conductors of the two orchestras; and so forth. The results have a kind of lively, organized, structured incoherence in which, nevertheless, a very clear relationship between the ideas and the actual form produced nearly always emerges. Not every possible performance—that is, every possible time-form realization —will be equally interesting or even equally valid in its own terms. But, in its best realizations, Brown's music grows out of not merely some particular notion of the realities of the performance situation, but also an encounter between the tension of fixed ideas and the vitality of structural decision-making (the opposite of traditional improvisation where the forms are fixed, ideas open), out of the intersection of music as a predetermined conceptualization and as an activity, of the interaction of fixed and free.

Another aspect of flexibility and freedom in the new performed music is the specific use of improvisation. In the chance or "aleatory" conceptions of Feldman and others, the propositions are put in such a way that all solutions are equally valid and there is no good reason for making one choice instead of another. Improvisation, however, runs the admitted risk of bad choice for a possible gain in spontaneity, in a certain immediacy of communication, in the chance for a kind of happy "discovery" and, most important, in the reaffirmation of creative music-making as a vital activity. Improvisation is, as it always was in the past, closely involved with specific performers and their style. The analogies with the old European tradition (now virtually extinct) and to jazz are obvious; a composer like Gunther Schuller has actually combined the techniques of modern jazz improvisation with the strict necessities of twelve-tone composition, the whole in a context of idiomatic and brilliantly conceived virtuosity. Schuller himself coined the term "third-stream"; and even his written-out twelve-tone music is informed by a kind of natural instrumental facility, which often relaxes specific temporal controls to allow for the image, if not the actual substance, of improvisation. "Third-stream" composers like Schuller, William Smith, John Eaton, Larry Austin and Peter Phillips are inevitably closely identified with performers and performance tradition; and modern jazz performers and performer-composers like Ornette Coleman, John Lewis, Lalo Schifrin, Cecil Taylor, and the late Eric Dolphy approach in their music—or their playing—the conditions of the new concert music.

There have also been a number of attempts to develop a non-jazz contemporary performance practice within which a new improvisation could develop. Interestingly enough, a great deal of this activity has taken place in California, the home state of Henry Cowell and John Cage and long an important source of new musical ideas. The San Francisco percussion ensemble group in the thirties was one of the few exploratory activities of that decade linking the new music of the twenties with the postwar period, and the San Francisco area has continued to be an important center of performance practice activity. The most important figure here, Robert Erickson, has been working out techniques both with performing musicians in controlled improvisational situations and in written scores which incorporate some of these techniques. Younger composers working along this line in the area include Larry Austin, Pauline Oliveros, Morton Subotnick, and Loren Rush.

The best known group in this field was the Lukas Foss Improvisation Chamber Ensemble, founded in Los Angeles several years ago. Since Foss has become musical director of the Buffalo Symphony, the Ensemble is essentially moribund; but Foss and the University of Buffalo are bringing a number of young musicians to Buffalo on a foundation-supported project which will undoubtedly be involved, in part at least, with a continuation of this kind of activity. The problem of improvisation, of course, is that the performers must improvise *on* something; in the absence of any performing tradition, Foss has attempted to invent the conditions— essentially the limitations—within which his players can operate. The problems inherent in all this are enormous; individual ideas may emerge with spontaneous vigor and may develop smoothly in a well-meshed ensemble, but the musical thread and ultimately the entire structures tend to spin themselves out in half-remembered finger motions and mental patterns of no particular significance to the conception at hand. In a way, the freer the schemes, the less the detail seemed to matter. The performances of a given scheme inevitably tended to solidify into a "composition" after a good deal of performing, yet the group never evolved any really distinctive means of expression; even over the relatively short period of its existence, it tended to be very fluid stylistically, moving along with Foss's own ideas from a kind of late neo-classicism into serial and post-serial modes.

Nevertheless, with all the shortcomings, the Improvisation Ensemble made a contribution, not only in matters of mere vitality and spontaneity, but also in demonstrating possible links between the performer and the composer realized through a conception of the character of the instruments and the skill of the players, both interacting throughout their entire range of possibility. Foss's recent written-out music—his *Time Cycle* (1960), in the version for soprano with the instruments of the Improvisation Ensemble (piano, cello, clarinet, and percussion) or for soprano orchestra with improvisations by the Ensemble, and his *Echoi* (1963) for the same quartet—grow out of the concerns of the Improvisation group. Both works, and especially *Echoi,* have the character of free and successful improvisations with the difference that the big forms are clearer, more consistent and coherent in detail, better controlled even where they are free, and not merely the result of performer reflexes but conscious, new and idiomatic.

Part of the charm of *Echoi* lies in the range of its activities which, in the manner of the Ensemble improvisation, includes loose serial techniques and formal devices roughly suggesting ideas of the German Karlheinz Stockhausen; coloristic, textual, and associative techniques resembling those of the Frenchman Pierre Boulez; action-and-gesture theatrics à la John Cage; open formal techniques parallel to those of Earle Brown and a chamber-instrumental style growing out of the Improvisation Ensemble, the whole unified in an assertive, even theatrical way by Foss's striking and individual sense of musical and dramatic gesture.

In the end, *Echoi* also relates to the character of much recent American music which grows out of the realities of the performance situation as expressed in a tension between performer and score—the precise act of intelligence controlling a muscular effort to put the right finger in the right place at the right time. Music like that of Elliott Carter grows out of the contrast between clock time and psychological time, between the metronome and the bar line on one hand and the cadenza on the other, between the necessities of complex precision and a rich play of free virtuoso colors. It is built on the individualization of the performers—in their "speech," in pitch, in rhythm, in color, even in tempo and space—with the capacities of each player extended to their limits. Rational control and carefully articulated structure are developed within a framework of great freedom and flexibility. The virtuosity is organic, no longer an embellishment on the surface of the music but conceived as a co-ordinated collection of actions and gestures which set up profound relationships and tensions—of a kind necessarily lacking in pure open-form, chance-and-choice music—which grow out of the performance situation and help to shape the music in on-going developing forms of real dramatic and psychological validity.

Key works in the development of this "new virtuosity" are Elliott Carter's Second String Quartet and his Double Concerto for Piano and Harpsichord. The former piece individualizes the players to the extent of giving them distinct musical personalities, the totality of the piece representing, so to speak, a confluence of divergent currents which retain their identity while contributing to the larger flow. The Double Concerto sets up the two keyboard instruments, each associated with its own instrumental ensemble, the whole framed in percussion. The two keyboard instruments with their characteristically percussive accent and attack mediate the opposition between pitched and non-pitched sound while always retaining separate modes of musical speech, individual expressive identities. Both pieces grow out of the tension between freedom and strictness, between different layers and levels of opposed sound, conceived in spatial, "stereophonic" terms and realized in the play of tone color and the richness of a great, intense, energetic virtuosity which darts and tumbles out to the furthest extremes of performer and listener comprehension.

Stefan Wolpe, like Varèse, is a composer who was born and trained in Europe, but his mature work has been accomplished here, and is essentially identified with American developments. Wolpe has long shown striking individuality in his choice of materials, in the character of his invention, in his insistence on ordered freedom and in his interest in new and organic forms. His recent work has, like Carter's, been involved, not only with the interaction of performers whose music intersects at different levels, but also with a complex interplay of oppositions: clarity and complexity, simplicity and density, careful articulation and great freedom. Works like his Piece for Two Parts for Six Players, his Piece for Flute and Piano, and his Piece for Two Instrumental Units outline new forms of great variety and power. Carter's forms are fluid

—they reveal themselves slowly in essentially dramatic articulations and structures which are constantly redefining the basic material which is open, fluid, arranged in parallel, linear, spatial structures. Wolpe's forms tend to accumulate as great static objects; the basic material is formed out of cell-like structures which are twisted, turned, combined and recombined, put together, taken apart, utterly destroyed and then resynthesized in patterns which can even take shape as literal recapitulations.

Varèse was perhaps the first composer to develop the idea of sound conglomerations composed as objects essentially remote from the possibility of traditional developmental and variational concepts. In the 1920's, in pieces such as *Hyperprism* (1923), *Octandre* (1924), *Intégrales* (1926), and *Ionisation* (1931), he had already created new forms out of the juxtapositions of great blocks of sound, defined primarily as color and accent and set into a new, imagined musical space. A composer like Ralph Shapey has carried forward the notion of fixed, invented musical shapes, set into great overlapping cycles and inter-related through statement and juxtaposition which constantly redefines and reinterprets the basic unyielding ideas. The effect is that of complex physical objects set in space, slowly rotated and seen anew from every possible angle. Whereas the basic characteristics of the new, on-going forms are asymmetry, non-repetition and aperiodicity, Shapey's forms—and, to some extent, those of Wolpe, of a work like Billy Jim Layton's String Quartet, of one or two of the younger composers—are important for their suggestion of new possibilities of symmetry, repetition and periodicity.

The "new virtuosity" is inevitably tied in with the remarkable development of performer skills in this country. There is now a whole generation of young American musicians with the techniques, intelligence and experience to deal with the complexities of even the most advanced new music and, indeed, a good deal of it has been written with their individual capabilities in mind. So many of these performers are themselves composers that one can almost speak of a "school" of performers-composers. Schuller is an excellent horn player and conductor, Foss, a fine pianist as well as director of the Buffalo Symphony; Shapey is active as a conductor; and there is a whole group of younger people whose performing and compositional activities are almost inseparable. The close relationship between the creative and the performing style of a young musician like Charles Wuorinen is typical: an exceptional pianist, he has developed an extraordinary range of piano activities and techniques. He sets the piano strings in motion in every conceivable way including brushing and slamming the keys with his fingers, palm and fist and manipulating the strings directly inside by plunking, brushing and scratching. All of these devices stem from Henry Cowell, but they are here used in entirely new ways. Wuorinen's own music (with or without a piano) has a highly improvisatory manner, expressive and free; even when open-form and improvisatory techniques are not used, the source of strength is the sense of controlled wildness. His structures, not unlike those of Carter and Wolpe, grow out of an on-going opposition between fixed and free, thrust and stasis, violent energy and intense calm.

Wuorinen is associated with an important concert series at Columbia and he has worked closely with the flutist Harvey Sollberger (for whom he has written an important *Chamber Concerto*). Sollberger's own music is also developing along lines suggested by the range of his own instrumental virtuosity and technical and musical achievement as well; *Chamber Variations* (1964) is a piece built on the opposition of extremes carried out and structured in virtually every dimension. A number of New York free-lance players, most of whom play contemporary music regularly, are themselves composers who, although perhaps not so well defined as creative personalities, attract attention because of the close association between their performing personalities and compositional ideas. Among them are Ronald Roseman, the oboist; Stanley Walden, the clarinetist; Easley Blackwood, an excellent pianist; Michael Colgrass, the percussionist; and Stanley Silverman, the guitarist. Especially impressive in this respect is the clarinetist William Smith, active in Europe and America both in jazz and all that non-jazz; Smith's astonishing range of technique includes double and triple stops as well as all kinds of other sounds previously considered out of the question on the instrument. The possibilities of instrumental technique remain wide open.

The tight relationship between expressive content and formal character (the two, now inseparable, become aspects of each other or perhaps inflections of some more basic imaginative unity) might be exemplified in a description of my own settings to the two-part song, "The Owl and the Cuckoo," from Shakespeare's *Love's Labor's Lost* (1962-3). The poem's two parts, "Winter" and "Spring," are parallel in structure, divergent in character and contents; the double structure and the opposition of poetic images and meanings determine the way the settings take shape. "Spring" is scored for soprano, flute, viola and guitar; "Winter" for soprano, clarinet, violin and guitar. Each song has its own instrumental color as well as its distinct musical character realized through a flexible vocal part and through the confluence of complex, running solo instrumental parts. The double image of parallel structure with contrasting content is set in a larger frame which includes a central guitar solo connecting the two songs, a brief instrumental tutti after the second song and a final bird-song vocalise at the end. The elaborateness of all the parts—soloistic and individualized with a series of cadenzas intended to articulate the form—invokes not only the continuity and texture of ensemble sound but also the continuity between the word sound, vowel and consonant rhythm (the instrumental parts range from pure pitch to highly unsteady attack and tremolo sounds to purely percussive rapping and clicking with and without pitch) and the close relation, as in Babbitt's *Philomel*, between the text and its setting.

These Shakespearean songs along with two others have been set for chorus and ensemble by another young composer, Salvatore Martirano, as a kind of cantata with a T. S. Eliot title: *O, O, O, O, That Shakespeherian Rag* (1958). Martirano extends the idea of solo virtuosity into a big choral conception. The chorus trills and hisses, whispers and shouts, it sings and speaks in tongues and puns, always with vitality and insistence. Martirano imposes on his performers, on his listeners, on himself in setting forth big dramatic conceptions which, in spite of the obvious planning underneath, have the impact and inevitability of a natural phenomenon. Composers like Martirano, Yehudi Wyner and Billy Jim Layton have retained an expressive freedom in their work which, although not necessarily reflecting the striking developments of the last few years, still suggests a growth out of instrumental resources and a chromatic vocabulary closely parallelling that of some of the music so far discussed. Wyner's *Duo for Violin and Piano,* with its carefully worked forms, and Layton's *String Quartet,* with its intensity developed out of a use of insistent intervals and its extended use (even redefinition) of structural repetition, have not yet had the creative follow-up that might have been expected; but they remain important works of the middle fifties which may yet be the predecessors of something still more remarkable.

It is curious that among all these composers involvement with twelve-tone technique remains the exception rather than the rule; outside of the composers grouped around Babbitt, only Schuller and Martirano have made extensive use of twelve-tone, serial technique. There is, of course, a middle-ground American twelve-tone music of great importance; the elder statesman in this department is Roger Sessions. Key works here are the Sessions *Solo Violin Sonata,* his *Idyll of Theocritus,* his *Piano Concerto,* his new opera *Montezuma* and his last symphonies. Aaron Copland's big serious works of recent years also belong in this category: his *Piano Quartet, Piano Fantasy* and *Connotations for Orchestra.* This quite abstract, conceptual musical thinking is already present in Copland's Piano Variations of 1930, and it carries over into a recent non-twelve-tone work like his *Nonet for Strings* (1960). The recent fascination with twelve-tone ideas, world-wide after the war, had a particular character in this country because of the presence of Schoenberg. Its most remarkable manifestation—one that can partly be associated with the American scene—has been the twelve-tone music of Igor Stravinsky, a composer who entered his third period under the "influence" of Schoenberg and Webern, but who has remained essentially Stravinskian in his esthetic outlook.

Nevertheless, in spite of the interesting large-scale organization of a twelve-tone work like *Threni,* Stravinsky remains basically a miniaturist who builds larger static forms through his personal techniques of juxtaposition and cumulative block-form. In contrast, the great significance of the twelve-tone idea in America has been its possibilities of new large-scale symphonic (i.e., directional-developmental, "narrative") forms without benefit of the old functional tonality. This tendency towards twelve-tone forms based on long-range linear motion can be seen in the twelve-tone work of a composer like Arthur Berger who, although originally under Stravinskian influence, anticipated and went beyond Stravinsky himself in the use of twelve-tone ideas applied to symphonic structures. More explicit development of twelve-tone symphonic forms can be found in the work of composers like Seymour Shifrin and Andrew Imbrie in California, George Rochberg in Philadelphia, Ben Weber in New York, and Kenneth Gaburo in Illinois. There is at least one case—George Perle—of a composer using complex twelve-tone techniques in the context of a non-twelve-tone, only partly chromatic music of great ingenuity; this is a kind of totally organized tonal music whose materials are known but whose forms are new and still organic. Leon Kirchner is perhaps the outstanding example of a number of composers who do not write twelve-tone music but whose work is a development out of chromatic expressionism; chromatic idioms (twelve-tone or not) using nineteenth century phrase structure and classicizing forms are the norm today just as "neo-classicism" and some kind of "neo-tonality" was ten and twenty years ago.

Many of the figures of the old American avant-garde are still active. Varèse is again part of the mainstream of new ideas; Henry Cowell, on the other hand, has turned away from the territory he staked out forty and fifty years ago to work translations of ethnic materials into symphonic guise. In his New England retreat, Carl Ruggles, now near 90, still paints and composes his rare, dense, personal chromatic music. The American tradition of eccentric individualism continues to produce originals working out their own ideas in isolation. Henry Brant, a former jazz arranger now teaching at Bennington College, long anticipated John Cage and his circle in creating open rhythmic structures in giant, freely coordinated spatial counterpoints (which derive ultimately from Ives). Brant is extremely sensitive to the character of instruments, to their disposition in space as well as to the acoustical properties of enclosed spaces. He will typically distribute his instruments around a hall with groups of them working individually on flexible material in a free, even uncoordinated stereophony. Harry Partch, now out on the West Coast, continues to work and develop his microtonal music with the special and remarkable instruments he has built for his purposes; micro-tonal materials (as distinguished from noise, "cluster" and glissando materials), although common in electronic music, have had only peripheral use in live instrumental music, and except in the case of isolated composers like Partch, remain essentially a secondary resource, not yet exploited systematically or organically.

These isolated currents stand in direct contrast to what might be called the New York Action Avant-Garde—the fashionable further-out far-out music of chance and changes, the Zen men, the indeterminates, the action and gesture music, the pop-art music and the neo-realism of a real-life, real-sound, real-object non-music music; American activities all, and those which most conveniently fit the old European dialectical idea of the nature of the avant-garde. The key figure here—the fountain-head, the source— is, of course, John Cage. Whether or not Cage can be considered as a composer or as a creator of works of art in the ordinary sense (he has, of course, done a great deal to change that "ordinary sense"), there is no question that he has been the most influential personality in the avant-garde arts since the war. In the thirties, he began with more or less conventional notes (rather ineptly managed) and then moved on to a percussion music (of an elementary kind) whose significance was its denial of pitch and rhythmic organization in the old sense. Cage's famous "prepared piano" belongs to this period; it was essentially nothing more than a piano with its insides doctored to make it function as a one-man percussion ensemble.

By the late forties and early fifties, Cage had abandoned not only pitch but also rational control over many aspects of composition. He used dice, a Chinese chance manual, random plottings on rough paper, haphazard spinning of radio dials, and a number of other devices to de-control the conscious manipulation of sound. His famous Music for Twelve Radios is—exactly like his tape music of the same period—essentially a random noise collage whose materials (including other music) are no more than aural objects, plucked from the real world by random, irrelevant methods, and put in random juxtaposition within a carefully defined time space. In essence, Cage's recent instrumental works function in the same way: the ensemble pieces, with parts written in handsome graphic, schematic or diagrammatic notations (invented for each piece) and which may be played together, separately or not at all. The natural sounds of the instruments may be combined with amplified sound through contact microphones attached to the instruments and transmitting impulses which may be randomly regulated by a performer at the controls right up to and even beyond the point of electronic distortion and the threshold of listener pain. Then, finally, there is silence—four minutes and thirty-three seconds of blessed, golden silence. Cage's famous silent piece of music may be taken as a frame for the natural sounds around us, the real world of accidental sound objects now become the exclusive subject matter; or it may be taken as an expression of the greatest piece of aleatory of all, the blessed and holy state of nothingness and death.

It might be imagined that once this ideal and sacred condition of inarticulateness had finally been reached, there would be nothing more to say and Cage, like Marcel Duchamp before him, could have packed his bags and gracefully retired from active competition. But 4' 33" was a purely literary idea which led Cage logically onward—with the dialectical precision which has always linked him to European tradition rather than to the Oriental ideas whose form he emulates but whose substance and condition remain foreign to his work—into purely literary-theatrical actions made up of meaningless, unordered slices of real life.

At one stage of this development, certain kinds of vestigial musical controls remain, functioning in a negative or reverse way.

This non-music music—we might call it "cisum"—takes everything that music does and does it backwards. Thus, whereas in music sounds are organized in relation to one another, there are works by Morton Feldman and Christian Wolff in which the sound content is as intentionally unrelated and disassociated as possible. Thus, where music may be defined as an organization of sound, a piece of "cisum" may consist of non-sound or silence; where a piece of music would be a finite event in time, there are compositions which imply an indeterminate or possibly infinite length; there is even a piece which consists of two notes with the direction: "Hold this for a long time." Where a piece of music would have a definable identity, a work of "cisum" might have none; there is a composition which consists of the direction: "Prepare any piece and play it." There is a piece which consists of the performers sitting on stage looking at the audience. La Monte Young, author of the above "compositions," made an appearance as a "violin soloist" which consisted of a ritual burning of the violin. We proceed in short, inevitable steps from Cage's "Indeterminacy: New Aspect of Form in Instrumental and Electronic Music"—essentially 90 tiny funny stories told by Cage—to his "Theatre Piece," a big collage of action and gesture, and from there to long sets of meaningless directions for meaningless and useless behavior and to the "happenings" and then on perhaps to meaningless, useless real life.

We need, as yet, no really new categories for the youngest composers. There has been a certain tendency among certain younger people to accept and extend transmitted ideas, even to the extent of regularizing and normalizing—one might almost say "neo-classicizing"—revolutionary notions of recent years. Composers like William Sydeman and Charles Whittenberg have been remarkably successful at domesticating for local consumption the music of European composers like Pierre Boulez and Luciano Berio and the recent visits of Stockhausen to this country have produced a small run of American Stockhanovites.

Some of the important younger composers who have been working with serial techniques have been mentioned and a number of the composers and composer-performers who can be loosely grouped around "The New Virtuosity" have also been discussed. Then there are the Indeterminists, the Happeningniks, the neo-Realists and the Popsters who take the slightly rearranged real world of sound for subject-matter and materials; they trade in on solid, real sound objects, ready-mades right to hand, artifacts from the real world—even the world of real music—which can be slapped into random place in any existentialist juxtaposition. There are a number of young composers—notably a group from Ann Arbor, Michigan (Gordon Mumma, Robert Ashley, Roger Reynolds) and several New York composers (James Tenny, Malcolm Goldstein)—who are developing and expanding a Cage-ian performance practice music using elaborately conceived live and live-and-tape techniques. Performers are often scattered around a hall; they sing, babble and squeak; they act on rather than perform on musical instruments which squeal and scrape at their outer edges; contact microphones are often attached to the instruments with amplified sound mixed with straight live and tape sounds in the form of brawling, scrambling and aural collages all realized within an amplifier-loudspeaker esthetic which mixes, transforms and distorts right up to the limits of perception. Sound itself is treated here as scrap material—useless, irrelevant and disassociated objects arranged and deranged. This is a junk music—a sound equivalent of junk sculpture made up of discarded bits and scraps from the junk heap of aural experience. The possibility of new significant forms—probably dramatic forms associated with other arts and disciplines—is by no means excluded. To the younger composers, Cage, chance, aleatory, open-form and the like are merely ways of doing business, serial or otherwise. It is perfectly clear that, win, lose, or draw, the old battles are finished. Four minutes and thirty-three seconds of silence may be nonsense or some kind of attempt to reduce esthetic distance or to bring in the real world; but *it can no longer pose any real issues*. The barriers are down, the old categories destroyed; the possibilities of utter silence or meaningless accident or total determinism have now been stated and there is no particular significance any more to the mere possibility of such statement. All relationships between creator, creation (if any), performer (if any), and audience (if any) are possible, including none; but this fact is hardly remarkable anymore except as redefined artistically in the context of total possibility. The new materials and ideas of the last decade or two are, to younger composers, just possibilities—raw materials like any other.

If, wherever we turn, we seem to be approaching extremes, that is merely in the nature of contemporary life which, for the first time, offers us the complete range of possible experience as material for artistic development. But what is important today grows out of not just the fact that any kind of perceptive experience can be established, but the exploration of the way heightened experience can be communicated throughout the range of human capacities—not the mere fact that it is possible to go up to and beyond the boundaries of perception, but the artistic exploration of those boundaries.

The old avant-garde in the early part of the century and its continuation in the late forties and fifties had indeed a clear historical role: that of widening our conception of musical experience and broadening our notions of the relations between experience and communication. But, in effect, the accomplishments of the Cage-ian avant-garde were achieved through a series of acts of renunciation: the renunciation of pitch, repetition, symmetry, periodicity in any form, specific sounds, connections between sounds, the conscious control of sound and, finally, sound itself. But these renunciations (or any others) can no longer be justified as intrinsic virtues or a result of historical necessity; eventually they turn out to be merely new forms of self-indulgence with, at best, only a private meaning or necessity.

The new range of potential experience has opened up new forms and new psychological validities whose potential seems limitless; the range of possible experience *is* the subject matter of the new art. The best new music is expressive in the sense that it is again "about" something: the quality and nature of heightened experience, perception, thought and understanding, all established through premises uniquely stated by each work of art. Thus, the new forms grow out of the range of activities and means suggested by the relationships, oppositions and juxtapositions of such aspects of experience as strictness and freedom, rational control and irrationality, fixed detail and improvisation, total unity and open form, symmetry and asymmetry, periodicity and aperiodicity, extreme register and extreme dynamic, motion and stasis, high and low tension, thinness and density, complexity and simplicity, confusion and clarity, intelligibility and incomprehension, pitch and noise, sound and silence, expressive-and-isolated detail and big-line-and-form, and so forth. This is no longer a music of fixed goals but of transformations which take place in every musical dimension and throughout the entire perceptive range. The transformations become ways of acting, experiencing and relating action and experiencing (i.e., of knowing) and they can alter and extend the quality of our experience, of the way we perceive and the way we relate and organize our perceptions (i.e., the way we know). In this music, we rediscover ourselves, our ways of experiencing, perceiving and knowing, altered and extended right up to the constantly expanding, redefined limits of our capacities.

SELECTED DISCOGRAPHY

(*indicates deleted recording. Where two numbers for a record are listed, the second is stereo.)

ANTHEIL, GEORGE: *Ballet mécanique (1924)* Urania 134; 5134

AREL, BULENT: *Electronic Music No. 1 (1960); Music for a Sacred Service (1961); Fragment* Son Nova; S-3
Stereo Electronic Music No. 1 (1961) Columbia ML 5966; MS 6566

ASHLEY, ROBERT: *In memoriam Crazy Horse* Advance 5

AUSTIN, LAWRENCE: *Improvisations for jazz soloists and orchestra* Columbia ML 6133; MS 6733

BABBITT, MILTON: *All Set (1957)* Columbia C21 31; C2S-831
Composition for 4 Instruments (1948); Composition for Viola and Piano (1950) CRI 138
"Du" (1951) Composition for 12 Instruments (1948) Son Nova 1; S-1
Composition for Synthesizer (1961) Columbia ML 5966; Ms 6566
Partitions for Piano (in recital of American piano music by Robert Helps) RCA Victor 2 LM/LSC 7042
N.B. Recordings of "Vision and Prayer" and "Philomel" are expected to be released in the near future.

BERGER, ARTHUR: *Polyphony for Orchestra (1956)* Louisville 58-4
String Quartet (1958) CRI 161
Chamber Music for 13 Players; Three Pieces for Two Pianos Columbia ML 6359; MS 6959

BLACKWOOD, EASLEY: *Chamber Symphony for 14 Winds (1955)* CRI 144
**Symphony No. 2* RCA Victor

BRANT, HENRY: *Angels & Devils—Concerto for Flute (1932)* CRI 106
Signs and Alarms (1953); Galaxy 2 (1954) Columbia ML 4956
Millenium II Lehigh University
Millenium IV Advance 2

BROWN, EARLE: *Music for Violin, Cello and Piano (1952); Music for Cello and Piano (1955); Hodograph I (1959)* Time 58003; 8003

BRÜN, HERBERT: *Futility (1964)* Heliodor 25047; 5-25047

CACIOPPO, GEORGE: *Time on Time, in Miracles (1964); Cassiopeia* Advance 5

CAGE, JOHN: *Amores for prepared piano and percussion (1943)* Time 58000; 8000
Aria (1958) with Fontana Mix (1958) Time 58003; 8003
Cartridge Music (1960) Time 58009; 8009
Fontana Mix Turnabout 4046; 34046
Indeterminacy: New Aspect of Form in Instrumental and Electronic Music (1959) 2 Folkways 3704

Sonata for Clarinet (1933) Advance 5

Sonatas and Interludes for Prepared Piano CRI 199

Variations IV Everest 58000; 8000

25 Year Retrospective Concert (1934-1958) George Avakian JC-1; JCS-1

See also Cages extensive notes to the *Retrospective Concert* and his *Silence,* Wesleyan University Press, 1961

CAGE, JOHN & LOU HARRISON: *Double Music for Percussion (1941)* Time 58000; 8000

CARTER, ELLIOTT: **Double Concerto for Harpsichord and Piano with 2 Chamber Orchestras (1961)* Epic LC3830; BC 1157

Eight Etudes and a Fantasy (1950) Concert Disc 1229; 229

String Quartet No. 1 (1951) Columbia ML 5104

String Quartet No. 2 (1960) RCA Victor LM 2481

Sonata for Flute, Oboe, Cello, Harpsichord (1952) Columbia ML 5576; MS 6176

Sonata for Piano (1946) Epic LC 3850; BC 1250; also Dover 5265; 7014

Variations for Orchestra (1955) Louisville 58-3

CHOU WEN-CHUNG: *All in the Spring Wind, Rondolet for Orchestra (1953)* Louisville 614

"And the Fallen Petals," Triolet for Orchestra (1954) Louisville 56-1

"Soliloquy of a Bhiksuni" (1958) Louisville 641

COLGRASS, MICHAEL: *Percussion Music (1953)* Period 743; S-743

Three Brothers Urania 106; 5106

COPLAND, AARON: *Concerto for Piano and Orchestra (1927)* Vanguard VRS 1070; VSD 2094

Connotations for Orchestra (1962) Columbia L2L 1007; L2S 1008

Orchestral Variations (1957) Vanguard VRS; VSD 2085

*Piano Fantasy (1957) Columbia ML 5568; MS 6168

Piano Variations (1930) Columbia ML 5568; MS 6168

Quartet for Piano and Strings (1950) Columbia ML 4421

*Sonata for Piano (1941) Lyrichord 104; CRI 171

Nonet (1960) Columbia (to be released)

COWELL, HENRY: *Ostinato pianissimo for percussion orchestra (1934)* Time 58000; 8000

Piano Music (1913-app. 1930) Folkways 3349; CRI 109

Toccata for soprano, flute, cello and piano (1938) Columbia ML 4986

Quartets Nos. 2-4 (1934-1936) CRI 173

DAVIDOVSKY, MARIO: *Study No. 2 (1962)* Son Nova 3; S-3

Electronic Study No. 1 (1960) Columbia ML 5966; MS 6566

Synchronisms 1-3 (1963-65) CRI 204; 20450

ERIKSON, ROBERT: *Chamber Concerto (1962)* CRI (to be released)

FELDMAN, MORTON: *Pieces for one, two, three and four pianos, violin and piano, string quartet (1951-57)* Columbia MS 6090

Durations (1960-61) Time 58007; 8007

Out of "Last Pieces" (1963) Columbia ML 6133; 6733

FOSS, LUKAS: *Improvisation Chamber Ensemble (1961)* RCA Victor LM 2558; LSC 2558
Time Cycle (1960) Columbia ML 5680; MS 6280
Echoi (1963) Epic LC 3386; BC 1286
GABURO, KENNETH: *Lemon Drops/For Harry* Heliodor 25047; 5-25047
Line Studies (1962) Columbia ML 5821; MS 6421
Two Advance 1
HAMM, CHARLES: *Canto* Heliodor 25047; 5-25047
HARRISON, LOU: *Canticle No. 1 for percussion (1940)* Time 58000; 8000
Canticle No. 3 for percussion (1941) Urania 106; 5106
Song of Queztecoatl (1941) Period 743; S-743
IMBRIE, ANDREW: *Legend for Orchestra (1959)* CRI 152
Violin Concerto Columbia ML 5997; MS 6597
Quartets Nos. 2 (1953) & 3 (1957) Contemporary 6003; 7022
IVES, CHARLES: *Choral Music: Harvest Home Chorales (3) 1898-1912* Victor LM/LSC 2676; Columbia ML 6321; MS 6921
General William Booth Enters Into Heaven (1914); Circus Band; Serenity Psalms 24, 67, 90, 100, 150; New River; December Columbia ML 6421; MS 6921
Quartets Nos. 1 (1896) and 2 (1913) Vox 1120; 501120
Sonata No. 2, "Concord, Mass., 1840, 1860" (1909-15) Time 58005; 8005. CRI 150
Sonatas (4) for Violin and Piano (1908-14) 2 Phillips WSm/s-2-001; 2 Folkways 3346/7
Songs Overtone 7; 2 Folkways 3344/5
Symphony: Holidays (complete) 1904-13 CRI 190; 190SD
Symphony No. 1 in D (1896-98); Unanswered Questions (1908) Victor LM/LSC 2893
Symphony No. 2 (1897-1902); "Fourth of July: (from Symphony: Holidays) Columbia ML 6289; MS 6889
Symphony No. 3 (1901-04); Central Park in the Dark (1898-1907); "Decoration Day" (1912) (from Symphony: Holidays); Unanswered Questions (1908) Columbia ML 6243; MS 6843
Symphony No. 4 (1910-1916) Columbia ML 6175; MS 6775
Three Page Sonata for Piano (1905); Anti-Abolistionist Riots (1908); Some Southpaw Pitching (1908); Three Protests (1914); 22 (1912); Theatre Set: In the Inn (1904-11) Folkways 3348
Three Places in New England (1903-1914) Meridian 50149; 90149. Columbia ML 6084; MS 6684
Tone Roads Nos. 1 (1911) & 3 (1915); Over the Pavements (1913); Hymn (1903-14); Indians (1912); Rainbow (1914); Hallowe'en (1911); The Pond (1906) Three Page Sonata for Piano (1905) Cambridge (1) 804
JOHNSTON, BEN: *Duo for Flute and String Bass* Heliodor 25047; 5-25047
KIRCHNER, LEON: *Piano Concerto (1952-53)* Columbia ML 5185
Concerto for violin, cello, 10 winds and percussion (1960) Epic LC 3830; BC 1157

Quartet No. 1 (1949) Columbia ML 4843
Sonata for Piano (1948) Epic LC 3862; BC 1262
KUPPERMAN, MEYER: *Line Fantasy from Infinities I* CRI 212
LAYTON, BILLY JIM: *Quartet in 2 Movements (1955-56)* CRI 136
LUENING, OTTO & VLADIMIR USSACHEVSKY: *Poem in Cycles & Bells, for Tape and Orchestra (1954); Suite from King Lear for Tape Recorder (1955)* CRI 112
    Rhapsodie Variations for Tape and Orchestra (1954) Louisville 545-5
MARTINO, DONALD: *Cinque Framment; Set for Clarinet* Advance 1, 4
MARTIRANO, SALVATORE: *O, O, O, O That Shakespeherian Rag (1959)* CRI 164
    Underworld Heliodor 25047; 5-25047
MILLER, LEJAREN: *Machine Music* Heliodor 25047; S-25047
MUMMA, GORDON: *Venezia Space Theater* Advance 5
PARTCH, HARRY: *Windsong; Bewitched; Castor & Pollax; Cloud Chamber Music: Wayward Letter* CRI 193
PERLE, GEORGE: *Quintet for Strings, Op. 35 (1958); Monody No. 1* CRI 212
POWELL, MEL: *Divertimento for 5 Winds (1956); Divertimento for violin and harp (1955); Trio for violin cello & piano (1956)* CRI 121
    Haiku settings (1960); Filigree Setting for String Quartet (1959); Electronic Setting (1961) Son Nova 1; S-1
RIEGGER, WALLINGFORD: *Concerto for Piano & Winds, Op. 53 (1952)* Concerto Disc 1221; 221. Everest 6081; 3081
    Romanza, Op. 56a (1954); Music for Orchestra, Op. 50 (1951) CRI 117
    Variations for Piano & Orchestra, Op. 54 (1952-53) Louisville 545-3
    Variations for Violin & Orchestra, Op. 71 (1959) Louisville 601
ROCHBERG, GEORGE: *Night Music (1949)* Louisville 623
    Quartet No. 2 with soprano (1961) CRI 164
    Symphony No. 1 (1949-55) Louisville 634
    Symphony No. 2 (1958) Columbia ML 5779; MS 6379
RUGGLES, CARL: *Evocations (1945); Lilacs (1924); Portals (1925)* Columbia ML 4986
    Organum (1945-46) CRI 127
    Suntreader (1932) Columbia ML 6201; MS 6801
SCHULLER, GUNTHER: *Abstraction (1961)* Atlantic 1365; S-1365
    Concertino for Jazz Quartet & Orchestra (1959) Atlantic 1359; S-1359
    Conversations (1959) Atlantic 1345; S-1345
    Music for Brass Quintet (1961); Fantasy-Quartet for 4 Celli (1958) CRI 144
    Seven Studies After Paul Klee (1959) RCA Victor LM/LSC 2879
    Transformation (1957) Columbia C2L 31; C2S 831
    Woodwind Quintet (1958) Concert Disc 1229; 229
SEEGER, RUTH CRAWFORD: *String Quartet (1931)* Columbia ML 5477; MS 6142

SESSIONS, ROGER: *Suite from "The Black Maskers" (1923)* Mercury 50106; 90103
"From My Diary" for piano (1940) Epic LC 3862; BC 1262. Music Library 7003
Sonata No. 1 (1946) CRI 198
Sonata No. 2 Dover 5265; 7014
*String Quartet No. 2 (1950) Columbia ML 5105
Sonata for violin solo (1953) Folkways 3355
Idyll of Theocritus for soprano and orchestra (1954) Louisville 57-4
Symphony No. 1 (1927) CRI 131
*Symphony No. 2 (1945) Columbia
SHAPEY, RALPH: *Evocation for violin, piano and percussion (1959)* CRI 141
Seven for Piano, 4 hands (1963) Friends of Four-Hand Music 1027
(None of Shapey's other important works has been commercially recorded.)
Rituals for orchestra has won a Naunburg Award and will be recorded by Columbia.
SHIFRIN, SEYMOUR: *Serenade for 5 Instruments (1955)* CRI 123; 123-SD
SMITH, WILLIAM O.: *Capriccio for violin & piano; String Quartet; Suite for violin & clarinet* Contemporary 6001; 7015
4 Pieces for clarinet, violin & piano; 5 songs for soprano & cello; Quartet for clarinet, violin, cello & piano; 5 pieces for Clarinet solo Contemporary 6010; 8010
SOLLBERGER, HARVEY: *Chamber Variations* CRI 204SD
STRAVINSKY, IGOR: Recent works:
Agon (1957) Westminster 9709. Columbia ML 5215; MS 6022
Cantata (1952) Columbia ML 4899
Canticum Sacrum (1956) Columbia ML 5757; MS 6357
The Flood (1962) Columbia ML 5757; MS 6357
In Memoriam, Dylan Thomas (1954) Columbia ML 5107
Movements for piano & orchestra (1958-59); Epitaphium (1959); Double Canon for String Quartet (1959) Columbia ML 5672; MS 6372
Septet (1953) Columbia ML 5107
Three Shakespeare Songs (1953) Columbia ML 5107
Threni (1957-58) Columbia ML 5383; MS 6065
A Sermon, a Narrative and a Prayer (1961) Columbia ML 6047; MS 6647
SYDEMAN, WILLIAM: *Concerto da Camera; 7 Movements for Septet (1958)* CRI 158
Orchestral Abstractions (1963) Louisville 644; 5-644
Music for flute, guitar, viola and percussion (1962); Concerto da Camera (1960) CRI 181
USSACHEVSKY, VLADIMIR: *Composition; Sonic Contours; Underwater Waltz* Folkways 6160

Creation-Prologue Columbia ML 5966; MS 6560

Metamorphosis (1957); Linear Contrasts (1958); Improvisation No. 4711 (1958) Son Nova 3; S-3

Piece for Tape Recorder (1955) CRI 112

VARÈSE, EDGARD: *Deserts (1954); Arcana (1927); Offrandes (1922)* Columbia ML 5762; MS 6362

Amériques (1926) Vanguard 1156; 71156

Arcana (1927) Victor LM/LSC 2914

Ionisation (1931) Columbia ML 5478; MS 6146. Urania 106; 5106

Octandre (1924); Intégrales (1925); Density 21.5 (1935) Columbia ML 5478; MS 6146

Poème électronique (1958); Hyperprism (1923) Columbia ML 5478; MS 6146

WEBER, BEN: *Prelude & Passacaglia, Op. 42 (1954)* Louisville 56-6

Serenade for Flute, Oboe, Cello & Harpsichord, Op. 39 (1953) Decca 10021; 710021

Symphony on Poems of William Blake (1952) CRI 120

WEISGALL, HUGO: *The Stronger (opera) (1952)* Columbia ML 5106

The Tenor (opera) 2-CRI 197

WEISS, ADOLPH: *Trio for clarinet, viola & cello (1948)* CRI 116

Variations for orchestra (1931) CRI 113

WHITTENBERG, CHARLES: *Electronic Study II with Contrabass (1962)* Advance 1

Three Pieces for Clarinet Solo (1963) Advance 4

Triptych for Brass (1962) Folkways 3651

WOLFF, CHRISTIAN: *Duo for Violinist & Pianist; Duet II for Horn & Piano; "Summer" for String Quartet* Time 58009; 8009

WOLPE, STEFAN: *Sonata for Violin; Passacaglia; Percussion Quartet (1948-51)* Counterpoint 530

Ten Songs from the Hebrew Columbia ML 5179

(None of Wolpe's works discussed here has been commercially recorded.)

WOURINEN, CHARLES: *Prelude & Fugue for percussion (1954)* Golden Crest 4004

Prayer of Jonah (1962) Cambridge (1) 416

Symphony No. 3 (1959) CRI 149

WYNER, YEHUDI: *Concerto Duo for violin and piano (1956)* CRI 161

Serenade for 7 Instruments (1958) CRI 141

—ERIC SALZMAN